HANDSWORTH: OLD & NEW

A History of
Birmingham's Staffordshire Suburb

BY

FREDERICK WM. HACKWOOD

EDITED BY ALAN A. VERNON

Brewin Books

This edition of 750 numbered copies published by
Brewin Books Ltd., Studley, Warwickshire B80 7LG, 2001

British Library Cataloguing in Publication Data
A catalogue record for this book is available from
The British Library

ISBN 1 85858 189 3

Made and Printed in Great Britain by
Warwick Printing Company Ltd.
Theatre Street, Warwick CV34 4DR

Dedicated to my wife Brenda, who has for the past 40 years been my constant help and support in all I have tried to achieve

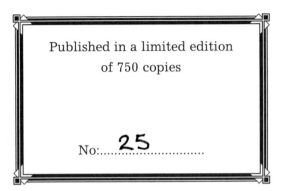

Published in a limited edition
of 750 copies

No:.......**25**..........................

FREDERICK WILLIAM HACKWOOD

F. W. Hackwood was born to Enoch and Sarah Hackwood on the 18th April 1851 at 69 High Street East, Wednesbury. His father, Enoch was a tailor, the family had settled in Wednesbury in the middle of the 18th century, the Hackwoods originally came from Stoke-on-Trent.

In 1868 he was admitted to St. Peter's Teachers Training College, Saltley and in 1871 he was appointed headmaster of St. Bartholomew's Church Schools at Wednesbury. In 1878 he was Headmaster of Dudley Road Board School, Birmingham and in 1888 he became Headmaster of Soho Road Board School also in Birmingham where he stayed until 1916 when he retired.

In 1874 he married Sarah Phoebe Simkin and they had two children, a son, Harold and a daughter, Louisa. He lived with his family at Comberford Lodge, Bridge Street, Wednesbury, until a subterranean fire at a neighbouring colliery forced them to leave the house and move to Handsworth. During the course of his life Frederick Hackwood wrote 28 books about Staffordshire and the Black Country, 'Handsworth Old & New' being one of them, published in 1908. Apart from writing on local history, he wrote books on a variety of other subjects including Natural History, Education, Church Lessons, Biography, Marriage, Sport and Food.

In addition to being a teacher and an author he was also a magistrate, a town councillor, a footballer, and the founder of several clubs and societies and was involved in creating open spaces like parks, allotments and re-afforestation of reclaimed colliery waste areas.

The last years of his life were spent at 2 Veronica Road, Balham near to his son, where he died on the 4th December 1926 aged 75 years.

ACKNOWLEDGEMENTS

I wish to thank the following for their help and assistance in republishing this volume. Firstly, to Alan Brewin, in agreeing to my suggestion to make this book available once more to a wider public. Reg Gower and members of Handsworth Local History Society for their advice and support in producing this reprint, John Maddison of Anvil Books, Halesowen for obtaining a copy of 'Handsworth Old & New' for me in the first place and finally my wife Brenda for putting up with working unsocial hours to produce this book.

BOOKS BY F. W. HACKWOOD.

Notes on Lessons on Moral Subjects. 1883.
Darlaston. 1887.
Tipton, 1891.
West Bromwich. 1895.
Some Records of Smethwick. 1896
Sedgley Researches. 1898
Handsworth Old and New. 1908
Annals of Willenhall. 1908
Oldbury and Round About. 1915
Story of the Black Country. 1892
Chronicles of Cannock Chase. 1903
Staffordshire Curiosities and Antiquities. 1905
Staffordshire Stories. 1906
The Birmingham Midlands. 1906
Staffordshire Worthies. 1911
Staffordshire Sketches. 1916
Staffordshire Customs. 1924
Staffordshire Glimpes. 1925
Staffordshire Miscellany. 1927. [posthumously]
Through the Midlands. 1905
Westward of the Wash. 1906
Story of the Shire. 1921
Olden Warwickshire. 1921
Notes of Lessons on Kindness to Animals. 1892
The Practical Method of Class Management. 1896
Natural History Reference Notes. 1897
Notes of Lessons on the Church Service. 1897
New Object Lessons [Animal Life] 1898
Chatty Object Lessons in Nature Knowledge. 1900
The Good Old Times. 1910
Old English Sports. 1907
Inns, Ales and Drinking Customs of Old England. 1909
Good Cheer, The Romance of Food and Feasting. 1911
William Hone, His Life and Times. 1912
Life of Lord Kitchener. 1913
Dragons and Dragon Slayers. 1923
The Bridal Book. The Lore, History and Philosphy of Love, Courtship and
    Marriage 1923
Wednesbury Papers 1884
Wednesbury Workshops 1889
Olden Wednesbury 1899
Religious Wednesbury 1900
Odd Chapters in the History of Wednesbury 1920
Wednesbury Notes & Queries. 3 Vols. 1902.
Wednesbury Ancient & Modern. 1902.
Pocket Guide to Wednesbury. 1908.

INTRODUCTION

When Frederick Hackwood wrote and published 'Handsworth Old & New' in 1908, he described Handsworth as 'Birmingham's Staffordshire Suburb'; but at that time, Handsworth was an Urban District Council and remained so until 1911, when it became absorbed into Birmingham. Handsworth like Smethwick had been part of the County of Staffordshire for nearly a thousand years. Many people living in Handsworth, as well as some of those resident in Smethwick would still like to be part of Staffordshire, seeing that the 'County of the West Midlands' has ceased to exist in all but name.

At the beginning of the 1900's when Frederick Hackwood lived in Handsworth after moving from Wednesbury, the suburb we see today was a very different place, the population of around 55,000 was small when compared to todays heavily populated area, with a rural aspect, fewer houses, business premises and people, The Rev. Stebbing Shaw described Handsworth in 1798 as 'an extensive and pleasant village'. Today's Handsworth can no longer be said to be a 'village' but parts are still pleasantly green, the "Old Town Hall' still retaining some of the 'Old Handsworth' character.

The original publication of 'Handsworth Old & New' was a limited issue of only 80 copies and this reprint will allow those interested in the history of Handsworth easier access to this very scarce volume

2001

CONTENTS

Chapter No.   Page No.

I.   Introductory – Making the Holyhead Road – Perry
        Castrum   1–5

II.   Romano – British Handsworth – The Roman Bridge
        at Perry   6–10

III.   The Founding of Handsworth – A Co-operative
        Community   11–15

IV.   Handsworth in Norman Times – 'Free Warren' in
        Handsworth   16–18

V.   Life in the Manor in the XII. Century – Handsworth
        Manor House...   19–22

VI.   Sir William De Parles, The Imperious Lord of
        Handsworth. The Advowson – Crusading Incidents.   23–27

VII.   Mediaeval War Taxes Collected in Handsworth –
        Inhabitants of Handsworth in 1327 – A Valuation of
        the Manor   28–32

VIII.   Handsworth Dominated by the Seigniory of
        Hampstead – The Transmission of the Manor –
        Advent of the Stamfords....   33–37

IX.   The Wyrley and Wyrley-Birch Families – Wyrley the
        Antiquary   38–41

X.   The Manor of Perry Bar   42–43

XI.   The Stamford and Gough Families – 'New Inn'   ...   44–47

XII.   The Old Water Mills of Handsworth – The
        Importance of Mill-Power – The Booths of Witton   48–51

XIII.   The Manor of Witton – Old Field Names – Vestiges
        of Old Customs...   52–56

XIV.	The Fabric of the Church – The Church Bells – The Parish Registers	57–62
XV.	Handsworth at the Reformation – A Puritan survey, 1586	63–66
XVI.	The Benefice – Handsworth Deanery – Handsworth Rectory Acts, 1891	67–71
XVII.	The Church Charities – The Workhouse – The 'Pious Resignation' of the Poor – The Separate Charities of Perry Barr – Missing Endowments... ...	72–82
XVIII.	A Well Endowed Parish – Kendrick's Pamphlet [1841] Almshouses	83–88
XIX.	Growth of Anglicanism – Church Rates – St. Michael's Church	89–94
XX.	The Replanting of Catholicism – New Oscott – Hunter's Lane Convent	95–100
XXI.	Dissent and Nonconformity – The Wesleyan College – The Free Churches	101–106
XXII.	The Bridge Trust – The Trust Rent Roll [1807] – Church Rates 'National' Schools	107–113
XXIII.	Diverted from Bridges to Education – Grammar School founded...	114–117
XXIV.	Warlike Handsworth – The Yeomanry – The Militia – The Volunteers	118–123
XXV.	The World of Soho – The Mint – The World – Fame of Soho	124–128
XXVI.	A Residential Oasis – Geology of Handsworth ...	129–132
XXVII.	Old Families and Names of Note – Prominent families	133–136
XXVIII.	Topography – New Inns – Old Residences – The Manwoods	137–142

XXIX.	The Turnpike Roads – Hamstead and Birchfield Roads – The Toll-Gates ...	143–147
XXX.	From Stage Coach to Tram Car – Horse Trams and Cable Traction – 'The Tramways Muddle' ...	148–153
XXXI.	Handsworth under Village Government – Watchmen and Parish Constables ...	154–156
XXXII.	Modern Local Government – Municipal Institutions – Perry Barr Authority ...	157–162
XXXIII.	Folk Lore, Customs and Habits – Institutes and Societies ...	163–165
XXXIV.	Miscellanea – Politicians, Inventors, Collectors, Etc.	166–169
XXXV.	Bibliography – Clerical and Medical Writers, Poets, Etc. ...	170–174
	Index ...	175–178

HANDSWORTH

OLD AND NEW.

I.—INTRODUCTORY.

Handsworth, not so long ago a pretty Staffordshire village, preserving its freshness and quietude midway between the Black Country and Birmingham, has now grown into a populous suburb of that city, with no less than 52,921 inhabitants (1901 census). It is not quite so large as Birmingham's Worcestershire suburb of Kings Norton, which with Northfield possesses a population of 57,120; but it is more than three times the size of its Warwickshire *faubourg*, Erdington, which has only 16,366 inhabitants. Handsworth remains almost entirely residential, except that recently a few of the factories typical of Birmingham's jewellery quarter, the adjoining district of Hockley, have begun to stray over the border into the Staffordshire area. It therefore would be hardly fair to compare this congeries of villas, cottages, and private houses with those busier outskirts of the great city which have attained, by virtue of their industrial activities, to the dignity of independent municipalities; the new Staffordshire borough of Smethwick having reached a population of 54,560, while the other daughter borough of Aston Manor, on the Warwickshire side, has no less than 77,310 inhabitants.

Handsworth being fortunate in the possession of a large acreage, has not been spoilt quite so much as many similar places have been by rapid building developments—an area of 7,680 acres allowing room for the making of many new streets of houses.

How rapid the development has been in this instance is difficult to realise. Till within the most recent centuries, the country lying to the north of Birmingham, right away through Handsworth and West Bromwich to the confines of Wednesbury, was mostly open heathland, a wild and desolate region of gorse, ring, and bracken, on one side of which lay the preserved precincts of the Royal Forest of Cannock, divided from it, between Aston and Wednesbury, by the course of the River Tame. Looking northwards, this open country was fringed on the left, beyond Winson Green and Birmingham Heath, by a dark line of woodlands, from Ladywood and Rotton Park to Bearwood; whence the western skyline was carried onward by the ridge of the Rowley Hills, the farther distance brought up by a panoramic view of Dudley Castle. On the other side, the line of the eastern horizon was bounded by the foliage of Aston Park and the uplands of Barr; while directly in front, and crowning the rise on the farther side of the little valley in which the old church nestled, was the sylvan screen presented by Handsworth Wood, an obstruction to the field of view that obscured but a portion of the neighbouring domain of Sandwell. The last vestiges of the wild heathland, with here and there bare patches on the sides of its hillocks that disclosed the dry gravelly nature of its soil, were to be seen till quite recently in front of the Handsworth (Great Western) Railway Station. Another remnant of the same stretch of wilderness may still be recognised near the Summit Bridge at Smethwick. It was from the elevation of Handsworth Heath that, like another Dick Whittington, William Hutton, a runaway boy from Derby, who afterwards became the historian of Birmingham, obtained his first view of the city of his adoption, in 1741; St. Philip's Church, then comparatively new (he says), being plainly seen through a clear atmosphere, "untarnished with smoke," and the view of it quite unobstructed by buildings, New Hall being the only house standing between it and the peeling eyes of the youthful spectator. Eighteen years later, "at Midsummer, 1759, Hutton took a lease of two acres of waste land upon Handsworth Heath, of Mr. Wyrley, for ninety-nine years, at twenty shillings per annum, to begin to build a mill." In 1768, we also learn from his diary, he purchased three more acres of land in Handsworth for £156. Obviously the eligibility of the place, a breezy upland, in close contiguity to a growing city, was beginning to dawn upon the commercial minds of Birmingham. Pye's "Description of Modern Birmingham," published in 1819, calls it the "elegant village of Handsworth, where, the common lands of the parish being inclosed by Act of Parliament in 1793, they have probably been as productive, if not more so, than others of a similar nature in any other part of the kingdom; for there are now at least one hundred and fifty respectable houses erected upon the ground, which before it was inclosed lay entirely waste; and plots of the same land have been sold from two hundred pounds to a thousand pounds an acre."

While land in Handsworth was thus being sold by the acre, many Black Country manufacturers, as well as numbers of Birmingham's fat citizens, began to establish themselves here in very comfortable residences, and some of them indeed in highly desirable domains. In 1841 the population had grown to 5,205, and in the next forty years it increased fourfold, reaching 22,896 by the year 1881. Perry Barr, the transpontine portion of the parish, has so far preserved its rurality, the population between 1891 and 1901 having increased only from 2,310 to 2,348.

For centuries the wide area of the parish had been intersected and traversed by a number of rough and ill-defined roads. most of them mere tracks worn by the traffic between this and the surrounding villages and towns. The road most frequented by the parishioners of Handsworth was the one on which the church was situated, the ancient highway to Walsall; which starting from Hockley proceeded along the line of Hunters Lane, passed over Hamstead Hill and away towards West Bromwich Church, and then over the Tame Bridge into Walsall. From Handsworth Church another beaten road doubtless struck off along the line of Wellington Road in the direction of Aston Church, its continuance along Church Lane in the opposite direction offering an alternative route into West Bromwich. The Crick is an ancient bridle-path; and of the other beaten tracks across this waste of scrub and heather one certainly went in the direction of Harborne, possibly along the line of Nineveh Road. Two important tracks converged near Villa Cross, a slightly elevated spot which a century or two ago was known by the name of Gallows Hill. The only properly constructed highway in Handsworth was that portion of the ancient Roman road which passed through it and took its way over Perry Barr Bridge.

The present main road through Handsworth and West Bromwich was for many centuries nothing more than a little frequented track across the lonely heath. In 1727 it was made and turnpiked as far as Wednesbury, on account of the growing traffic in coal, which hitherto had been carried from the coal pits there, to the busy hearths of Birmingham,, in panniers slung across the backs of horses. But it was 1752 before the usefulness of the road was recognised for fly-wagons and stage coaches, at which date the compilers of road books suddenly became alive to its directness and many other advantages for the through traffic from London towards Shrewsbury, Chester and Holyhead, now that the rising importance of Birmingham compelled coaches to travel by way of that town, instead of giving it the "go-by" on the old Coventry and Castle Bromwich route. In this new departure what Castle Bromwich lost became Handsworth's gain.

Another aspect of the place in the sleepy centuries of bygone times which must not be lost sight of, was the part played by the little river Tame and its feeders. These insignificant streams, though entirely useless as a means of communication, were utilised to their fullest capacity to supply motive power for the primitive industries of the locality. By the seventeenth century iron mills and furnaces had located themselves at somewhat short intervals along every available stream in the vicinity. Engaged in this important local industry in that and the succeeding century were the well-known families of Jennens, Foley, Fowkes, and Parkison. The iron ore had to be carried considerable distances from the pits, and when the exhaustion of the timber in the locality led to the use of mineral fuel, so had the coal. It was this heavy traffic in the conveyance of minerals from the pits to the furnaces which led to the wearing of that track at Hamstead, now known as Rocky Lane, and which doubtless effected a junction with the old Aldridge Road. The Jennens had their ironworks at Lozells, the Foleys at Perry Barr, and the Fowkes family at Little Aston. The common lands of Handsworth, Perry, and Oscott, which in the aggregate comprised no inconsiderable tract of waste, came together at Holford iron mill. Hamstead Mill remained a grist mill, but everywhere around Birmingham there was a great demand for water-power, to work blade mills. slitting mills, and polishing mills in connection with the local iron trade. At Witton were established two iron mills, besides a rag or paper mill.

The epoch which marked the awakening of Handsworth from the sleep of centuries was that at the close of the eighteenth and the commencement of the nineteenth centuries. First came the selection of Soho—a mere rabbit warren at that time—as the site for that marvellous hive of industry, that pioneer establishment of organised labour, Boulton's factory. And next, more important still, Handsworth was brought at last under the stimulating influences of the outside world through the adoption of one of its roads into the system of the country's main arteries of communication; for not only was the fast coach traffic developing everywhere at that time, but after the Union of 1801, and as the result of Parliamentary agitation, this particular road was specially reconstructed, shortened and straightened, to Holyhead, so that the new Irish members might be relieved in their tedious journey, and particularly of being compelled to change coaches at Chester. How the making of the Holyhead Road shifted the centre of Handsworth's population when it began to grow, may be seen in the erection of its earliest public building, the present "Parish Offices," erected at the end of Baker Street in 1830, quite remote from the church, but close to the new arterial flow of life and trade. Then it was so many of the residences in the old Georgian style were put up.

And here one important incident in connection with the Holyhead Road must not be omitted. When Telford was constructing this great national coach road a great lawsuit arose concerning the portion of it passing through Soho. At the Stafford Assizes of 1824 Matthew R. Boulton (son of Birmingham's eminent "captain of industry") brought an action against Stephen Falknor Crowther, a nominal defendant, by reason of his being Clerk to the Trustees of the Wednesbury and Birmingham Turnpike Roads. In making the improved coach road, Telford, as appointed engineer and acting through the local Trust, had raised the level of the valley at Hockley Bridge by six feet, and lowered the Soho Hill section a further seven feet by means of a cutting. It was complained by Boulton, whose residence stood in fifty acres of land on the crest of the hill, that the levelling had interrupted the access to his pleasure grounds, had deprived him of a spring of water which supplied his garden tanks, and had permanently injured the estate as prospective building land, deteriorating it to the amount of £1,800, and necessitating an immediate expenditure of £900 to put its drives and roads into proper order again. One gate at Hockley Brook, opening on a footpath to the Soho Factory, was said to have been completely blocked. Damages were laid at £10,000. There were produced in court an extraordinary number of plans and models of the estate, showing its landscape features, its levels, and elevations, all made quite realistic by the addition of numerous figures of men, and cattle, and vehicles. In fact all the mechanical resources of the famous Soho Factory seem to have been called into requisition, till the opposing counsel ridiculed the whole display as a mere "puppet show." On the other side evidence was given of the considerate treatment that Mr. Boulton and his interests had received all through the proceedings. James Frost, roadmaker, said due notice of the work was given, and the operations were obligingly commenced on the Hockley Hill, the rise on the further side of the brook, in July 1823. On behalf of the plaintiff, Jonah Robins, a well known local surveyor, said that "the town of Birmingham was travelling very fast towards Handsworth," and this estate would become very valuable building land. The parish surveyor, Kempson, thought the estimated amount of the damages had been placed too low. But the defence was that the work had been done under the direction of Mr. Telford, who was fully authorised under the General Turnpike Act of 3 George IV. A special jury had no hesitation in finding a verdict for the defendant, the work in their opinion, having been done properly and with all due care.

II.—ROMANO-BRITISH HANDSWORTH.

Perhaps the most hoary relic of antiquity in Handsworth is the portion of the Roman road from St. David's to Northumberland which passes through it, over Perry Barr bridge—the great Ryknield Street. This ancient military highway came along the line of Monument Lane, crossed the brook at Hockley, and passing on, presently entered Handsworth from near Chain Walk. Taking a fairly straight course past Well Head it crossed the Tame at Perry Pont, and so on along Holly Lane, till it entered Sutton Park, where its well-defined line is still easily to be traced. Chronological precedence, however, would have to be given to the Aldridge Road if, as some writers have claimed, it is part of an ancient British trackway. It certainly runs along an elevated ridge, as, in an age of undrained fen and bog, available roads were bound to do; and it went directly towards Barr Beacon, a commonly recognised centre of Druidical activity. Tradition hath it that here these astrologers of old scanned the heavens which

> Studious they measure, save when meditation
> Gives place to holy rites; then in the grove
> Each hath his rank and function. Yonder grots
> Are tenanted by bards, who nightly thence
> Rob'd in their flowing vests of innocent white,
> Descend, with harps that glitter in the moon,
> Hymning immortal strains..

Some interesting discoveries relating to this far-away period are reported in a paper contributed to the Birmingham Archæological Society (1906) by Mr. G. Bernard Benton. While admitting that the locality shows a dearth of Celtic remains, he reports the finding of a few chipped flint instruments at Perry Barr and Sutton.

After reading Mr. Benton's paper one cannot fail to be thrown back upon the reflection that the study of existing evidences of man's earliest energies in this immediate neighbourhood has not received that close attention it deserves. Mr. Benton's contribution to the subject is extremely valuable, and his rather original views excite a new interest. And though Handsworth merely touches the fringe of the area of his investigations, his references are far too important to be passed over here in silence.

Mr. Benton, by the way, claims Key Hill to have been the site of an ancient British fort; he says it was originally known as the Kay Hill, "Kay" (? Caer) being merely Welsh for "castle." But what is more important his paper is illustrated with a plan of the Perry Castrum of the Romans, "an enormous square camp large enough to contain one of those great double consular armies which assembled when all the legions in Britain, raised to double strength with their auxiliaries, were mustered for some great enterprise." The camp was approached by the Ryknield Street which passed along the southern end of Well Head Lane. "I place," says our authority, "the southern face of this [earth] work at a line of dykes and pits extending across the isthmus of Perry Barr from Well Head House to Holford Farm; other works on either bank covered the Witton Ford of the Tame."

Then follow the somewhat technical details and precise figures of the measurement of this once important Roman camp, which is said to have had a wall of great breadth within the north-moat at Perry. "Some of the farm buildings [in the vicinity] contain much stone dressed with Roman scappling, and one shows faintly a letter or two of inscription. It has been the custom for some considerable time to speak of the Bridge as Roman. Against this I felt originally the strongest prejudice. It seemed to me that if the Ryknield Street had a bridge here, as it most certainly would have, it should be sought on the direct line of the street. It seemed possible that its present fame was due to the discovery of Roman stones reused in its piers. But now I have not any doubt that the deviation of the high-road was made under the Empire, and that the bridge was permanently built in its present position at a time when a magnificent station was set up in the north-west angle of the works.

"The ruins of this establishment choke the gardens of Perry Pont House with thousands of tons of stone, while all the materials common in the hypocausts . . . have been utilised in the vinery and other parts of the buildings. There are, too, inserted in the numerous grottoes, more than a dozen grotesque heads carved in stone and exhibiting the characteristics of some of the best Roman work of this character found in the provinces. I saw also one small head of a portrait type with beard and whiskers of the Antonine period. Again the decorations of one of the grottoes suggests that its builder had excavated mosaics on this site, and was moved to imitate the effect.

"Among the debris I distinguished three stones which, fitted together, formed a portion of a small round arch showing the triple faciæ of the classic architrave carried around it."

Now, whatever scepticism may be aroused by a closer examination of the sculptured fragments, the presence at Perry Pont of so many hundreds of tons of stone, much of which has been tooled and worked by the mason, can scarcely be accounted for by any other theory; so vast a quantity was certainly never conveyed there for the mere purpose of constructing garden "rockeries," or even to be half-buried in the foundations of walls. It must not be forgotten that Roman coins have been discovered in this vicinity, William Hutton recovering one of Vespasian in 1765. If the foundations of the present bridge were examined beneath the level of the bottom of the stream all doubt would probably be set at rest.

After proceeding to account for the deviation of the road and the present position of the Bridge, Mr. Benton proceeds: —"Beyond the bridge, roads to Aldridge, Windley Green. and Welshman's Hill were distributed, and then the Ryknield Street proceeded by way of Holly Lane to the Roman's Field: near here the Tumulus of King's Standing seems to have been a roadside tomb, for the labourers obtained a considerable treasure of silver chains when the wood was cleared. "The original Tumulus is said to have been destroyed in ignorance by a new tenant clearing the land; and the present landmark was thrown up and enclosed by him as soon as he learnt from his neighbours its historic interest as the place where Charles I. had reviewed his troops. Our authority traces the continuation of this great military road, as it passes eastward of The Parson and Clerk Hotel on its way through Sutton Park, Little Aston. and beyond, where we have no need in the present instance to follow. More to our immediate interest is the writers description of the Chester Road or Ridge Way, which comes along here past the King's Standing, from Coventry and Castle Bromwich (having left the Watling Street at Weedon) which he states was not only the main line of march for Roman legions passing between London and the north of Wales, hut was the route always used by mediæval armies, and the one certainly indicated by Shakespeare as that used by Sir John Falstaff on his way from Coventry to Shrewsbury, when he is represented to have halted at Sutton Coldfield (1 *Henry IV.* 4-2.)

Another ancient military road indicated by the writer is Sandwell Lane. He correctly notes that it was the line of march adopted by Queen Henrietta when she came from the east coast through Lichfield and Walsall, crossing Tame Bridge at the Delves, and so on by Smethwick, Harborne, and Kings Norton—in fact along the line of the Icknield Port Road. It remains only to cull from our interesting and highly original authority his note that he unearthed at Booth s Farm, Great Barr, a portion of an old quern—presumably one of Roman workmanship.

There is nothing inherently improbable in Mr. Benton's theories. As the Ryknield Street passed through the line of country between Gloucester, Worcester, Birmingham, Derby and Chesterfield it would have to cross many streams and small rivers, an engineering feat which presented no difficulties whatever to the Romans. From a study of this extensive system of Roman bridges, however, it is not to be understood that every one was a round-arched bridge; piers of size and strength sufficient to withstand the thrust of the waters were occasionally spanned by massive timbers. This however, was done only when the requisite spring of the arch would have raised the road to an inconvenient height.

The Anglo-Saxons, not being builders or engineers, were careful to preserve all the bridges they found existing here, the charge of them being thrown upon the Hundred or the County. There can be little doubt that nearly all the bridges remaining here at the Norman Conquest were of Roman origin and construction. The present Gothic bridge at Perry, erected in mediæval times, probably preserves a number of Roman-worked stones in its foundations. As to the branching of the roads on the northern side of the bridge, it is a fact that the central districts of Roman-Britain were traversed by a net-work of roads other than the great military highways; there were branch roads (*viæ vicinales*) country roads (*agrariæ*) and bye-roads (*deviæ*), to say nothing of the number of saltways leading out of Droitwich. One of the last-named perhaps passed on its way through Selly (Sale-ley) and Saltley if the names of these places really betray their origin; another possibly passed through Oldbury and Wednesbury, where their course in both these old towns is still called the Portway. It is scarcely necessary to mention that the Roman towns, Manduessedum on one side of Perry Castrum, and Eteocetum on the other, were not on the Ryknield Street, but on that greater national thoroughfare, the Watling Street; the former being now known as Mancetter, situated on the Anker, in Warwickshire, and the other as Wall, near Lichfield, in Staffordshire. It is not difficult to imagine cohorts of the famous Tenth Legion, so long stationed at Chester, maybe their armour gleaming in the sunlight of a British summer day, marching southwards to Wall, and there wheeling to the right along the Ryknield Street, and in a tramp of a few more miles through Streetley taking up their quarters in Perry Castrum. Whether this was one of the later *castra stativa*, or permanent camps for keeping a district in subjection, or as is more probable, one of the *castra exploratoria* pitched during the earlier period of conquest, its location in close proximity to Barr Beacon is significant.

For while so much of the country remained undrained, this camp would possess the ample security of high embankments in the midst of a wide watery lowlying swampland; a civilised stronghold in the very heart of a wild country of "blue savages and black forests." With the fall of darkness at the close of each day the security of such massive earthworks would need only the simple military device of *tessera,* a square tablet of wood on which was engraved the watchword for the night, to be passed round among the centurions on duty. Consistent with a theory that the ultimate sanctum sanctorum of esoteric Druidism was to be found here in the heart of the country, to wit in the almost impenetrable primeval forests which anciently clothed the classic heights of Barr, a playful fancy would have little difficulty in reconstructing a scene which might indeed have occurred on the Roman bridge at Perry—a scene of one of the earliest peace negotiations attempted between the supreme leaders of the Britons and the accredited generals of the invading forces. On the one hand, marching out through the north-west gate-pit of the great camp, the tall Roman officers, with bright helmets, and cuirasses of beaten bronze inlaid with silver scroll-work, below which the skirts of their fine cloth tunics fell to the knee, the dress elaborated with richly ornamental straps of metalled leather, and the equipment of arms as complete as a military civilisation could make it; and on the other, emerging from the gloom that distinguished the heart of the mystic oak forest, the stately procession of the College of Druids, their majestic figures clothed in flowing garments, and their stately steps measured by the white wands of office they carried in their hands. An imposing sight, truly; and the occurrence of such an incident is not so far beyond the bounds of possibility as some may think.

III.—THE FOUNDING OF HANDSWORTH

Whether Key Hill was ever the site of a Celtic fort, or Perry of a Roman Castrum, it is certain that Handsworth village had its roots in the settlement of a Saxon family. Most of our villages, towns and political divisions received their names from the early English—there were exceptions to this rule one of which will be noted presently. The name Handsworth is made up of the personal name of the Anglo-Saxon chieftain who headed that family of pioneer settlers; followed by the Anglo-Saxon suffix "weorthig," common to many place-names, as in Tamworth, Lapworth and Kenilworth.

The founder's name may have been Hand or Honde, but more probably was Hun, Hune or Huna. The name of the place has appeared in many forms; for instance in Domesday Book it was Honesworde. in the next century it was spelt Hunesworth and Honesworth; and in the thirteenth century it is found written Hunnesworth. The signification of the terminal "worth" is *property* or *farm, so* that the whole name means "Hune's estate." or maybe "Hune's farm".

Isaac Taylor, an eminent authority on placenames, says—"The Anglo-Saxon 'weorthig,' which appears in English names in the form of 'worth.' . . . denotes a place *warded*, or *protected*. It was probably an inclosed homestead for the churls, subordinate to the tun," or town. If the surmise of Dr. Taylor be correct it makes Handsworth the secondary settlement of that tribal group of Saxon adventurers, who at the end of their voyaging and wanderings, selected this situation for their new home. The chief seat or actual residence of the leader himself was fixed on the brow of the hill on the other side of the wood, and was distinguished as "the" homestead, now called Hamstead. So that while the community of dependents, the population, were settled at Handsworth village, Hamstead was a mere domiciliary settlement with the usual number of ancillæ, and other indoor domestics attached to the lord's household. This view is practically corroborated by the subsequent history of the two places; for in the time of Edward I., when the lord of Handsworth and nearly every other landholder in England were striving to make good their claims to the rights and privileges of lordship over their tenants, the then holder of Hamstead could not by any stretch of conscience say that such feudal rights had ever been exercised on that estate.

There was yet another community established in the wide area which was afterwards formed into the parish of Handsworth; it was on the farther side of the stream, itself a feature which would be one of the considerations influencing the selection of the settlers, and became known as Perry Barr.

The name Barr is one of the exceptions in our system of place-naming to which reference has just been made. There can be no doubt the name by which the mystic region of Barr, the very heart and centre of Druidism, had been so long known, was a name of import which clung to it in spite of the deeply rooted custom of these English new-comers to "call their lands after their own names."

Barr is a survival of Ancient British nomenclature and means "a hill top" or "a summit." Perry is from a Middle English word *pirie* signifying "a pear-tree;" the addition of Barr was no doubt made to distinguish the place from other Perrys. The peopling of Perry Barr was probably a little later than that of Handsworth and Hamstead, not being effected perhaps till the superstitious fear of the Druid-haunted recesses of Barr's frowning Beacon had been lost sight of. The Celtic name, it will be noted, dominated the place after its dread traditions connected with human sacrifices and other occult mysteries had faded away. It must not be forgotten that on their arrival in this country the Anglo-Saxons were themselves pagans, to whose polytheism we still bear witness in the names of the days of the week we use, and of which we sometimes find traces in place-names; as in those of Tutbury, Wednesbury and Thursfield, three in this county of Stafford alone.

* * * * * * *

For the better understanding of the social conditions prevailing at that remote period in a village like Handsworth, a digression may be permitted here to explain, in the briefest manner possible, the evolution of the English manor, or lordship.

In these days of Socialistic tendencies it will be interesting to observe how the free institutions of a liberty-loving people gradually fell away into a system of servility under recognised lordships. During the Roman occupation of Britain private villas and family estates were found, though no doubt at long intervals, and at certain favoured spots along the arterial flow of their great highways; for the Roman system of taxation seems to have been based upon personal wealth and land ownership.

Under the Anglo-Saxon polity society was rigidly graded in rank from Earl and Thane to Ceorl, to dependents and slaves, all bound together by the mutual tie of protection and service. It was a system of patronage which gave Saxon society a personal aspect. It consisted of a political grouping of households, kindreds, and tribes which eventually divided the land into Hundreds, and supplied the machinery of justice, taxation and defence. The Early English everywhere formed the Tun (or large village) for the purposes of cultivation and defence; and the aggregation of tuns grew into the groups of the Hundred and then of the Shire. The Tun, however, was not the unit, for it grew out of the Household, and was defined by rights and duties, according to the occupation of definite shares—that is, of hides or ox-plough fractions—which composed the area of the Township. Local illustrations of these territorial divisions will be suggested by the names Aston and Sutton—the "East-tun" and the "South-tun"; and found in the Hundred of Offlow and the Stafford-shire, in which divisions Handsworth is included. The unit of occupation was the Household, the members of which had a measure of rights in the dwelling and close (or homestead), in the arable land and meadow, in pasture, wood, and water. Every householder co-operated in the village husbandry.

Every house had a common and undivided use of the waste-land, of which there was a large area surrounding every Saxon township. Portions of waste might be reclaimed, for exclusive use, only under certain very restrictive rules. But most important parts of the township were the arable lands, which always lay in scattered strips; and in the cultivation of these everybody was bound to conform to the same rules, and the same rotation of crops. The parish was, as it were, one farm occupied and tilled by a group of persons. The individual holdings were not compact, but were spread over the parish in small strips and each farmer farmed his strips according to the method prescribed by common agreement; the ancient English village being virtually a co-operative community. In Handsworth the position of these arable lands of the ancient village community is indicated by known place-names, such as Heathfield, Broomfield, Middlefield, and perhaps in the locality re-named the Birch-field. Field names are often pregnant with meaning, if rightly understood. The unit of arable holding in a village community was the yardland (sometimes also called the virgate); in the same connection was derived the term "Long acre," meaning the long strip of cultivable land allotted to each villager, a not uncommon place-name, as found in Nechells and many other localities.

The system of agriculture was the same, where the village was half servile under a lord, as where it was a village of socmen or other free people. All this was enforced by a common consent which became the "use" of the manor—otherwise the manorial custom or law of the locality. There was no individual ownership of land, either for pasture or cultivation, in early times. But there were rights of use for every one. The Householders elected overseers for every class of work; one man to look after the woods, one to supervise the dykes, another the roads, and so on for every executive office. Similarly they appointed constables, coroners, reeves and other administrative officers.

In fact the unit of the Householder evolved the whole Anglo-Saxon system of government. There was the Folk Mote for the Township, then the Hundred Court, then the Shire Court, and, lastly, the King's Court. The Saxon Manor it will be seen was originally communistic in form, and directly characteristic of a freedom-loving people. The decadence of manorial free institutions may be attributed in large measure to the exigencies of military organisation; the Anglo-Saxons having constantly engaged in internecine wars till such time they had united themselves into one nation; and then finding themselves called upon to fight as constantly for the preservation of that national existence against Danes and Norsemen. The old-world aspect which Handsworth preserved to so late a period, of a village or cluster of dwellings surrounded by a wide margin of common-lands, is traceable to another trait in the character of the Saxon invaders. They disliked and distrusted stone walls and fortifications. To them the breath of freedom was to be found only in the open air. They held all courts of law and public assemblies under the shelter of some mighty tree; and as they disdained walled cities, they surrounded all their "tuns" and villages with a "mark" or very broad belt of open heath. This was the early English substitute for a defensive wall; no stranger might cross it to enter the village without first giving notice of his approach by the blast of his horn, or such approach was tantamount to an act of hostility. But what was of greater importance, no man among them might appropriate any of this land; it remained open and free to all the world, came they in peace. The men of the village collectively had the use of it as free grazing land— such was the origin of our common-lands.

The enclosure of the common lands by which the poor were despoiled for the benefit of the landowners commenced during the Tudor period, but the bulk of the Enclosure Acts were passed in the half-century 1790-1840, the date of the Handsworth Act being 1793. Under these Acts not only these common-lands, or the "lord's waste" as they came to be miscalled, but the common-fields, the communistic arable lands, came to be enclosed and appropriated.

With the advent of the Normans a purely military class arose. Small landowners dropped into a dependent class because they could not afford to bear arms according to the Feudal System. The Township gradually became a Lordship; the town officials became the lord's officers. The Norman based his system on a tenure of land, and thus feudal manors were created where none had existed before. The English Manor, speaking generally, was in its organic fulness in the year A.D 1000; and it held complete sway as the basis of all local government for a thousand years, say from A.D. 500 to the year 1500.

The history of Handsworth as a feudal manor, after the free institutions of its founders had been gradually lost in the development of the amateur militarism of the Middle Ages, will be traced in the succeeding chapters.

*　　*　　*　　*　　*　　*　　*

The name Handsworth is not unique; there is another Handsworth in the West Riding of Yorkshire. To prevent confusion in these bustling times the Post Office authorities now permit "Handsworth, Staffs." to pass as one word in telegraphic communications. Oscott, sometimes spelt Auscott, a hamlet in Perry Barr, obtains its name (according to Mr. Duignan) from Osa, or some Saxon personal name like Oswald; to which is affixed *cot*, the Anglo-Saxon for "cottage." Queeslet, a hamlet in Great Barr, derives its name from *queese*, "a wood-pigeon," and *slade*, "a little valley"; it lies in a hollow and was once probably the haunt of these wild birds.

IV.—HANDSWORTH IN NORMAN TIMES.

Our first real glimpse of Handsworth is obtained from the entry relating to it in the Domesday Book—the great national land register in which the Norman Conqueror took stock of his new dominions. The date of the Domesday survey is 1086; it took twenty years after the Battle of Hastings to consolidate the Norman position in England.

From this great national document we learn that before the Conquest, about the year 1041, Handsworth was an estate divided between two Saxon thanes, Ailverd and Alwin, who are stated to have held it "with sac and soc," in other words, with very extensive powers and jurisdictions over the inhabitants. Not improbably this Alwin was the same who also held the manor of Birmingham at that time, "a thousand summers back," near about the period when lived (as Tennyson has it)

Godiva, wife of that grim Earl who ruled,
In Coventry.

After the Conquest, when William I, had divided the whole of England among same 700 of his chief barons and most loyal supporters, Handsworth is found among other manors in the Hundred of Offlow, forming part of the possessions of William Fitz-Ansculf, the puissant lord of Dudley. As Fitz-Ansculf was seated in his baronial castle at Dudley, Handsworth like his numerous other manors, was let to a tenant. The tenant of Handsworth in 1086, was a vavasor named Drogo, who is stated to have rented one hide of land here. The hide was a variable quantity of land, according to its quality and productiveness; but from the fact that its dimensions are quoted in these terms it is known to have been arable land. In fact a hide was generally about 120 acres, and supposed to be so much cultivable land as would support one family, and employ one plough. The other inhabitants of Handsworth are stated to have been six villeins and four bordars; and taking their families to be of average size, the whole population at that time, might have reached 50 souls at most. It was probably less. The Villeins (a name connected with the words villa and village) were men who held land by a servile tenure, and who owned a little live stock of their own; they paid their rent partly in "kind," and partly in service, being liable to render three days service per week to the lord of the manor (and also at other times for special payment), cultivating their own lands in the remainder of their time.

Though the holding of a villein was never his absolute possession, the enjoyment of it and the passing of it to his heirs, was seldom interfered with, so long as the customary services for it were loyally rendered to the lords of the manor; villeins became customary tenants, in after times known as copyholders, though once on a time called "serfs of the folkland." Reference to the last chapter will show how feudalism gradually usurped most of the rights of communism —how a people originally free became largely servile. The Bordars (or boors they may perhaps be termed) were inferior villeins; they were something like squatters on the land, having been allowed to build their own cottages and cultivate a small patch of land, each in return for the privilege making a small return to the manorial magnate by supplying him with eggs, poultry, and similar small foodstuffs, all of their own produce and sometimes designated "bord."

The Domesday register proceeds to inform us on a number of other points very material to an agrarian community. For instance, we are told there were two ploughs in Handsworth, and naturally enough two carucates of arable land, one of them stated to be "in demesne." A carucate was so much "carved" land as one plough could till; and one of these being in the "domain" of the lord of the manor, or as we should say now-a-days, reckoned in the homefarm, it has to be accounted for outside the hide already mentioned as belonging to Drogo; for the demesne lands were never estimated in hides, but according to the number of "carucae," or plough-teams employed on them. After the arable land ranked the "meadow" land; that is land capable of irrigation and therefore of being mown. Of this there were stated to be 2 acres. Next in enumeration came "a wood half a mile in length and the same in bredth," say 360 acres. Lastly there was a water-mill, turned no doubt by the little stream which now runs through the public park and joins the Tame at Perry Barr, the value of which was estimated at 2 shillings a year, the annual value of the whole manor being set down at 20 shillings, a very desirable estate when the relative values of money, then and now, are taken into consideration. But Drogo, it may be added, also held under William Fitz-Ansculf, the manor of Perry, and an estate in Barr. There were two Domesday Manors of Barr (or Barra). One, now called Great Barr, was associated with, and a sub-tenure of Adridge; the other, Little Barr (Barr Parva) was associated with Perry and Handsworth.

Of the 7,680 acres in Handsworth, less than one half are in Perry Barr; and taking the two carucates as two hundred acres, there remain at least three thousand acres unaccounted for so far. And admitting that a vast area in those times was occupied by the "waste," which served as a mere grazing ground for the cattle of the lord and his tenants, is not this discrepancy too serious to be passed over? Why, the area of the whole manor of Wednesbury, which now constitutes the modern municipal borough, did not exceed 2,000 acres altogether. Has the area of Hamstead been omitted from this entry? Grave errors have been discovered in these Domesday returns.

The Domesday commissioners made their primary reports on loose leaves or rotulets, and these were arranged according to counties and hundreds. In due course these leaves were sent *en masse* to the King's Exchequer to be transcribed and codified by exchequer clerks, who were not the same as had been round the country, and whose lack of topographical knowledge must be held responsible for a large number of inaccuracies.

To take a local illustration; it was thought, till the closer researches of recent years had dispelled the error, that Domesday Book contained no entry relating to West Bromwich. Yet the manor was known to have been held, with Birmingham and Handsworth on one side of it, and Dudley on the other, in the barony of Fitz-Ansculf. But the explanation is simple enough. It would appear that the West Bromwich survey was made in regular form; the loose roll containing it was sent to the government office in London; there it was duly examined, checked, and registered, and then instead of being classified with similar returns like that of Handsworth, in the Hundred of Offlow, in the County of Stafford, it was erroneously kept, along with other rolls relating Fitz-Ansculf's holdings there, among the Northamptonshire returns.

Now, as one would scarcely look for West Bromwich in Northamptonshire, who would think of searching for a moiety of Handsworth in Oxfordshire ? Yet there can be little doubt that the following entry in the Domesday survey of Oxfordshire relates to Handsworth in Staffordshire:

"Land of William, the son of Ansculf, in Dorchestre Hundred—

"William, the son of Ansculf, holds of the King, and Walter of him, five hides in Hunesworde. Land to five ploughs; now in the demesne, two ploughs; eight villeins have one plough and a half. There is a mill of eight shillings, and twenty acres of meadow. It (the manor) was and is worth £4 by the year."

There can be no doubt whatever that this return, which, be it noted, is of a larger and more valuable estate the one correctly scheduled as being the Handsworth of Offlow Hundred, relates to the other portion this manor. The name "Hunesworde" distinctly identifies it; moreover it is in the tenure of the same baron, though who the sub-tenant, Walter, may have been, cannot be hazarded. But it is evident that Handsworth was in two separate manors one held by Drogo, and the other by Walter.

V.—LIFE IN THE MANOR IN THE XII. CENTURY.

From the earliest times, as we have seen, Handsworth was divided into two estates. A century after the Conquest the chief manor, or at, least the one which had given its name to the parish, was held by Peter de Birmingham, house steward to the baron of Dudley. He was called Dapifer, which literally signifies "feast-bearer"; but his office in the baronial household was one of honour and responsibility, and his name or title of Dapifer was as honourably derived as was that of the royal house of Stuart—otherwise "steward."

The other manor was in the tenure of William Fitz-Wido, probably a son of the Wido (or Guido) de Hamstede, mentioned by the county historian, Shaw, as a witness to the frank-marriage (that is, a marriage with gift of land for dower) of Margaret, daughter of Pagan de Parles, and Alice his wife, with Andrew de Bromwich. Of the Parles family more presently; but first of Peter Dapifer.

Peter de Birmingham as his territorial surname stands, was seated at that place, and not in Handsworth. He held altogether nine knights' fees (that is nine separate holdings of land, each accounted sufficient to support and equip a knight for the field); among them, one in Birmingham, one in Perry Barr, a half-fee in Little Barr, another half-one in Handsworth, and one in Oxfordshire, all in the barony of Dudley. Peter had probably acquired his estates by inheritance, because he is found in possession of all his nine fees in 1135, when he was quite a young man. When Civil War broke out in Stephen's reign, through the Empress Maud claiming the throne, Peter doubtlessly followed the fortunes of his overlord, Ralph Paganel, baron of Dudley, a supporter of the Empress. It was then he erected his "castle" at Birmingham. "a bowshot west of the church"; and we may picture him during these troublous times, as Paganel's leading knight and most powerful vassal, keeping a tight rein on the neighbouring knights who held Edgbaston and Handsworth; in harrying the surrounding manors held by men of the opposite faction; making hasty levies of his lord's Staffordshire retainers for the garrisoning of Nottingham castle, of which stronghold Maud had made Paganel the governor; and leading generally that life of warlike excitement and constant danger men of his calibre were inured to.

After Stephen's death, when Maud's son had succeeded to the throne as Henry II., that King among other favours, granted to Peter the right of "free warren" in both Birmingham and Handsworth; that is, at a time when hunting rights were valuable and strictly guarded (particularly on the outskirts of the royal Forest of Cannock) he was given the privilege of taking the smaller game on his own land. He might chase the, hares and conies with his dogs, and fly his hawks at the pheasants and partridges; and in such pleasurable pursuits was no doubt often to be seen riding forth from his gates, and taking his way in a northerly direction across the "coney-gre" of Birmingham; or farther afield over the wide moorlands of Handsworth.

It was Gervase Paganel, the successor of Ralph, who in 1166 made Peter his "dapifer"; and as holder of this honourable and responsible position as head of his lord's retinue, he would be almost constant in his attendance at Dudley Castle during the ten or a dozen years he held it. It will be noted he was never at any time resident on his Handsworth manor. Of a resident lord on the manor of Handsworh no record exists for a century after the name of Drogo (? or Walter) is recorded as such in the Domesday Book. About the close of the reign of Henry II. Pagan de Parles is found in possession of the manor, and about 1194 he seems to have erected a substantial manor house and resided in it. Two brothers, Baldwin de Parles and Pagan de Parles, presumably Normans, married two English sisters and coheiresses; Juliana the elder, brought to her husband, Baldwin, the manor of Great Rollright, Oxfordshire, which was in the barony of Stafford; Agnes, the younger, bringing to Pagan as her portion, the Staffordshire estate of Handsworth, held under the great feudal baron of Dudley In 1194 the Paganels were succeeded in the barony of Dudley by the Somerys, and according to Dugdale's "Warwickshire," Pagan de Parles held Handsworth under a grant from Roger de Somery, baron of Dudley.

The site selected by Pagan de Parles for his manor house was certainly not that occupied by the building known as Handsworth Hall demolished late in the last century, and which gave its name to Hall Road. Not improbably it was on the site occupied by the old Rectory, close to the church, and now included in the Victoria Public Park. Its moat could have been fed by the little stream which still trickles through the hollow there. We know it had a moat, and that this moat was spanned by a drawbridge, because of an incident recorded as occurring there in 1270, about a century after the place had been built, and when one William de Parles had succeeded to the manor.

The incident referred to, which well illustrates a phase of life at that distant period, is worth recounting. It would appear that the drawbridge which formed the defensive entrance to Handsworth Manor House was insecure, or in some way out of proper working order; and a man named John Eleford fell from it into the water and was drowned. The procedure of the law in such cases of sudden or violent death was peculiar. The "first-finder" of the dead body was attached; if any one fled he was suspected; and suspicion lay all around till the coroner's inquest had cleared the air. In this case it was reported that the first-finder was dead—it may be readily understood that it was inconvenient, if not actually dangerous to be the first-finder of a dead body. The next point to be dealt with, was the actual instrument by which a sudden death, accidental or otherwise, was brought about. If a cart-wheel went over a man and killed him, the wheel was called "deodand," or the cause of death, and as such it was valued, and its value had to be paid by the owner as a fine to the king.

In this Handsworth case the jury brought in a verdict of misadventure; accounted the drawbridge of William de Parles' "deodand," and valued it at three shillings. It is difficult to convey any accurate conception of the actual and relative values of money at that time; but it is manifest that the drawbridge had been wilfully undervalued, perhaps in fear of the overbearing and unscrupulous lord of Handsworth. The rolls of a higher court have it left on record that in consequence of the jury having falsely appraised the deodand, all the "vills" from which the offending jurors were drawn, namely, Onesworth (so Handsworth is spelt in this instance), Perry, Harborne and Bromwich, were all heavily fined. And this was another way in which the law at that time endeavoured to make persons and communities mutually dependent upon each other for the preservation of order; to make each man feel a definite responsibility for the good behaviour and integrity of his neighbour.

There was a somewhat similar case in 1292, in which a man killed himself in his own house at Handsworth. The first-finder presented himself, was not suspected, and a verdict of "Felonia de se" was returned. But again the Handsworth jury undervalued the goods, and were accordingly fined.

It may safely be assumed that Handsworth was not the only seat of this family; and that the Parles's lived sometimes on one manor, sometimes on another. The retinue of such a mansion would include house-cleaners, seamstresses, breweresses, a cook, a baker, and other indoor domestics. The farm servants would consist mainly of carters and farriers, while the bulk of the farm work would be done by the rent-labour of the numerous born-serfs or bondsmen of the manor; men who had no choice but that of abiding on their native soil from the cradle to the grave, and rendering so much bodily service to their feudal lord for the privilege of living. Perhaps they were not overworked, nor deprived of their hours of recreation; but they were serfs none the less. Over every one of them the lord practically held full and complete sway; they were his servants in time of peace. his soldiers in time of war—

> Every vassal of his banner
> Every serf born to his manor
> All these wronged and wretched creatures

—in fact, every dependent inhabitant of Handsworth he held in the hollow of his hand, almost to the arbitrament of life and death.

A more privileged class of confidential domestic would include the huntsman and the falconer. For among the strong and straggling outbuildings of Handsworth's ancient manor house not the least important would be stables for the horses, mews for the hawks, and kennels for the hounds. Everything out of doors was in the hands of a bailiff, who was responsible for production; all indoors was controlled by a house-steward, who accounted for the consumption of his master's substance. When the household migrated the bailiff of the manor was left in charge of everything upon it. Bread was baked every Saturday. The neighbouring stream provided trout and the moat or fish-stews supplied eels, salmon in its proper season might sometimes be sent from somewhere on Severn-side. The only sea-fish procurable at a place far inland would be salted stock-fish. Even fresh meat was to be had only for about half of the year, because root crops and other winter fodder were as yet unknown to the English agriculturist. So it came about every November that the salting tubs of the household were filled with every variety of flesh to be preserved for winter consumption, sheep and swine particularly being salted down, with the necessary salt brought from Droitwich. The hides so largely produced at this great Martinmas slaughtering were tanned after a very rude manner; parchment and vellum, too, were sometimes prepared; while all the superfluous fat of the beasts was converted into home-made candles. This brief outline will perhaps give some faint conception of life as it was lived in Handsworth during the twelfth and thirteenth centuries.

A feature in the life of this period was the scarcity of money. A coinage was scarcely needed; the simple life led by the common people enabled them to produce all the necessaries; and luxuries were unknown among them. From this feature may be traced the origin of those quaint tenures so characteristic of mediæval transactions. A little later than the period just dealt with some Handsworth lands were held by the tenure of rendering a pair of gilt spurs every year; in another transaction a Handsworth landed proprietor remitted his claim to a mill at Rushall, not for so many pounds, shillings, and pence, but for a Sparrow-hawk.

VI.—SIR WILLIAM DE PARLES, THE IMPERIOUS LORD OF HANDSWORTH.

So far as the fitful pictures can be discerned through so great a distance of time, there emerge from the half-lights and hazy shadows of musty 13th century records, a series of scenes, of which Handsworth forms always the background, typical of the feudal landlordism of the period. In the reign of Henry III. Sir William Parles, knight, was head of his family, and also sub-tenant of Handsworth under the king's tenant-in-chief, the Baron of Dudley. He is stated to have held "the town of Honesworthe," owing "suit to the two great Hundred Courts" for the privilege of holding a free court there outside the jurisdiction of the Sheriff of the county, with the manorial rights of "frank-pledge" and "waif." The Frankpledge was the peace-pledge which every man on a manor had to take, to observe its customs for the promotion of law and order. In the old Saxon police system of mutual responsibility, every man was bound to belong to some manor, hundred or tithing, and every landless man to have a lord to answer for him in the courts of the land. By the right of Waif was meant that goods waived, that is, stolen stuff thrown away by a thief in his escape from the "hue and cry," became the property of the lord of the manor, if the real owner thereof did not come forward to make good his claim, within a year and a day. Lost property and strayed animals, after being cried in the market, or published in the church, might similarly become forfeited to a lord of the manor who possessed this extended privilege. These are but a few of the ancient manorial customs incidental to life in Old Handsworth.

The Parles's held in this vicinity not only Handsworth in Staffordshire, but the contiguous estate of Nechells in Warwickshire. In 1235 a dispute arose concerning the boundary line between Aston in Warwickshire and Handsworth in Staffordshire; whereupon the king ordered the sheriffs of the two counties to hold an inquiry into the matter at Lichfield, on the Sunday next after St. James's day, then and there to swear a jury of twelve discreet and lawful knights to establish the proper line of demarcation; which was accordingly done, but whether the line now running through Lozells was the one then settled upon cannot be authoritatively stated.

It has been said of the Parles family that they were "always at law or at war" with their neighbours; and although they were unquestionably a contentious and turbulent lot, they were probably very little worse than their contemporaries in the same position of life. It would perhaps convey a much truer impression if it were said that the lords of Handsworth were typical of the times in which they lived.

Let it not be forgotten that the age was a comparatively lawless one; the law's delays being so many and vexatious, a man who was at all high-spirited seldom hesitated to take the remedying of his wrongs into his own hands, and forthwith might became right. A resolute man, too, lightly risked the consequences of law-breaking when it was possible to minimise them by intimidation or, as was sometimes done, by subornation. As a matter of fact the rolls of the law courts of the period are full of cases in which the landed gentry of this country figure repeatedly as guilty of overriding their neighbours and infringing tile rights of their fellow-subjects "by force and arms"—this is the phrase that occurs in thousands of pleas for redress.

Of the quarrelsome and litigious nature of William de Parles certainly not a few of the old court rolls have been left to testify. In 1254 he and his wife, accompanied by a number of his more intimate neighbours and supporters to keep him in countenance, went to Weddington and proceeded summarily to eject the parson of that Warwickshire parish from his residence, and then to carry away the unfortunate man's goods and chattels, to the very considerable value of £20. What may have been the merits of this quarrel cannot be judged at this distance of time; but when brought to book in the courts, both William and his wife were unable to offer any effective defence. As befitted his knightly rank the lord of Handsworth was a man of wide interests: that is to say, of landed interests; for then, as practically ever since, the prevalence of land hunger betrays the fact that real estate is the ultimate bed-rock, the source and foundation, of nearly every worldly interest. For though, by the prevailing system of subinfeudation, he held his lands merely as a subtenant under one of the king's tenants-in-chief; and though feudal landholding incurred the liability to bear every burden which at that period the state had to impose; it was manifestly the fierceness of his land hunger which led him so often into the turmoil of the law courts.

Attached to the manorial estate of Handsworth was the advowson of the parish church; and in this interest, probably over a presentation to the living, Sir William de Parles became embroiled with his neighbour, the Prior of Sandwell. If the irascible knight had little respect for the law, he had less for the church: accompanied by his friend, Adam, the lord of Perry, and other supporters of his cause, and with a following of retainers at his back, he proceeded to Sandwell where he encountered the Prior and his men, attacked them with arms and soundly thrashed them, the Prior himself only escaping after a long chase which ended in his barricading himself securely inside the doors of his own monastery (1254).

This piece of ecclesiastical patronage came into the family about 1230, when John de Parles, heir to William de Parles (and father to Sir William) secured it in exchange for a certain "messuage in Birmingham". Disputes arose from time to time over it, usually over the right of presentation. John de Parles, as soon as he became patron, presented the living to "William, his clerk," who was ecclesiastically instituted, and died seventeen years later "Parson of Handsworth." Then the Prior of Lenton made a claim to half the advowson; and as this was "warranted" by no less a personage than the Prior of the Hospital of St. John of Jerusalem in England, the court to which appeal was made, ordered that the rights of presentation should be exercised alternatey by the two claimants.

This decision, fair as it seems, did not put an end to the disputations between the two parties, as was immediately apparent whenever the living fell vacant. John de Parles had presented Hugh de Alvechurch, who was formally instituted, and held the living till his death. Then Sir William de Parles, the successor to John, had the usual wrangle with the Prior of Lenton, and the case was sent for trial; but a special reservation was made that the jury was not to be selected from the Hundred of Offlow, in which De Parles at that time held a preponderating influence. When the case came on for trial, however, the plaintiff Parles withdrew his plea; and a few years later (1279) the Prior of Lenton ceded his half rights in the church of Handsworth to the Dean and Chapter of Lichfield, in lieu of a fine of 1,000 marks imposed upon him for "spoiling" the tithes of Peak. To make this account of the advowson less disconnected, the life story of Sir William has been somewhat overrun; and, while dealing with matters ecclesiastical, it may be added that a very similar grant between the same two parties (the Prior and the Chapter) had been made 20 years previously; and also that for 10 years at least the Dean and Chapter had been in receipt of "pensions" from the churches of Handsworth and Harborne.

Going back a few years, to the outbreak of the Civil War (1264) the waspish nature of Sir William de Parles was seen in the attitude he assumed during that disturbed period. It was quite to be expected of him that he should array himself with the rebel barons against Henry III., particularly as his own superior, the baron of Dudley, remained loyal to the King,

> When face to face, and limb to limb,
>   And sword with sword inwoven.
> That stubborn courage of the race
>   On Evesham field was proven.

When the Baron's War was over, and every Handsworth man who survived the campaign had got back to his home again, De Parles was punished for his defection. He was deprived of his manor of Handsworth, the confiscated property being handed over to Roger de Clifford; and worse than this, while Sir William was languishing in the prison of his outraged suzerain, Roger de Somery, at Dudley, he was forced under pain of torture, to sign a deed divesting himself of many other rights. This nefarious practice came to light when, a year or two later, the restored De Parles contested the cutting down of his woods in Handsworth by virtue of the fraudulently obtained document; or at least, it was fraud which the indignant lord of Handsworth alleged.

That William de Parles was fully restored to the royal favour would appear from the fact that Henry III. not only re-instated him in the possession of Handsworth, but granted him (1275) superior rights in the whole Hundred of Offlow. Again he seems to have abused his trust. In the succeeding reign of Edward I, the Sheriff of Staffordshire declared De Parles to be disobedient to the King's precept, which he said could not be carried out in the Hundred. The Sheriff stated that Sir William had arrogated to himself the perquisites of the View of Frankpledge, and the Sheriff's Tourn, which were worth 100 shillings a year, and a loss accrued to the royal revenue by that amount. De Parles denied that he had appropriated the Sheriff's Tourn (the right to hold a Criminal Court in the Hundred twice a year) while as to the View of Frankpledge, it was customary, he said, to render the King the fixed sum of 20s. 6d for it.

Another serious broil into which Sir William de Parles was drawn related to the custody of a ward named Hamon FitzHamon, who lived in his guardian's house at Northampton. Many very substantial rights accrued to a feudal guardianship, involving the forfeiture of some of the ward's property to the guardian, if the ward failed to comply with certain legalised requirements of his properly appointed custodian. It almost appears as if the youth had not been so compliant as his strong-willed guardian thought he had a right to expect from a minor. It may be the youth had refused to marry the lady which it had been to the best interests of his legal custodians to provide for him; the upshot of the affair was a double attack made by the family and connections of the young man upon the property and authority of the autocratic Sir William de Parles. As if by concerted action one party under Hamon of Wyleston and William of Arden made an armed raid on the Handsworth mansion, carrying away with them a large amount of valuable property; while another party, led by other knightly sympathisers marched to Sir William's house at Northampton and abducted his ward, Hamon Fitz Hamon, who was evidently kept as a prisoner there.

The other William de Parles, ancestor of Sir William, had in 1208, laid claim in the courts of law to a similar wardship, with all its accompanying perquisites, of William de Rushall; and this litigant in a case which came on three years later, contended with all his might for a jury of Staffordshire knights—the significance of all which cannot fail to be apprehended in the light of what has gone before.

It will have been noticed in passing that Sir William had another residence in Northamptonshire; while in a suit of the year 1224 the former William de Parles is recorded to have been resident in Warwickshire.

Trouble, most of it of his own seeking, accumulated so heavily upon the head of the doughty knight of Handsworth that by 1265 he had fallen irrecoverably into the hands of the Jews. Sampson, a usurious Hebrew of

Lichfield, being himself unable to recover from the debtor, with the king's permission sold the debts to Sir William's overlord, Roger de Somery, who by virtue of the King's writ and in due process of law, took possession of the manor of Handsworth and all the goods and chattels upon it, which had been given in pledge for these debts. The fiery spirited bankrupt did not submit to all this quite tamely for with the aid of his son John and his staunch friend and neighbour, the Lord of Perry, he organised a raid on his forfeited property; and one dark night in the year 1271 he broke into the Park at Handsworth, and drove off sixty head of cattle. For this daring exploit Sir William de Parles was promptly arrested by the Sheriff, and cast into prison. On emerging from prison a man of broken fortunes a splendid opportunity for the repair of those fortunes seemed to present itself in the possibilities offered by the new Crusade which was just then being vigorously organised. So joining himself to this, the seventh and last great expedition to the Holy Land, he left England in 1271 determined to make the most of his opportunities. This purposeful enterprise being followed with more success than strict honesty, it was not long before his career was brought to a sudden stop by a charge of felony, for which this bold and adventurous knight was incontinently hanged (1277). A life of lawlessness and turbulence terminated by a malefactor's death! The ignominy of such an end was realised even by Ancient Pistol at the Battle of Agincourt, who when his friend the bragging Bardolph was ordered to execution for robbing a church, exclaimed—

> A damned death!
> Let gallows gape for dog, let man go free,
> And let not hemp his windpipe suffocate;
> And let not . . . vital thread be cut
> With edge of penny cord, and vile reproach.

VII.—MEDIÆVAL WAR TAXES COLLECTED IN HANDSWORTH.

When the news of Sir William de Parles' death by summary execution at the hands of a provost marshall at last reached England, Roger de Somery, the Baron of Dudley, proceeded to act on the principle that the property of a felon is forfeited; he therefore took the manor of Handsworth into his own hands after the usual lapse of a year and a day. A claimant for the sub-tenure of the manor promptly appeared in the person of John de Parles who, though a son of the felon Sir William, preferred to make his claim through hereditary descent from Agnes, the original heiress who brought the property into the Parles' family by her marriage. Prolonged litigation followed, John trying to strengthen his claim by asserting that the manor had been conveyed to him as a gift by Sir William in his life time and before his conviction as a felon.

Matters were complicated in 1291 by the death of Roger de Somery, who was succeeded in the barony by his son and heir, John, a boy 12 years of age, and in wardship; when the manor of Handsworth, together with Weoley in Worcestershire, and another estate in Berkshire, went to dower his widow, Agnes. As to the Parles' family no member of it ever again resided in Handsworth after the notorious Sir William; nor indeed was there ever any other resident lord of the manor, for Handsworth was subsequently retained in the hands of the superior lords. It may be mentioned that while Agnes de Somery was in possession of this estate, she was summoned to attend the Coronation of Edward II. in 1308, shortly after which she died. John de Somery, her son, became a gallant warrior; and though a "baron bold" who added to the defences of his Castle at Dudley, he too had presently to succumb in his fight with the King of Terrors—

> In this fight was Death the gainer
> Spite of vassal and retainer,
> and the lands his sires had plundered,
>   Written in the Domesday Book.

He died, the last of his line, in 1322, his lands being divided between his two sisters, Handsworth with Warley, Northfield and Weoley fell to Joan. Joan was the widow of John de Botetort, and as their chief seat was Weoley Castle, Handsworth Manor fell into desuetude, and gradually into decay.

In the year 1300 John de Parles was in the law courts complaining that he had been unjustly dispossessed of his manor of Handsworth by Agnes de Somery; at the same time he was suing the Prior of St. John of Jerusalem, presumably for the advowson of the church, pertaining to the said manor. Little more transpires with regard to the Parles family, whose chief seat was in Northamptonshire. There is a record that John de Parles did hold one-fifth of a Knight's fee in Handsworth in the time of Edward I., although in 1327 the manor had again been seized by the superior lord, and litigation for its possession was continued (1341) by Walter de Parles, the son of John. Ralph de Parles is named as in possession of Handsworth in 1384, and the last male of this line to hold the property was John de Parles, whose daughter and heiress, carried it, in the time of Henry VI., to her husband John Comberford, the son of her guardian.

The participation of Sir William de Parles in a Crusading expedition, was not the only influence the Wars of the Cross had upon Handsworth and its history. During the Middle Ages the papal Exchequer received regular contributions from the English Church in the shape of "first-fruits," otherwise the first year's income from ecclesiastical benefices or church livings; and again in the shape of "tenths." In 1288 the spirited foreign policy of Pope Nicholas IV. induced him to grant the tenths to Edward I., for a period of six years, towards defraying the expenses of a Crusade; it was the papal ambition to fire men with the belief that

> The brave who sleep in soil of thine
> Die not entombed, but shrined, O Palestine.

No Crusading was done, but the exactions were made all the same. In order that the tenths might be collected at their full value, the king caused a Roll to be prepared which took three years to complete; and so well was the work done it has served as the basis of many taxings ever since 1291. An excellent copy of this Roll is preserved in the Chapter House at Lichfield. The "Valor Ecclesiasticus" held good for all taxes due from benefices, both to our kings, and to the popes, and regulated all such payments till the Reformation (1536). Then the "first-fruits" and "tenths" ceased to be forwarded to Rome, and were transferred to the Crown; in 1700 these receipts were appropriated to the augmentation of poor livings, and formed into the fund now known as Queen Anne's Bounty—a more righteous diversion of public moneys than often takes place.

Let us see how Handsworth was taxed for this proposed Crusade. Reckoning the mark at 13s. 4d., it will be seen the decima or "tenth" to be paid was exactly as moneyed out, in the second column, from the assessable value of the living at 21 marks. A transcription of the entry of 1291 appears thus—

Decimal

Hunnesworth..........xxi *marc* ....*ii*. marc x vi. *d.*

A few years later new War taxes were levied; no pretensions to a "holy war" this time, but the rousing of patriotism and the loosing of purse-strings were effected by the time-honoured device of an invasion scare. Whether the danger was real, or whether the invasion was to be provoked, matters not here; it is more to the purpose of this work that the collecting of these taxes gives us an insight into the social and economic life of Handsworth at that time.

When the throne of England was ascended by the youthful Edward III. in 1327, the Scots determined to take advantage of his minority to invade England. The danger was immediately countered by the English Parliament granting the king a subsidy to carry on a war of national defence. This subsidy was a tax assessed at the value of one-twentieth of the movable goods in every household; and the fact that villeins were taxed equally with the freemen (wherever the movable property could be assessed at not less than 10s) indicates the gradual emancipation of the serf. Assessors were appointed and sworn in every parish, and bearing in mind that Parliament had made certain exemptions, we get an idea from this return of the numbers and status of the inhabitants of every town and village in the country. The exemptions from taxation were characteristic of the times. In an age when the army of national defence was supported solely by those who held the land, to exempt armour and cavalry horses was perfectly justifiable; but when the plate and the robes and jewels of gentlemen and their dames had also been exempted from this taxation, it was attempted to balance this class privilege by allowing all agricultural implements, and the tools of workmen, to go free, though how any balance could possibly be struck on an *ad valorem* basis, it is difficult to divine. The list shows that 12 persons paid the tax in this manor:—

HONESWORTHE,

	s.	d.	
De Joh'a Botetort	ij	vj.	
Hugone at Atteberge	iij		
Joh'e del Squier		xviij.	
Joh'e del Bredeheth	iij	vj,	
Will'o Coco	ij	vj.	
Agnet Attenbrugg-ende	iiij	vj.	
Joh'e Atte water	ij	vi.	
Joh'e le Westerne	iiij		
Sibilla del Heth	iij		ob. qu.
Steph'o Monnyng	ij	vij.	ob. qu.
Will'o Coco	ij	vj.	
Will'o atte putte	ij	ix	ob.
Summa	xxxiiij	viij.	Pb.

The account is correctly cast to 34s. 8d., and the total (or "summa") is carefully audited (pb. being the abbreviation of "probata" or proven; "ob." the short method of expressing "obolus" or halfpenny; and "qu." that of indicating the "quarter" or farthing). The 12 inhabitants of Handsworth in a position to be taxed may be compared with—

75 persons in Birmingham taxed to the amount of			...		£7	0	6
11 ,, ,, Perry	...	...	...	...	...	...	1	17	2
14 ,, ,, Erdington ...	...	...	...	...	...	1	11	3
9 ,, ,, Aston	...	...	...	...	...	...		14	11
5 ,, ,, Witton	...	...	...	...	...	...		19	2

The comparison is interesting as showing the importance of Perry Barr. This manor lay just outside the boundaries of the Forest of Cannock and the Chase of Sutton; it was well watered and well wooded, was favourable for cultivation, had several water-mills, and lay on the Ryknield Street which gave it easy communications with the surrounding country.

Now to examine the names of the Handsworth list of taxpayers. The scribes, after the fashion of the time, have attempted to Latinise and contract the Christian names, but have been discreet enough not to make the same attempt on the good English surnames. It will be noted that Joan Botetort, although she heads the list as the King's tenant-in-chief, is not the largest taxpayer in this particular vill; the explanation is that she was scarcely ever resident in Handsworth, and the manor house would therefore be poorly equipped and furnished. Hugh de Atteberge came of a substantial family; in 1312 Thomas de Attelbergh and his servant were both feloniously slain in Handsworth; and in 1321 Roger, "the parson of the church of Handsworth" was administering his estate as the appointed executor.

John the Squire may possibly have been the founder of the Squire family so long resident in Handsworth at Ley Hall; John at the Broad Heath, Agnes at the Bridge-end, John at the Water, Sibyl at the Heath, and William at the Pit, all derived their names from the quarter of the parish in which they resided. Sibyl Heath (as we nowadays should more tersely put her name) is described as Sibyl de Hondesworth when in 1332 she paid her next war subsidy as a resident of Essington. The Cook family are represented by two householders, both bearing the same Christian name, William.

It is noteworthy that there is no list for Hamstead, although there is one for Barr, and another for "Pyrie et Parva Barre" The name of John de Perry heads the latter, that of John de Barr coming second, followed presently by a Richard de Perry, who is the largest taxpayer. Allusion to Hamstead is made in the returns of the previous Scotch War; that of Edward II. who marched into Scotland only to meet with disastrous defeat at Bannockburn (1314), from which returns it appears that William de Hamsted and Robert de Hamsted were serving in this campaign under the banner of their superior lord, John de Somery, baron of Dudley, and during their absence from England on active service had Letters of Protection—writs issued by the king to protect them and their property from legal process, which implies that personal actions were then pending against them in the courts.

Six or seven years after the Subsidy of 1327 the goods of the commonalty were assessed on almost similar lines for the expenses of another Scotch expedition; the exemptions including one robe for each man and each woman, and also their bed. The tax in towns and cities was levied at one-tenth. while in vills and parishes outside the towns it was only one-fifteenth. The Subsidy Roll of 1332 for this manor now included only 11 taxpayers—

HONNESWORTHE.

	s.	d.	
De Joh'na Botytourt	v	iiij	ob.
Rob'to de Wyrley	iiij		
Joh'ne fil' Henrici	iiij		ob.
Joh'ne Atte hull	iij	iiij	qu.
Joh'ne Otheheeth	ij	x	ob.
Steph'o Mounynge	iiij	vj.	
Guyd Alewyne	iiij		
Rob'to Atte venue	v		
Rog'o le Kokes	ij		
Will'o le Kokes	iiij		
Will'o Moldun	iiij		

Joan Botetort paid for the "capital messuage", of Handsworth; Robert de Wyrley, a scion of the knightly house of Hamstead, appears as resident in this manor, while the name of his father, John de Wyrley, is found in the Perry and Little Barr schedule paying as much as John de Perry, lord of that manor; there being no mention of Hamstead in any list. Of the names which appeared in the former list, we note the recurrence in 1332 of William the Cook (spelt "le Kokes," although the Anglo-Norman form was "Cocus"), Stephen Mouning, and John Heath. Of the new taxpayers William Moldun was probably the miller; John had his residence on the Hill; and Robert dwelt near the venu or village recreation ground. Guy Alwyn seems to be of Saxon extraction, and John the son of Henry we should nowadays dub John Harrison.

The taxpayers got something for their money, if military glory may be taken into account. At the battle of Halidon Hill, the Regent Douglas, four earls, the prime of the Scottish nobility, and 30,000 Scotsmen were left dead upon the field; and in the following year (1334) the warlike Edward III. received the submission of Scotland.

> Nor mountain targe of tough bull-hide
> Nor lowland mail, that storm may bide—
> Woe, woe to Scotland's bannered pride!

VIII.—HANDSWORTH DOMINATED BY THE SEIGNIORY OF HAMSTEAD.

Here it will be useful to go back, for a moment, to the death of Handsworth's superior lord in 1291. When a baron or any holder of feudal lands died, there was always an Inquisition into the amount of territory for which he was responsible to the King in the scheme of national defence. The inquiry into the extent and value of the great barony of Roger de Somery was a piece of business that extended itself into several counties, but we are concerned here only with that relating to Handsworth. This particular inquest was made 30 November, 1291 before a local jury which included Thomas de Attelberge, John de Barre, and one John Turnpeny Wido described as "of the Head of the Bridge," and who declared on their oaths that the Manor of Handsworth was holden as the fourth-part of a Knight's fee, and was of the total annual value of £23 19s. 10d. This amount was made up, among other items, of the "chief edifice" worth 12d., one carucate of plough-land 30s., and meadow 6s. The herbage "in severalty," that is, of which he was the sole tenant, was worth 10s., and a fishery 12d. The sale of underwood in the park of Handsworth was worth, "if cut without waste," 20s.; the herbage of the said park was valued at 20s. Among the remunerative Franchises of the manor, the rents or revenues derived from freeholders and copyholders at the Assizes were valued at £11 8s. 6d. a year, the Pleas and other perquisites of the Courts adding 13s. 4d. more. The Advowson of the parish was set down as being worth 30 marks (a mark was a silver coin then in use of the value of 13s 4d.)

Almost immediately upon coming into possession of this particular dower portion, Agnes de Somery took steps towards improving the value of the property; for 1293 she laid claim to a number of valuable franchises in Handsworth. She claimed the right to hold Pleas of the Crown (a kind of limited criminal jurisdiction), Gallows, Waif, Free Warren, Fairs and Markets. A jury of the Hundred of Offlow before whom the case was tried, declared that the warrant for holding such feudal privileges was unknown.

Whatever precedent there may have been for holding some of these franchises, it is certain there was none for markets and fairs; for at no period of its history has Handsworth ever been a market town.

As the right to erect Gallows for carrying out the extreme penalty upon convicted criminals, it is interesting to note that the lord of Little Barr and several other landlords in the vicinity made similar claims at this period, and in most cases failed to substantiate them. The right of Free Warren had undoubtedly been exercised (as we have seen) by Peter Dapifer, and that this right together with that of Waif was revived may be gathered from the record of what took place more than half a century later.

A successor of Agnes de Somery (John Botetort) being then in possession, Henry de Morwode, the parson of Handsworth, was attached on a charge of forcibly breaking in the Free Warren of that place, in the year 1362, and taking a number of hares and rabbits; and also with taking a strayed mare on the same estate, which the lord of the manor (Botetort) claimed as a Waif. The parson in defence proved that the mare was his, that it had been stolen from him, and then allowed to stray; and he denied altogether the charge of trespassing in pursuit of game. The proceedings in this case were exceedingly prolonged, and a fresh charge was brought against the parson that he had broken into the Park at Handsworth (Botetorts) and taken thence a number of bucks and does. The deer stealing was apparently proved against the defendant, and a fine of 10 marks imposed for it. The reputation of this clerical gentleman could not have stood very high in the neighbourhood, as in 1369 he was compelled to prosecute Roger Wyrley of Hamstead and John Dymmok of "Wennesbyrie" (Wednesbury) because, as he alleged, they had conspired to have him falsely indicted for another felony.

As indicated above, the overlordship of Handsworth had in the meantime passed from the Somery family to the Botetorts. This was on the death of John de Somery in 1322, when the manor with other large possessions went to Joan, his second sister and a coheir, she being at that time the widow of Thomas Botetort, of Weoley Castle. Handsworth on this occasion was returned as being of the annual value of £24 11s. 4¼d. Joan Botetort had to go to law in 1330 to recover the right of presentation to the Handsworth living from the Dean and Chapter of Lichfield. On the death of Magister Hugh de Alvechurch, the Prior of Lenton had presented John de Derby. This rector resigned the living during the time Roger de Somery was in possession of the manor (to which the half advowson was legally appurtenant) through the felony of Sir William de Parles, and the baron of Dudley presented William de Hamelton. On the resignation of Magister William de Hamelton, the Dean and Chapter of Lichfield presented Roger de Grutwych to the living of Handsworth; and it was on the death of this cleric that Joan had to substantiate her right to the next presentation.

Although the Botetorts had their demesne in Handsworth, they are not to be found much in residence here. John Botetort lived at Meer, a manor which with Clent, was long linked with that of Handsworth, where only a small establishment was maintained.

The superior-lordship of Handsworth in 1393 passed by hereditary succession from the Botetorts, to a cousin of the family, Sir Hugh Burnell, of Weoley, who held the manor and advowson, together with two other Staffordshire estates, Clent and Mere. We read of Sir Hugh being troubled by the ploughmen of the parish, who were in the habit of breaking into his Park at Handsworth and taking his game (1428). From the Burnell family the manor devolved upon John Butler, Earl of Wilts, a zealous Lancastrian during the Wars of the Roses. Taken after the battle of Towton, attainted and beheaded as a traitor at Newcastle by the victorious Edward IV., his estates were forfeited to that Yorkist monarch, who very appropriately utilised them to reward one who had fought as strenuously on his side. Th.is was Sir Walter Wrottesley, who thus acquired two-thirds of the manor in 1462, with a reversion of the other third on the death of the widow of Fulk Stafford, to whom the property had been previously granted, and who had no issue. The reversion fell in 1466, when the manor and advowson of Handsworth passed entirely into the hands of the Wrottesley family.

From the time of Henry VI to the middle of the Tudor period the manor was held under the Earl of Arundel by the family of the Earls of Ormond, Lady Anne St. Leger, a daughter of that noble house, dying possessed of it in 1553. A portion of the manor, with a mansion known as Bayshall (not a "capital messuage" or manor-house) with some 400 acres of land, a water-mill and an iron-mill called a hammer-mill, constituting 1-30 of a Knight's fee, with a rent of 15s. 8d., a heriot and reliefs, was valued at £6 8s. 0d. a year. In this enumeration, with mention of "hammer- mills" and "heriots," we have a curious blending of modern commercialism and ancient feudalism. Shortly after this, Sir John St. Leger, lord of Bordesley, sold the manor to William Stamford of Gray's Inn.

*　　*　　*　　*　　*　　*　　*

We now turn our attention to the northern portion of the parish which extends itself to the riparian boundary of the River Tame, and is known as Hamstead. Hamstead has practically remained a hamlet to the present day; it derived its name from being the site of the "homestead," or chief seat of the family first settled upon its soil, as suggested in Chapter III. As the story of the place unfolds itself, it will be observed that the centre of gravity, as it were, appears to shift; that while the manor of Handsworth, through absenteeism and the lack of any centre of social life, declines in civic status, Hamstead, on the other hand, rises into importance. It is not the lord of Handsworth who dominates the life of the parish, and whose private chapel and family tombs adorn the parish church; it is the lord of Hamstead.

The earliest family recorded as being seated at Hamstead came from Little Wyrley, and although some of them were at first designated by the territorial title "de Hamstede," the, finally adopted the name "de Wyrley." Robert de Wyrley held Little Wyrley in the time of Henry II.: his grandson, Guy de Wyrley, was also known as Guy de Hamstede; while Guy's son combined both territorial names in the style and title "John de Wyrley, of Hamstead."

When in 1293, that determined monarch, Edward I., was compelling every one of his landed subjects to show by what title they held their lands, and by what rights they exercised any of the rights of feudalism over their tenants and retainers, Thomas de Hamstede (a younger son of the above-mentioned John) forswore all claim to any franchise of manorial lordship in respect of Hamstead; a fact to which attention has been drawn previously. It does not appear that in the earlier generations at least, the head of the family always resided in Hamstead, as the Wyrley's at that time held a large estate at Swynfen. In the twelfth century Thomas de Hamstede gave a portion of a manse in Swynfen to enrich the Prebend of Weeford, and also a number of rents in Lichfield to benefit the cathedral of that city.

The Wyrleys continued to hold Hamstead, generation after generation, acquiring as time went on estate upon estate, till they had not only absorbed all the seignorial rights in Handsworth, but by the period that feudal land-holding had been superseded by absolute landowning, they were amongst the most considerable landowners in the neighbourhood.

The life led by the Wyrleys at Hamstead was not in its earlier period unlike that which has been described of the Parles family; for though not by nature so turbulently disposed as the latter, the Wyrleys were at times not above taking the law into their own hands and righting their wrongs by main force. Holding their estates by military service, and every man on their land being an amateur soldier, there was perhaps some excuse in days of old for such high handed behaviour.

Not only the anomalous tenures by which lands were held, but the numerous rights and privileges which were claimed as appurtenant to such land-holding in feudal times, led to endless law proceedings. To add to the litigious troubles of this family one De Hamstead in the middle of the thirteenth century made two outrageous marriages; the first wife, whom he abandoned because she was found to be within the prohibited degrees of consanguinity, managed to outlive him, and then claiming to be his legitimate widow, sued for a third of the manor of Swynfen as her dower. It was essentially an undisciplined age, in which men frequently gave way to passion, and salved their consciences afterwards by making rich votive offerings to the church

In 1293 Thomas de Hamstede sued William le Mouner (that is "the miller") of Handsworth for a mill in Handsworth which had been left to him by Guy de Swynfen, his grandfather. About a century after this—in 1382, to be precise—John Botetort the overlord was summoned for illegally taking away from a place called Haylond, in Handsworth, four oxen and four cows belonging to Cornelius de Wyrley. The defendant admitted the seizure of the animals, but said Cornelius held certain lands in Handsworth of him by Homage, Fealty, and Scutage (the last-named was a "shield tax" of £3 which a Knight might pay in lieu of rendering military service); by performing service at his Court every three weeks (that is, if called upon—an almost universal method of acknowledging suzerainty); by a Heriot (or death due), namely, the best beast, after the death of every tenant of the tenements so held; and by a rent of 15s. annually. De Wyrley pleaded that he held by Fealty only, and the payment of 7s. 6d. yearly in lieu of all services; and that nothing was in arrear. Sworn evidence of this kind is useful as showing the nature of the tenure by which such estates were held. Cornelius de Wyrley is described as "of Handsworth", his father, Eudo de Wyrley, is described as "of Handsworth, Hamstead, Barr, and Oscott." The numerous family deeds printed in Shaw's "History of Staffordshire" show that the Wyrleys at one time or other, were in possession not only of Handsworth and the three Barrs, but of the adjoining estates of Witton and Aston (both described as in "Colefield" which, therefore, identifies the latter as Little Aston) Hillehoe in Sutton, the manor of Tipton, and a manor in Leicestershire.

At the commencement of Elizabeth's reign William Wyrley, Esq., died possessed of "Handsworth manor, or capital messuage, called Wyrley's Hall; another messuage called Hallford, held of Robert Stanford, Esq., by fealty; two watermills, with a pool and moor and a fishery in the Tame; four cottages, 300 acres of land, 40 of meadow, 500 of pasture, 40 of wood, 100 of heath, all valued at £15 19s. 4d. A moiety of the manors of Perry Barr, Hamstead and Oscote; 4 water-mills called Blade mills; 12 messuages, 10 cottages, 200 acres of land, 40 of meadow, 300 of pasture, 100 of wood, and 20s in rent, held of the Queen, *in capite*, and worth altogether £26 7s. 6d. Likewise the Manor of Tipton," etc., etc. A chancery suit was tried about this time before the great Lord keeper, Sir Nicholas Bacon, in the matter of a claim to the tithes of Handsworth by the Wyrleys.

IX.—THE WYRLEY AND WYRLEY-BIRCH FAMILIES.

By 1561, in the spacious times of Queen Elizabeth, the Wyrleys had given their own name to the chief seat in Handsworth, where they were the chief tenants of the Crown; and they were deriving a considerable portion of their wealth from the rising hardware industries of the district, through their proprietorship of water-mills profitably engaged in the iron trade.

William Wyrley was "buried under a fair monument in Handsworth Church," which also commemorates his wife, Elizabeth, a sister to Sir Ambrose Cave, a former Chancellor of the Duchy of Lancaster. It is an interesting monument of the Elizabethan period, which has been thus described by Shaw: "On an altar tomb of free stone, a man in the same kind of armour as the former (namely, plated like scales on the arms, and like flounces on the body), in hard blue stone; and gauntlets, hair cropt, bare headed, lion at feet looking up, sword and dagger, crest on a helmet; a women by him in a close cap, ruff, long sleeves, close gown, dog under her feet."

The son and heir of William was Thomas Wyrley! to whom allusion is probably made in this inscription upon the tomb: "Here lyeth buried the bodies of Thomas Wyrley, Esquier, and Dorothy, his wife, daughter of Hugh Harmon, Esquier; the said Thomas died in March, Anno Domini 1583, and the said Dorothy in January, 1597, and they had ten sons and eleven daughters between them". The alliance with the Harman (or Vesey) family, of Moor Hall , Sutton Coldfield. is interesting—the benefactor of Sutton, Vesey, Bishop of Exeter, being brother to the said Hugh Harman.

Of the Stamford family, of Perry Hall, some particulars will be given in a subsequent chapter; in the meantime note must be taken of a Bond given in 1583 by Robert Staunford (or Stamford), Esquire, of Perry Barr, to the above-named Thomas Wyrley, on the close of an arbitration in a law suit between them. The Bond runs—

"4 February 25 Elizh. (1583).—Know all men by these presents That I Robert Staunford of Puryhall in County Stafford Esquire am held and firmly bound to Thomas Wyrley of Hampstead in said County Staff. Esquire in £100," &c., &c.

The condition is that "if Robert Staunford do perform and fulfil &c. all such award Arbitrament &c. of Edward Leighe Edward Holte Clement Fisher and Richard Reppington Esquires Arbitrators indifferenty elected upon all manner of causes quarrells suites &c. &c. and now depending in variance from the beginning of the world to the present time &c then these presents shall he void &c. ROBERT STAUNFORD.

"Sealed and delivered to Edward Henstote to the use of Thomas Wyrley Esq. in the presence of Thomas Selman William Bothe John Stoneley Edward Henstot and Henry Worsey."

Another memorial inscription in Handsworth Church threw further light on the family pedigree of the Wyrleys. It was on a flat stone of alabaster, with portraitures cut in black lines, of a man in plated armour, ruff, helmet under his head, a lion looking up at his feet; and of a woman lying on a tasseled cushion, in a veil head-dress, flowing gown, and laced petticoat; the words round the verge being:—"Here lyeth buried the bodys of John Wyrley, Esquier, and Goodith, his wife, daughter of Humphrey Peyto, Esquier; the said John died in February Anno Domini 1594, and the said Goodith in November 1622, they had between them eleven sons and seven daughters." John Wyrley was succeeded in the Hamstead Estate by his son Humphrey, in 1594.

There is extant an interesting Deed of the year 1646. relating to the Wyrley possessions in Great Barr, worded thus—

"10 November 22 Charles.—Indenture of Lease Humfrey Wyrley of Hampsteed Esq. to John Belcher of Hounsworth gent. and Judith his wief of All Messuage or Mansion House commonly knowen by the name of the Motte House with the orchard gardens yaords &c. Also those two leasowes pastures and grounds called the Lawrence feildes the Lawrence Hill feilde the well crofte the orchard feilde the Chappell feilde with meadow thereunto the rough Marrians the playne Marrians the ground called the great flaxalls and lyttle flaxalls &c. scituate lyinge and beinge in Great Barre &c. if Humfrey shall so long live and John and Judith or either of them shall be then lyvinge. To pay £33 6s. 8d. and the chief Rent to the Lordes or Lord of the fee and also two good Capons at the feaste of All Saynts and two good henns upon the 8th day of January yearly. "Covenants as to maintaining mounds ditches and fences and as to manuring, tilling, ploughing, &c.

Humphrey Wyrley for his second wife married a connection of the family, Knightley Wyrley by name: and in due time he was succeeded by the eldest son of this marriage. This son was John Wyrley, knighted at Whitehall in 1641, by Charles I.

Sir John Wyrley was accounted a very "learned gentleman," proud of his ancestry, and always a staunch Royalist. In 1685, when all the non-conforming Governors of King Edward's School, Birmingham, were ousted under a charter newly granted by James II., he and his neighbour, Sir Henry Gough, of Perry, were placed upon the "reformed" governing body of that institution, to act under the congenial chairmanship of Sir Charles Holte, of Aston Hall. When Sir John died, in 1687, at the ripe age of 80, leaving no issue, he was succeeded by his nephew, Humphrey Wyrley, whose father had been a prothonotary in the Court of Common Pleas.

Of the four children of Humphrey, two died unmarried; the other two, daughters, introduce new names and new interests into the history of Handsworth. Mary married Captain John Lane, of Bentley, grandson of the celebrated Royalist Colonel who saved the life of Charles II. after the battle of Worcester, the other, Sybil, married the Rev. Peter Birch, D.D., a prebendary of Westminster, and a member of an ancient Lancashire family. The Rev. Peter and Sybil Birch had two sons. Humphrey, the elder, adopted the ancient name of Wyrley, and died unmarried in 1746. The estate then devolved upon his brother John, who also adopted the name of Wyrley, and though he married twice, taking as his first wife Knightley Wroth, and for his second Jane, eldest daughter of the aforementioned John and Mary Lane, he too died childless; whereupon the estate passed by will to a distant relative, George Birch (son of Judge Birch), of Harborne. John Wyrley-Birch was buried at Handsworth, 1775.

This branch of the Birch family were long landowners and residents in Harborne. In the old church there was a quaint epitaph to Thomas Birch and Sarah his wife——

A greabler couple could not be,
Whatever pleased he, always pleased she.

The manor of Harborne which the family had acquired in 1710, was sold by George Birch soon after his marriage into the Wyrley family and on his becoming possessed of the manor of Handsworth and the joint lordship of Perry Barr. Esther, daughter of Judge Birch, married the Rev. Thomas Lane, rector of Handsworth.

At the close of the eighteenth century the manor of Handsworth was sold to the Earl of Dartmouth; and the Wyrley-Birches now reside at Wretham in Norfolk. In times past four members of this old local family have filled the office of Sheriff of Staffordshire; Humphrey Wyrley in the 10th year of Charles I.; Sir John Wyrley in the 17th of Charles II.; John Wyrley-Birch in 22nd George II.; and John Wyrley-Birch in 44th George III.

*   *   *   *   *   *   *

It has been mentioned that the Wyrleys once possessed an estate in Leicestershire; this was Nether Seile; and from the branch which settled on this manor came William Wyrley, a famous herald and antiquary of the Elizabethan era. He was born in Staffordshire, a grandson of William Wyrley of Handsworth, in 1574; his great work, "The True Use of Armoury, shewed by History, and plainly proved by Example," was published in London, 1592. It was a very learned treatise, written in French. He was also the author of a poem dealing with the exploits of Sir John Chandos.

William Wyrley in 1604 become Rouge-Croix in the College of Arms; he acted as amanuensis to Sampson Erdeswicke, the earliest historian of Staffordshire; he accompanied Burton, the historian of Leicestershire in his survey of the churches of these two Shires; and even while he was an undergraduate of Oxford, employed himself in collecting arms and inscriptions from monuments and painted windows in old churches; so that his MS. collections became both voluminous and valuable, particularly his '"Church Notes," many of them preserved to this day, some in the Herald's College, others in the Sheldonian Library. This being so, it is not surprising that a very full pedigree of the Wyrleys of Hamstead should figure in Shaw's "History of Staffordshire" nor that the Wyrley arms should have been freely sculptured about Handsworth old church.

Strangely enough there are two curious points to be noted in connection with the heraldic devices borne, by this family. The Wyrleys have not kept constantly to one coat-of-arms, as is the almost invariable practice of families entitled to this distinction; on one of the shields they have used the chief part of the device has been three bugle horns, on another it has been two lions passant, crowned, and each holding a fleur-de-lis in its paw; on a third, the shield showed a chevron between three lions rampant; while yet another blazon in Handsworth Church displayed six golden fleur-de-lis. The family crest is a wing.

The other curious point to note has reference to the second coat-of-arms, which (it is stated) "was given by a friend, in whose memory they bear it." It would appear that in the reign of Edward III. John, son of Sir Thomas Heron. ville of Wednesbury, granted to his dear friend, Roger Wyrley, a certain coat-of-arms "that he had by descent"—which is the usual way such dignities come to one. (This incident will be found dealt with at greater length in the present writer's "History of Tipton." p. 7. It is interesting to note that two silver lions crowned with gold, on a black shield, constitute the chief part of the Wednesbury borough arms to this day.)

X.—THE MANOR OF PERRY BARR.

As William Stamford purchased Perry Hall and the landed estate of some 500 acres accompanying it, about the same period (1546), it will be necessary here to review briefly the history of that portion of the parish lying on the opposite bank of the Tame, and adjacent to "the Colefield" In 1240 there was a dispute as to the boundary line between Perry and Witton. The ancient manor of Perry Barr (as we have seen) was at the Domesday survey of 1086 held under Fitz-Ansculf, baron of Dudley, along with Handsworth and Barr, by Drogo. Later, when it became the principal seat of the holder, it gave its name to the manorial proprietor; thus in John's reign there was a "Henry de Pirie," and in Edward I.'s time, William de Perry is recorded as holding it as a knight's fee under Roger de Somery. A knight's fee may be defined as so much land of inheritance as was esteemed sufficient to maintain a knight with suitable retainers, the money value of which, about this time. was reckoned at £15 per annum. This particular fee was held by sub-infeudation of the lord of Birmingham, under the baron of Dudley.

Yet, curiously enough, about the same time we read of Perry Barr—if not the manor, large lands in the place—being willed by a Wyrley to his son and heir. However, what is more important, is the record of an Inquisition taken at Dudley in 1347 (*tempo.* Edward III.) from which it is gathered that John de Perry held his manor under William de Birmingham by service of a knight's fee.

There is a vague tradition that while Perry was under the dominance of the lords of Birmingham, some "castle" or fortification was put up near the bridge. The probability is that the present bridge was erected, to replace an older and less adequate one, about this period. Old Perry Barr bridge is distinctly Edwardian, and there is some probability it was rebuilt in its present style soon after its predecessor was found to be totally inadequate for its purpose in flood time. The proper-name Tame signifies "flood water," and a bridge at that point had frequently to do more than to span a running stream; it had to afford after a heavy rainfall a dry-shod path across the adjoining low-lying marshes.

The inadequacy of the bridge there in 1380 is disclosed in the report of a law case which has nothing whatever to do with Handsworth. It appears that Roger, son of Sir Roger Hillary of Bescot, appealed against a verdict which had been given against him through default of his appearance at the Assizes held at Lichfield in the year named. In his appeal he stated that as soon as he had received the notice of the trial, he had started from the manor of Stretton-on-Fosse in Warwickshire, which was 30 leagues distant, on the Wednesday before the Thursday of the trial. But when he arrived at Handsworth, which was in the direct line to Lichfield, about the hour of vespers, he found "the water called Teme" had suddenly risen to such a height, it was impossible to pass either by the bridge or by boat; and he had to return and make a circuit of six leagues, seeking for a passage the whole of Wednesday and up to the middle of the night, and it was impossible to pass without peril to life before the first hour of Thursday, when the water was going down, and he was then able to pass by the Ford at Handsworth. Before he could reach Lichfield, however, the default had been recorded against him. He therefore appealed, as the delay was unavoidable. It is not on record how the case terminated, but the reference to Perry Bridge is particularly interesting; the bridge was certainly on the ancient streetway which crossed the Tame somewhere near its junction with Hol Brook. "Bridge Meadow" is mentioned in a deed of 1590 as situated in "Perry Barre lying neere to Perry Bridge."

In Chapter II. allusion was made to the deviation of the old Roman road, and the moving of the bridge in consequence. The original bridge probably crossed the stream some 200 yards to the east of the present one. In 1309 the road by the bridge was called the Hol Ford Bridge, an Inquisition of that date defining Sutton Chase as extending "as far as the Holebrook and as far as the Thame, and as far as the Hol Ford Brugge, and as far as Schrafford Brugge," the latter crossing the Tame at Gravelly Hill. The Holebrook is the stream which joins the Tame near the village.

In the time of Henry VIII. Eustace Fitz-Herbert was lord of Perry Barr; one of his daughters and co-heirs carried this manor and Sutton Coldfield to Thomas Smith, son of Sir Thomas Smith, a baron of the exchequer, who sold it to William Stamford, aforementioned (1546). An old altar tomb in Handsworth church has been attributed by Shaw to a member of this family, apparently identified by the fact that among the armorial devices upon it are to be found a barry shield, and a gauntleted hand armed with a sword. Writing in 1798 the county historian described it as a "fair raised tomb" standing in the body of the church towards the south side, "whereon is the figure of a man in armour. It is said to be for William Stamford, sometime of Perry Hall, in this parish, esq.; but of the epitaph there now remain no more undefaced than this:

"Sic mors seva rapit . . . . juvenesque senesque. . . ." Underneath this monument is fixed a cadaver, one of those emaciated skeleton figures in a shroud, wont to be carved on old-time tombs as fitting reminders of man's mortality. The main effigy is that of "a man in plated armour, like scales on the arms, and like flounces on the body, the head resting on a helmet." The tomb now stands at the east end of the south aisle, and the tablet with the above fragmentary inscription is set in the tower wall just above it. But which of the Stamfords it commemorates is uncertain.

The division of the Perry lordship is peculiar. It is not improbable that at an early period there were two distinct lordships—Pirie and Little Barr; and that one came down to the Stamfords undivided, for some lands, including Holford Mill, were held by the Wyrleys by fealty. The divided manors were probably Hamstead, Perry Barr, and Oscott. It was about the time of the Stamford purchase that the manor come to be designated Perry Barr *alias* Little Barr.

XI.—THE STAMFORD AND THE GOUGH FAMILIES.

Who were these Stamfords (or Staunfords, as they were sometimes called) who now began to loom so largely on the historical horizon of Handsworth ?

The purchaser of Handsworth and Perry was the son of a prosperous London mercer, though his father hailed from Rowley, in this county. William Stamford himself was born at Hadley, in Middlesex, in 1509. After being educated at Oxford, he entered Gray's Inn, in due time becoming a sergeant-at-law, and being appointed Attorney to His Majesty's Court of Surveyors, under Henry VIII. He was highly learned in his profession, and published two authoritative works, one entitled "Pleas of the Crown," and the other "The King's Prerogative," his erudition bringing him fame and fortune. Being a zealous Roman Catholic, he was raised to be a Judge in the Common Pleas by Queen Mary (1554), some eight years after his purchase of Perry Hall.

Sir William Stamford did not live long to enjoy his honours, dying in 1558, at the early age of 49, and finding interment in Hadley Church. (Salt, Vol. viii., pt. 2, p. 40, states that "William Stamford, Knight, died 1547," which appears to be erroneous. The date 1547 is not improbably that of the erection of the tomb described in the last chapter; the custom being to put in cadavers during the life-time of the person commemorated, to serve as a sort of *memento mori.)* As Sir William died so soon after becoming lord of Handsworth and Perry, and while yet a busy man with many appointments in London, he could have spent but little of his time at Perry Barr.

Sir Robert Stamford, Knt., of Perry Hall, his eldest son, succeeded to the Manor of Handsworth and a moiety of the Manor of Barr Parva, or Perry Barr. To these possessions he added a fine old mansion, called New Inn, Handsworth, which he purchased of Thomas Groves, brother of Edward Groves, of Bromwich. Both Sir Robert and his father always signed their name "Staunford."

(This last item of information is culled from the MSS. of William Booth, of Middle Temple, 1641, who was probably a gentleman closely connected with the locality; the surname of Booth is an old one in Handsworth.)

The second son of Sir William was Henry Stamford, who, was parson of Handsworth till he surrendered the living to Mr. Furnaby (or Fulnetby). In 1607 Edward Stamford succeeded his father, Sir Robert, in all the aforementioned properties, including Perry Hall and the advowson of Handsworth; together with the Manors of Rowley (near Stafford) and

Packington, and also the house he was residing in, Rea Hall, an old family mansion at Newton, West Bromwich, in recent times used as a farmhouse, but where a William Stamford was residing as late as 1660. Edward's brother, Charles Stamford, lived at New Inn, where he died suddenly in 1638. Edward Stamford's eldest son was William, who in 1630 was fined for disregarding the summons to appear at the Coronation of Charles I. to receive the expensive honour of knighthood. The last of the family to hold the estate was his grandson, Edward Stamford, who came of age the week his father died. On the outbreak of the Civil War he became a Colonel in the Royalist army, but in 1647 was forced to "compound" with the victorious Parliament for his "delinquencies." He was treated as a recusant, and his lands were sequestered; when, however, his wife, Mrs. Dorothy Stamford, pleaded that she was "destitute of a house. it was ordered she should have the house called Perry Barr Hall upon rent." Shaw, the county historian, states that the gallant Colonel "took the covenant" in 1646, but it is difficult to imagine so staunch a Royalist as a covenanter and a turncoat. The Stamfords remained resident owners for five generations, and in 1659 Perry Barr, together with Handsworth, was sold by Colonel Stamford to a wealthy London bookseller of Grays Inn Gate, named Richard Best, by whose sons Handsworth was sold to the Wyrleys, and Perry Barr to Henry Gough (afterwards Sir Henry Gough), by whose descendants it has been held since 1669.

*   *   *   *   *   *   *

The Goughs trace their ancestry from a Welsh chieftain named Innerth Goch, who flourished at the time of Henry II. Always loyalists, one member of the family lost his life in the cause of his King during Jack Cade's insurrection (1450, temp. Henry VI.); another, a rich woolstapler, of Wolverhampton, made a voluntary loan of a large sum of money to Charles I during the latter's visit to that town at the outbreak of the Civil War. The local tradition is that the wealthy merchant went unceremoniously to his royal master, produced a bag of gold containing £1,200 from under his cloak, and pressed the money upon the King for the good of the Royalist cause.

It was for this generous act that his grandson, the above-named Henry Gough, was knighted years afterwards by Charles II. Sir Henry's son, Walter, became a great traveller and a learned writer, succeeding his father in the Perry estate in 1724. He was succeeded in 1730 by his son Walter, and he in 1773 by his son John.

This "Squire Gough," as he was generally called, was somewhat eccentric, though otherwise kindly and liberal minded; and Shaw, the eminent county historian, has left it on record that when he came to deal with Perry Hall he was prohibited from making an inspection, even of the exterior, of this old moated mansion. In 1828 the old "Squire" was succeeded by another John Gough, at whose death this line of the family became extinct. In a vault in Handsworth Church lies buried Jane, the relict of Walter Gough, of Perry who died in 1781, in her 69th year.

The present possessors, the Gough-Calthorpes, sprang from Richard, the second son of Sir Henry Gough. Richard Gough became a great traveller, and "Gough's Passage," a strait near Chusan, in the China Seas, is said to have derived its name from him. He amassed a large fortune by trade, and was knighted by George I.; in 1717 he purchased the Manor of Edgbaston, formerly the estate of the Middlemore family. In 1796 the family was ennobled under the title of Calthorpe.

Perry Hall is a picturesque Elizabethan mansion, bearing the date 1576; it is in three storeys, gabled on its north, west, and south fronts, and encloses a small courtyard. It is fairly hidden from the road by a cluster of trees, and is approached by a fine avenue of chestnuts. The moat which surrounds it is broad and deep, and is spanned by a bridge, which carries the porch to its west entrance; on other sides it encloses large lawns and ornamental gardens. General the Hon. John Somerset Gough-Calthorpe, brother of Lord Calthorpe, now resides there.

General Gough Calthorpe is a descendant of the staunch old Royalist, though not in the direct line. He has had an eventful and interesting career, being an honoured veteran of the Crimean War. The present Lord Calthorpe, before his succession to the title, resided at Perry Hall, where in the year 1885 he had the honour to entertain our present King, then Prince of Wales, during his visit to Birmingham to open the Art Gallery and attend the Cattle Show.

*   *   *   *   *   *   *

A few words of explanation may be offered on the name "New Inn" for the mansion occupied by Charles Stamford. However appropriate the name may be for the hostelry to which it has been so long applied, it is evident that it was the name for a private family mansion on that site long before it was used to indicate a public-house. It is well known to students of history that the term "inn," in ancient times, was frequently applied to numbers of mansions, like the French term "hotel." This was particularly the case in London; thus Clifford's Inn was originally the family mansion of the De Cliffords, as Lincoln's Inn was the town house of the Earls of Lincoln.

The practice was seldom followed in the country, though hospitality to travellers was offered just as freely in many of the country mansions which stood on a much frequented highway. The difficulty in arriving at any satisfactory conclusion for the naming of a Handsworth mansion "New

Inns," is the fact that it was not situated on the line of any well frequented route. The only mediæval road which passed it was Sandwell Lane, a continuation of Icknield Port Road, towards Walsall and Lichfield, via Tame Bridge at The Delves. However, that the precursor of the present well-known licensed house and tramway centre known as New Inns was a private family mansion in 1638, is an indisputable fact; and a name so applied most likely originated in the fourteenth century, when "inn" accommodation had to be provided in private houses, owing to the lack of it elsewhere.

Rea (or Ray) Hall, at Newton, probably derived its name, as did the River Rea in Birmingham, from the Anglo-Saxon "ea," signifying running water.

About the same time Robert Stamford, another member of this family, was residing at the Lamb House, in Bull Street, Birmingham. This residence was probably a commodious burgage house, such as wealthy citizen merchants were in the habit of building for themselves; its name may have originated from the sign of a golden lamb, such as a woolstapler would display when, in an illiterate age, houses had to be identified by signs, the numbering of houses being as yet unknown. and many streets remaining unnamed.

XII.—THE OLD WATER MILLS OF HANDSWORTH

In feudal times land-holding involved the cost and responsibility of providing the national defence; in these later centuries it has conferred almost a monopoly in the sources of production. It will be interesting to note how riparian landlords hereabout have found streams and water courses a source of wealth.

The River Tame in its upper course had a number of mills, even before it passed through the immediate vicinity of Handsworth, where its banks were well wooded, and where it was also favourably situated for working mills without the expense of storing large bodies of water in pools and dams. It is surely appropriate, and well within the eternal fitness of things, that the parish in which lay the pregnant possibilities of Soho, from which in due time was to issue forth the greatest motive power known to modern science, should have had its embryonic industries quickened by a plenary supply of water-power.

FINCHPATH MILL, at Wednesbury, was perhaps the first; also the other feeder had one at Walsall, known as New Mills. Perhaps more ancient than any was Bustleholm Mill at The Delves, near Stone Cross, which is still working.

Another was the OLD FORGE in Sandwell Lane, anciently a corn-mill attached to Sandwell Priory, but soon after the dissolution converted to an iron-mill. The lane is sometimes called Forge Lane; and the adjoining lands were long known as the Hammer Mill Meadows; they were open fields in which various persons possessed doles.

HAMSTEAD MILL, for centuries the manorial grist mill, is still a prominent feature on the landscape. After leaving Hamstead the Tame flows through Perry Barr, feeding the moat of Perry Hall, in which a considerable body of water is stored. Immediately below this point once stood the manorial corn mill of Perry, close to the present site of Perry Barr railway station. The overflow water was carried by a fleam running across the meadow towards the present Walsall Road, the dry channel of which is still to be seen; while the river itself makes a sudden bend in the same direction.

The next was HOL-FORD MILL, long used as an iron forge; it was held by the Wyrleys of the Stamfords under an old tenure involving the performance of fealty.

The PERRY MILL was used for grinding grain, and was equally the property of the Wyrleys, who held one portion of the manor, and of the other owners of the manor who succeeded to the interests of the Pirie or

Perry family, as did Eustace Fitz-Herbert, in 1512, and William Staunford, in 1546.

Thanks to the researches of Mr. J. H. Stone, some leases relating to Perry corn mill are available. They are full of interest, because, as he says, the Wyrleys in the seventeenth century were working their corn mill at Hamstead with very considerable profit to themselves, and at the same time were exhibiting a determination to suppress, as far as lay in their power, any competition with it.

Hence the restrictive clauses in the following lease:—

"This Indenture made the three and twentith daye of Marche in the years of the raigne of our soveraigne Lord James the 30th and of Scotland the 49th (1632) Betwene Humphrey Wyrley of Hampsteede Haule in the county of Stafford Esquyer on the one parte and John Curtler of Walsall &c. on the other parte being a]ease for eleven years of:—

"All that moitie or one halfe parte of the Water Mylle called Perry Mylle scituate and being in Perry Barre in the foresaid countye of Stafford with the water and watercourses running to and from the same Mylle.

"And the moitie or half parte of the mylle howse to the said mylle belonginge and of the mylle poole fleames dammes and stancks easements liberties &c. At a yearly rent of £6 payable at the annunciacon of the blessed vergine Mary and St Michaell th' archangell.

"Curtler to sufficientlie upholde repaire &c.

"Wyrley to find sufficient Tymber.

"Proviso that Curtler shall not keep any loade horse to the said mylle nor fetche nor carrye any corne or grayne to or from the said Mylle unless it be from Walsall aforesaid, or from the mylles at Wednesbury, which the said Curtler now holdeth.

"That if Wyrley should paye or lawefullye tender to Curtler sixpence at or in the said mylle howse the lease to determine at the years ende."

Witnesses—HENRY COOKES, THOMAS ADDYES, THOMAS BLAKMORE.

It is clear that corn milling was a profitable business in those days, observes Mr. Stone, if Curtler could convey his grain from Walsall and Wednesbury to Perry Barr to relieve the strain upon his mills at those places, although the greater and more reliable water power at Perry would doubtless be an advantage.

Deprived of its natural source of profit it is not surprising that the old mill was falling to decay. A later lease shows how absolutely the starving process had ruined the old place.

Indenture made the 1st February 1650 betwene Humfrey Wirley of Clements Inne in county of Middlesex Gentleman and William Spencer of Honnesworth county of Stafford Yeoman being a lease for 25 years of

"The moyety of All that Milplace or parcell of ground whereupon formerly stood a Corne Mill situate lyeing and being in Perry Barre in the county of Staff, formerly called or knowne by the name of Perry Mill with the waters and watercourses milpooles floodgates and scutgates milfleame damms waies and passages to and from the said Milplaice or parcell of ground nowe or formerly used occupied or belonging lyeing and being between the land of Edward Stanford Esquire the land of Sir John Wirley and a little lane there leading from Perry towards the said Milplace on all parts."

Reserving to Sir John Wyrley free lilberty of fishing with the said Spencer in all the waters milgates and milfleames.

At a yearly rent of £3.

Covenant by Wyrley that Spencer may erect build or set up at his own charges any building whatsoever except a corne mill and a paper mill on the said grounde where formerly stood a corne mill and to repair same and all floodgates and damms and to ridde scour and cleane the milpoole milfleame and other watercourses.

Not to assigne except to wife or wives child or children without written lycence but may underlet so that he be accountable for the rent.

Witnesses—WILLIAM WYRLEY, ANNE WYRLEY.

A deed, dated 24 March, 1657, in which there is a noteworthy allusion to Handsworth Park, discloses the same policy of binding custom to the manorial mills—this time to Hamstead Mill. The reference to the hat making and the nail making trades in Handsworth is interesting; the Smallwoods were a family of yeomen who have been attached to the soil of Handsworth for several centuries, and are still represented here. The deed of 1657 runs:—

Indenture between Sir John Wyrley of Hampsteed Hall Kt. and William Smallwood of Hansworth, Hatter, being a lease of House and barne and other buildings and a little plot of ground or pindle in quantity about an acre formerly parcel of the Ground called the Hayes with all those parcels of land lying in Hansworth parke all lately in occupation of Thomas Dutton, Naylor, or heretofore of John Mason deceased excepting all trees woods &c. and with liberty to Sir John to cut down same. For seven years at a Rent of £7 10s. to be paid at the dwelling house of Sir John Wyrley called Hampsteed Hall and there also every yeare two fat capons on 1st November. Smallwood to grind all corne and malt used in his house at the Mills of sayd Sr. John Wyrley called Hampsteed Mills within the said parish of Hansworth being there well used and to pay all levies lones and taxes assessed and charged by vertue of any Lawe or authorite whatsoever. Witnesses Roger Wyrley, Wm. Smallwood, Roger Harrison.

Owing to the rising importance of the local iron and hardware trades at this time there was a great demand for mill-power in the vicinity of Birmingham and South Staffordshire. There were Blade Mills—did not Birmingham supply 15,000 swords to the Parliamentarian Army ?— Slitting Mills, and Polishing Mills, and presently when they begun to substitute mineral coal for charcoal in the smelting furnaces, the operation of blowing was at first performed by large bellows, moved by means of a water-wheel.

Before 1655 the Holford Mill was leased by the Foley family to be used as an iron works, the fuel for which was supplied by the adjacent woods, the timber of which they felled rather freely. It was one Thomas Foley who established this Forge by the side of the Tame which found employment for a considerable number of hands, many of whom lived in Perry Barr, then no doubt a populous and thriving village. Subsequently the establishment became a Blade Mill, and a century ago was in the occupation of Messrs. Woolley and Co., of Birmingham, who were then using it for the grinding of sword blades. On the opposite side of the parish, near to Bromwich forge, was a Slitting Mill, belonging to Messrs. Wright and Jesson.

Going back to the seventeenth century, there were other rising trades besides those of iron and hardware, which aided and abetted Hamstead Mill in retaining its monopoly as a Corn Mill. There was a Fulling Mill at Penns, Sutton Coldfield. By 1648 the Wyrleys had established a Paper Mill at Perry Barr, and thirty years later (1681) Sir John Wyrley leased to Samuel Jerrom the elder, of Perry Barr, paper maker, two Paper Mills on Perry Wood-brook, for eleven years, at the rent of £20 and four fat capons yearly, in addition to which Jerrom was to deliver to his landlord "five quire of his greatest paper, five quire of the middle sort, and tenn quire of the least sort" each year.

Again, in 1736, John Wyrley Birch acquired water rights in a stream at Witton, running to Sir Lister Holte's "Ragg Mill," otherwise a Paper Mill. Then, says Mr. Joseph Hill, in his "Old Birmingham Bookmen" (p. 125). William Hutton erected a Paper Mill at Handsworth in 1759, perhaps at Birchfield, upon land belonging to Mr. Wyrley, but gave up the venture in 1761.

Commonly the tenants of a manor were compelled, as a feudal obligation, to have their corn ground at the lord's mill. An interesting point in the foregoing leases is the retention in Handsworth to a comparatively late period of the old feudal tenures of fealty and the rendering of capons as part payment of rent.

XIII.—THE MANOR OF WITTON.

Of the manorial history of Handsworth but little remains to be said; the manor and the greater part of the property was purchased by William, Earl of Dartmouth, in 1819, from Mr. Wyrley Birch, some portion of the estate having been acquired before that time, and the copyhold having been previously redeemed by the vendor. No reminder of old manorial institutions has been left in the place for a century or so, except perhaps the Pound or Pinfold, the site of which has very recently been thrown into the playground of the old Church School adjoining.

*   *   *   *   *   *   *   *

Here it becomes necessary to introduce an allusion to Witton, the history of that place, though in Warwickshire, having become involved, at one time or other, with the chronicles of Handsworth and Perry. To Mr. Joseph Hill belongs the credit of unearthing much of this history.

The Manor of Witton, one of the smallest of the group lying around Birmingham, formerly written Witone and Wicton, was from the earliest times connected with the greater lordship which comprised Aston, Erdington, Water Orton, Nechells, Bordesley, etc., and was therefore an inferior Manor in much the same way as Edgbaston was to Birmingham.

Large portions of Witton manorial land had as early as 1350 been sold away to the Lord of Pyrie. The lordship was subsequently held for a long period by the Easts of Yardley, but eventually (temp. Hen. VIII.) was sold to Bond of Coventry (of Bond's hospital celebrity). This family, connected in some way with Birmingham and its neighbourhood, acquired other local estates, particularly that part of Little Bromwich known as Ward End, where a considerable park was made. Both Ward End and Witton passed to Bond's son-in-law, Edward Kynardsley, whose son John passed it to William Booth, Esq., a Birmingham barrister (temp. Elizh.). William Booth who resided in the manor, was a large landowner in Birmingham, Bordesley, Witton, Edgbaston, Sutton, Perry, Handsworth, and other lordships. William Booth Allestry was the last of the family (who had held it during 150 years), and he shortly before 1736, sold the lordship to Theophilus Levett, the town clerk of Lichfield, who by the following deed of 1736 conveyed the same to John Wyrley Birch of Handsworth.

The Booths during their lengthened ownership of the estate, and their residence at Witton Manor House, acquired a number of valuable properties in the neighbourhood. The following deed of 1736, although in a condensed form, is highly interesting on account of the insight into the topographical and territorial history of the locality afforded by its unusually descriptive details:—

"31 January, 10 Geo. II.—Indenture between Theophilus Levett of the City of Lichfield, Gentleman, and John Wyrley Birch of Handsworth, Esquire: Conveyance of

"All that the Manor and Lordship of Witton with all Royalties Cottages demeasne Lands Quit Rents Commons Wast Lands Services Court Leets Court Barons and whatsoever to Court Leets or Court Barons belongeth Waifes Estrays Deodands Felons Goods Fisherys Warrens Waters Franchises Customs Liberties Privileges Pools Ponds Brookes Mines, &c., belonging.

"And also that the Manor House of Witton wherein William Booth Allestry did lately, and Walter Tippin doth now, inhabit and dwell, with barns stables &c.

"And also the Fishery or right of fishing, late of W. B. Allestry and now of Levett, in the River Tame and other rivers and brookes adjoining to or running through the manor.

"Also those closes, leasows &c. lying near to the Manor House, Beech Nutt piece, Three homestalls and Pitt Hill meadow, late in possession of Wm. Walker, now of Wm. Tippins.

"Also the land lately enclosed out of the common field of Witton called the Broomfield late in occupation of Allestry now Richd. Goode and W. Tippin.

"Also two pieces of land called The Hilaries in Erdington (late Allestry, now Tippin).

"Also two new inclosures of another common field in Witton, called Heathfield, near the Manor House, part occupied by Thos. Hopkins.

"Also Glumsmore and Glumsmore Meadow in the parish of Handsworth [the location of this was the corner of Witton Lane and Aston Lane].

"Also that house or tenement in Witton and Erdington, with two meadows, formerly of John Phillips, late Allestry, now Tippin.

"Also that Warren House called the Lodge, upon the Waste called Witton Heath, with stables and barns.

"Also that warren of rabbitts and coneys, usually set with the same Lodge.

"Also several parcels of inclosed lands called the Newlands, near the same Lodge.

"Also those pools of water called New Pool otherwise East Pool, the Middle Pool, Fishers Pool otherwise Kendall's Mill Pool, and Lane's Mill Pool otherwise Banks' Mill Pool, in Witton and Erdington, with the streams dams fleams, floodgates, &c.

"Also that house in Witton, late of Wm. Culladine, with croft and other lands.

"Also that messuage house in Erdington, late Joseph Bawden, with 5 little crofts called Broomey Closes.

"Also that messuage in Witton late of Richard Whitehouse, with other lands.

"Also that messuage farm house &c. in Witton, late Wm. Hodgetts now Josiah Short, with the following lands:

"The two Broomy orchards, the Well Meadow, Crab Tree Meadow, Gibbons Meadow with the Rushy Pleck, the Horse Moor, the Ox Moor, Golds Moor, Baches Meadow, Little Meadow. Two pieces of Moorish Ground called Wilkins Hayes, 17 acres or days work of land, lately inclosed upon the Middle Shute out of Heathfield, Witton, and, 21 and a half acres or days work lately inclosed out of Middlefield in Witton, all in Witton and Handsworth (late Hodgetts now Short).

"Also seven closes in Erdington called the Blake Hills (late Hodgetts now Tippins).

"Also three closes in Erdington called Tibbins Hills (late Hodgetts now Richd. Goode).

"Also messuage farm house in Witton (late Thomas Hopkins) with the following lands:

"The croft or back side of the house Bridge Meadow, Glumsmoor, Cranes Moors, divided into 3 parts, Hodgcock Meadow, Flaxlands Meadow, Willets Meadow, and Coal Meadow, in parish of Handsworth.

"Also that house called Hardings House with Chetwynds Croft, and a croft fold yard, Hem pleck Garden Place, whereon a house formerly stood wherein one Richard Whitehouse did formerly dwell. Also 71 acres or days work inclosed into 3 parts out of Middle Field, and 13 acres or days work inclosed out of Heathfield on the south side towards the common, and 12 acres or days work out of Heathfield adjg. to the new land south, and the moor lands west, and 7 acres out of Heathfield upon the Middle Shute, the lane through the said field lying on the east, and the lane leading to Witton Bridge on the south, all late Thomas Hopkins.

"Also messuage house in Witton (now Francis Whitehead) with barn stables orchard &c.

"Also the closes &c. called the Marches in Erdington (late Thomas James now Tippin).

"Also messuages house &c. in Witton (now Thomas Norris) with the barns &c. Two crofts and meadow lying near River Tame and 19 acres or days work of field land *lying dispersed* in the common fields in

Witton (all now Norris).

"Also several closes lately enclosed out of Heathfield, now John Standley.

"Also house in Witton, late John Partridge, with garden and two crofts.

"Also messuage house in Witton, with the Mill thereto belonging, formerly Barnsley now Richard Goode, and commonly used as a Blade Mill with barns &c. &c.

"Also the moorish ground let with Mill called Tom Moor, also one large inclosure out of Broomfield lying near the house, and Mill and four closes Tibbins Hill closes, Erdington, formerly John Woodcock now Goode.

"Also that new erected Ironwork standing upon or near the River Tame in Witton called a Slitting Mill, with pools dams streams floodgates stanks &c. (now Thomas Stanton and Joseph Stanton).

"Also house garden &c. thereto belonging now Stanton.

" Also two Blade Mills in Witton and Erdington called Upper Mill or New Mill, and Browne's Mill but now called Jordins Mills (now William Jordin) and all dams pools floodgates &c. and cottage tenement thereto belonging in Erdington set with the said mills.

"Also little house with two crofts in Witton (Widow Goode)

"Also that watercourse in Witton running to Sir Lister Holtes' Ragg Mill (Peter Clarke).

"Also house in Erdington orchard garden croft &c. (John Wells).

"Also acre and a quarter meadow in Bate Meadow, Erdington (John Wells).

"Also large parcell of waste ground within Manor of Erdington, purchased by Willm. Booth Esquire grandfather of Wm. Booth Allestry from Sir Robert Holte Baronet and Dame Mary his wife and Stephen Smith Esq.

"Also that grant of *Two Bucks* and *One Doe* yearly out of the parke of the said Sir Robert Holte called Nechells Parke.

"Also all other grants made to the said Wm. Booth or any of the ancestors of W. B. Allestry of any fishery, game, venison, royalty, or other liberty in or near the Manor of Witton.

"Also the rent of 3s. out of close meadow in Witton, the inheritance of Willm. Gibbons, and rent of 2s. out of Hewell Meadow occupatn. of Nicholas Bache, the inheritance of the Feoffees of the parish of Handsworth.

"And all other messuages, lands, mills, &c., in Witton Erdington Handsworth and Perry late of Booth Allestry. The several estates purchased by Levett in Sutton Colefield Edgbaston Bordesley and Birmingham only excepted.

"also the meadow in Witton called Smallwood's Meadow adjoining the River Tame, purchased by Levett of John Gibbons, Gentleman.

"And all the rivers, pools, fishings, warrens, woods, wasts, mines, quarrys, royalties to the Manor belonging."

(Signed by THEOPHILUS LEVETT and witnessed by RICHARD SIMCOE, JOHN ROGERS, and ROGER AUSTIN.)

A few notes in explanation of the foregoing may be useful. "A "Pleck," in Warwickshire, was a field, generally an enclosed one, although in other parts of the country the term was employed to denote waste land. A "Croft" was an enclosure of land adjoining to a dwelling-house. A "Shute" was a steep hilly piece of land. "Newland" was virgin soil recovered from the common waste land, and recently brought under cultivation. The reference to "Feoffees of the Parish" evidently refers to lands held by and for the use of the whole parish. In the terms "Flax land" and "Hemp pleck" we have Handsworth testimony to that piece of futile legislation (24 Henry VIII) by which it was foolishly attempted to enforce the cultivation of these particular crops by an enactment of Parliament. The "Coal Meadow" mentioned could not have derived its name from being the site of a coal pit, as it might have done had it been in the Black Country; at that time coal-mining was accomplished by a mere scratching of the surface, and whatever coal may exist in this parish it is many fathoms deep, as at Hamstead Colliery. The "Coal Meadow" here mentioned was probably the place where the charcoal burner produced his vegetable fuel, so extensively used for iron-smelting before the invention of the blast-furnace. The "Day's Work" measurement of land was apparently an acre in this locality, though in many parts of England it was only three roods; it was so much land, the cultivation of which would occupy one servile labourer for one day when he was fulfilling his rent contract with his landlord. (See Chapter IV.). The grant of "Bucks and Does" from Aston Park was one of those quaint oldtime bargains similar in character to those feudal tenures mentioned in Chapter V. Other feudal terms here quoted in the deed of 1736 have been previously explained; as the franchise "Waifs and Estrays," in Chapter V.; and the fine "Deodand," (or the forfeit given to God, as it literally signifies) in Chapter V. The "Common Fields," or various strips of arable land cultivated by the village community in ancient times, and their wide dispersion over the area of the Manor, have been fully described in Chapter III. It only remains to emphasise the value of the Water Rights belonging to these river-side manors of the Upper Tame, the importance of which was noticed in the last chapter.

XIV.—THE FABRIC OF THE CHURCH.

From the manorial we now turn to the ecclesiastical history. The church, which is dedicated to St. Mary, although not exactly built on a hill, stands upon the side of a knoll which looks towards the east. The ancient structure was of brown stone in the Gothic style of architecture; the most striking feature of which was the unusual position of the tower. In most churches the tower is found either at the west end, or when the plan is distinctively cruciform, in the centre; here it is placed at the south side of the nave, a very exceptional position in which it resembles the old parish church of Claverley in Shropshire.

The tower is the oldest portion of the fabric, and dates from the time when the manor was in the hands of the Parles family; the great thickness of the walls, the narrow pilaster buttresses which sufficed to strengthen its outer angles, and the deeply-splayed window piercings of the lower stages being easily identified as twelfth-century work.

It has been surmised that as the original tower of the church of West Bromwich showed Norman work of noticeably similar design, these neighbouring edifices were erected by the same builders. The upper portion of the Handsworth tower was 15th century work, showing belfry windows on three of its faces, the whole being surmounted by battlements with pinnacles at the angles added in more recent times. An octagonal staircase turret runs up the eastern side of the tower. A drawing of the tower (which has undergone many changes) is given, as it appeared before the last alteration, in Lynam's "Church Bells of the County of Stafford" (plate xxi). The foot of the tower, once used as a vestry, is now thrown into the body of the church by means of a massive arch, on the inner side of which can still be seen deep grooves in the old stone-work which were worn by the ropes during the centuries the bells were rung from the basement floor. The south aisle was built, or rather re-built, against the tower in the 14th century, to which period the old chancel also belonged. This 14th century work disappeared at the last restoration in 1876, when under the direction of the well-known Birmingham architect, Mr. J. A. Chatwin, the church was re-built in its present form, at a cost of £8,000.

Previous to that renovation a notable scheme of rebuilding had taken place in 1819, when the Rev. T. Lane Freer was rector; the parishioners who signed the minutes of the meeting which decided upon the work of restoration being Wm. Haughton, James Underhill (Churchwardens), E. J. Clarke (Curate), Samuel Dawes, T. H. Hasluck, Joseph Grice, Z. Walker, Sol. Smith, Thomas Rhodes, and Leonard Tyson. At that date doubtless passed away many interesting features of the church's ancient architecture; there were left but few traces of the original nave, which opened into the south aisle by two arches of plain construction—it was shorter than the opposite site by one span, owing to the space occupied by the tower—work dating from the period when the Somerys held this and the surrounding manors, and when Aston and Birmingham churches were built; also the arcading on the north side of the nave was removed, and in the rebuilding the west end was extended outwards.

Tacked on incongruously to this old Gothic structure was a south porch in the debased style of the Georgian period; it had above its arch a tablet on which the churchwardens responsible for it had not been ashamed to record their names, and the year 1759, economically carved on the back of an appropriated gravestone that bore the date 1675.

During the progress of the work in 1819 a wish was expressed that the old north arcade should be retained, but this was successfully opposed, no less a person than James Watt, the most illustrious parishioner Handsworth ever had, adding his opposition and giving expression to his opinion in the startling phrase that it would be "like pitching the word of God through a keyhole!" Ruthlessly was the fine old architecture of the 14th century swept away to give place to that more in consonance with the utilitarian ideas of the early nineteenth century. Shaw has briefly described that ancient edifice as consisting of "a nave with three arches, a little clerestory opposite to the pulpit, two arches and a chancel." That which replaced it had attenuated stone columns of bad proportions, making pretence to sustain an imitation vaulted roof, constructed of sham groining in lath and plaster; and, greatest sacrilegious anachronism of all, was the insertion of an iron column in the venerable Wyrley Chapel, a fifteenth century chantry. The large space added on the north side was neither transept nor aisle.

Mr. Chatwin's reconstruction in 1876-8 remorselessly cleared out all these inartistic crudities of "churchwardens' architecture"; the ungainly north transept was re-modelled, and an extra north aisle built out; the roof was raised and the galleries removed; the Jacobean pulpit with its heavy hexagonal sounding-board which stood on the south side, and the old high-backed pews curiously arranged to face it, finally disposed of; while the Wyrley Chapel was opened into the chancel by two fine arches, and an organ chamber placed on the north of it.

Shaw describes the font of 1799 as "a grey stone basin, hexagonal, on a pedestal of niche work." This old relic seems to have been lost sight of for many years, probably since the alteration of 1819; but strangely enough during the next restoration in 1878 it was found in a farmyard at Newton doing duty as a horse trough, when it was promptly recovered, carefully repaired, and re-instated at the west end of the church. Two other pre-Reformation relics have been carefully preserved, namely, two piscinas, or shallow-stone basins provided with drain-holes to run off the water used in the ceremony of the Mass. One probably stood beside the high altar, and the other near the altar of a chantry or side chapel; and both have been replaced in appropriate, if not in their original situations, one in the chancel and other in the Wyrley Chapel. Two ancient sedilia-seats for the priest and his assistant—mentioned by Shaw, were removed when the entrance to the Watt Chapel was made. The existing sedilia are modern.

The Watt Chapel on the south side of the chancel balances the Wyrley Chapel on the north side. It was put up by the trustees of James Watt, and is maintained by a fund provided by them; the floor is of marble and the roof of stone, and it contains Chantrey's magnificent life-size statue of the great engineer, elevated on a pedestal, and facing the only window, which is in the east wall. The appearance presented by the interior of the church since the last restoration is that of a rather complex scheme of aisles and arches, columns and chapels, the meaning of which it is difficult to arrive at in the dim half-lights supplied by its ineffective fenestration. The addition of a second north aisle had made the building disproportionately wide, and seemed to call for clerestory windows over the south aisle, had they been found possible.

There were formerly in the coloured windows of the ancient church many coats of arms of the local families; they were fully recorded by Dugdale in 1663 and will be found somewhat fully described in Shaw. Not a vestige of this old heraldic glass remains.

Of the more ancient monuments something has already been said (chapters ix-xi); though coarse in execution, and artistically incomparable with those in the neighbouring church of Aston, they are none the less interesting. That of William and Elizabeth Wyrley originally stood in the northeast of the chapel bearing the name of this family and marked by old carvings of the Wyrley arms. The tomb of John and Goodith Wyrley has long since disappeared.

The mural monuments in the church are numerous; they include one of Flaxman to the famous Matthew Boulton of Soho, and one to the memory of the inventive William Murdock, by Chantrey. There are memorials to the Goughs of Perry Hall, to Henricus Geast Dugdale (1840), to Watt's son who died at Aston Hall in 1848, to Anne Maria Sacheverelle of New Hall, Sutton Coldfield; and others, to which reference will be made later.

The noblest memorial of all is that to James Watt, supposed to be Sir Francis Chantrey's masterpiece, depicting the great inventor in a seated attitude, a sheet of paper in his left hand, and a pair of compasses in his right, the eyes intently gazing forth in abstract thought, the whole figure all but breathing the breath of life. A colossal figure, it may be noted, also from the chisel of Chantrey, immortalises the memory of Watt in Westminster Abbey.

Handsworth Church viewed from the exterior is a very different building from that before the addition of the Watt Chapel and the extensions of 1876-8. The enlargement is best realised by a glance at the two plans given by Mr. Allan E. Everitt in "The Transactions of the Birmingham and Midland Archæological Society (1876)," and the perspective drawing accompanying. The transformation in size and feature embraces the prolongation of the west end, erection of a new north aisle, with rebuilt porches and vestries in the Gothic style; while in place of an eastern elevation presenting a chancel with high-pitched gable, there is substituted a chancel elongated towards the east, which as well as its flanking chapels distinguished respectively by the heraldic cognisances of James Watt and the Wyrley family, are all topped by embattled parapets and decorated with crocketed pinnacles. The whole edifice has been well knit together, and taken in the mass leaves a very pleasing impression on the mind. When the corbels, crockets, finials, and other decorative embellishments of outline, so many of which have been left merely "blocked out" in the rough, have received the final touches from the hands of the carver, the church will present a somewhat lighter and more graceful appearance.

In the belfry is a peal of six bells, and regret has been expressed by some that it has not been increased to eight. Their inscriptions (in order) and their respective diameters (in inches) are as follows: 1. "Good will towards men" (27)—2. "Peace on earth" (30)—3. "Glory be to God in the highest" ($32\frac{1}{2}$)—4. "God preserve the Church of England as by law established" (33)—5. Thomas Okes rector John Piddock Thomas Osborne churchwardens 1701 (38)—6. "Quarta fui, nunc sexta, sono modulate tonabo" (40). The first five were cast by Joseph Smith, of Edgbaston, in 1701, being the first peal sent out from his foundry. The sixth is of earlier date; and the inscription on it—which may be rendered, "I was fourth, now sixth; I will ring with a sweet sound"—recalls that at the Reformation inventory of the year 1552, there were only four bells in the peal.

*   *   *   *   *   *   *

The Handsworth Parish Registers commence with the year 1558, twenty years after the issue of the earliest mandate for the proper recording of births, deaths, and marriages. Very few parish registers were kept from the first year of this ordinance of Henry VIII.; and, as will be observed, those of Handsworth did not begin till the first year of Elizabeth's reign. The first volume is "a catalogue of the names of those who, from the twenty-sixth day of the month of November, 1558, and year I., of the reign of our lady Elizabeth, were baptised, married and buried in the Parish Church of Handsworth, County of Stafford, and Diocese of Coventry and Lichfield. "It is signed at the foot of every page, from 1570 to 1603, by Rev. W. Walter, incumbent; it is written in a bold courtly hand, though some of the ink is fading and parts are fast becoming illegible. The earliest entries, copied from an older register (according to the rigorous requirements of a mandate issued in 1597, making it imperative that every parish should provide a register of stout parchment, and not of paper) have the usual old Latinised forms and contractions, and are the work of a scholar. Volume I is of sound parchment skins, each leaf measuring 16 inches by 8, in a modern binding between stout boards: there are at the end a number of blank leaves, and it is doubtful if those containing its later entries have been properly collated. Thus, following some faded entries of baptisms for 1618 there is a blank skin, and then the register resumes with 1604 marriages. This, of course, may have occurred through the method of arrangement, because another page has a few marriage entries at the top, and then come underneath all three classes of entry under their respective headings "Christenings 1622," "Burialls 1621," and "Marriages 1621." After this the registers seem to be more methodically kept, separate pages for Burials being headed with the year date. The last item written in the volume is—"1627. Sampson Walker, gent. and Goodith Wyrley, daughter of Humphrey Wyrley, esquire, married ye third day of July."

Volume II. is also of parchment, though the skins are of a different size, being 14 inches by 9. This book has the appearance of having suffered rough usage at some remote period; it is torn lose from its original cover of thick skin, and is clearly only a fragment of what it was. It does not resume with the year 1627 or with 1628, but commences at 9th September, 1631, and runs on to 5th September, 1653. At the end is a memorandum, which appears to have been written in 1780, and reads as follows:—

"1620. The Regesters from this date to the 26th March 1699, wear Destroy'd by Vermin Getting into an olde chest in the church, where they wear Deposited.

"Soloman Smith,
"Parish Clerk."

A subsequent Memorandum on the same page adds—
"Found to 5th September 1653, 24 leaves of "the Book cut out."

This second volume contains all three classes of entry. Thus near the end are to be found a record of the burial of the "butler to Sr. John Wyrley of Hampstead, ye 17th day of Aprill, 1652"; next but one comes a marriage solemnised on "Aprill ye 28th"; and presently an entry of the baptism, on May 27th 1653, of "a son of William Osborne, bellowsmaker."

The hiatus during the Commonwealth, during which the registration of births, marriages, and burials was performed by a civil registrar elected by the parishioners, is common enough. The minister had nothing to do with the registration between 1654 and 1662, while marriages were regarded as civil contracts, and were solemnised before Justices of the Peace. The clergyman who held the living after St. Bartholomew's Day, 1662 (by the

Act of Uniformity) might have recovered the civil register, but apparently did not do so. The next (or third) Handsworth Register does not commence till 1699, and bears the following imprimatur of one who was evidently a very painstaking clergyman, perhaps newly appointed to the living:

"A Register of all the Christenings, Marriages, and Burials with in ye Parish of Handsworth. Anno Dom. 1699.

"THOMAS OAKES"
"Rector."

Under an Act of Parliament of 1812 (known as George Rose's Act) the whole system of Parish Registers was altered; an Abstract of the old ones to that date was ordered to be printed by the House of Commons in April 1833. According to that official Abstract those of Handsworth were in seven volumes: viz.—

Regr. No. I — Baptisms, Burials, and Marriages from 1558 to 1627.

„   No. II — Baptisms and Burials from 1699–1774: Marriages 1699–1753.

„   No. III— Baptisms and Burials 1775–1812.

„   Nos. IV. to VII—Marriages 1754–1812.

From this it will be observed that the fragmentary Register, which should come between No. I. and No. II., is omitted from official cognisance. The modern Registers, crowded as they are with the vital statistics of a large and populous urban district like Handsworth, are admirably kept by Mr. W. H. Price, the Registrar in strict accordance with present day requirements.

XV.—HANDSWORTH AT THE REFORMATION.

The exact period of the foundation of Handsworth Parish Church has been lost in the mists of antiquity. Although no mention of a "presbyter" or priest resident in Handsworth is made in Domesday Book, such omission is by no means proof that a church did not exist there at that time. A small timber-built church may very possibly have stood there from Saxon times. Anyway it is quite certain there was a very substantial stone-built church in Handsworth within a century of the date of the Domesday records because vestiges of Norman architecture have been recognised in the oldest part of the building. Internal evidence points to the fact, as recorded in the last chapter, that the earliest portion of the present structure was erected in the twelfth century when the manor was held by the Parles family.

From our earlier chapters are to be gleaned a number of items of interest in the ecclesiastical history of Handsworth. In chapters VI.–VIII. it may be read that John de Parles acquired the advowson in 1230, and presented to the living "his clerk William," who held it for seventeen years (p. 24). On William's death, the Prior of Lenton claimed half the advowson, and a quarrel ensued in which the Prior of Sandwell seems to have become involved (1254). Whatever claim the monks of Sandwell may have set up it is clear they had to relinquish it to De Parles. The right of presentation seems to have been again exercised by John de Parles, who gave the living to Hugh de Alvechurch on whose death the Prior of Lenton presented John de Derby; on his resignation Roger de Somery presented Magister William de Hamelton. On the resignation of this parson Roger de Grutwych was presented by the Dean and Chapter of Lichfield, into whose hands the advowson had been ceded by the Prior of Lenton in 1279 (p. 34).

In 1324 Joan Botetort, by virtue of her rights in the manor, received the advowson from the Dean and Chapter of Lichfield; and in 1466 it passed, as appurtenant to the manor, to the Wrottesleys. In the meantime note was taken in chapter VIII. of Henry de Morewood, the notorious poaching parson of Handsworth. In the same chapters it was also recorded that the living was valued at 21 marks in 1288 and at 30 marks in 1291; also that in 1559 the Wyrleys laid claim to the tithes of this parish.

The nearness of Sandwell Priory could not have been without some considerable influence upon the religious life of Handsworth during the Middle Ages. It was a Benedictine house established by the lord of the manor of West Bromwich in 1180, and was suppressed in 1526. The present writer has dealt with Sandwell Priory and its story, at some length, in his "History of West Bromwich;" it is not therefore proposed to say anything further on the subject here, except to reiterate that no traces of the ancient monastery remain—this notwithstanding that Miss L. J. Selwyn has professed ("Chronicles of Sandwell" 1875) to be able to identify portions of the old cloisters; and that Murray's Handbook declares "some portion of the original foundation to be still visible to the antiquarian eye, behind the house and among the offices."

From the ancient Episcopal Registers of Lichfield it is made evident that in the fourteenth century the Wyrleys had private chapels in their family mansions; not only at Handsworth, but also at Tipton, of which manor also they held the lordship. The Kalendar for January 1360 records that the Bishop had granted to Roger de Wyrley a licence to celebrate mass in his oratories or household chapels at Honnesworth and at Tybinton for a term of two years. Without such permission, the formal granting of which was intended as a safeguard against the celebration of the Mass in the households of unworthy persons, Mass could not be said or sung in any private oratory.

Another entry in the Episcopal Register, under date April 1364, records leave of absence for one year granted to the Rector of Handsworth, with permission to let his church to farm to an ecclesiastic. Under cover of this a properly qualified ecclesiastic would arrange to pay an agreed amount to the Rector, and during the specified time would perform all the duties as minister of the church, receiving for himself all the rectorial tithes, dues and fees.

A third entry, dated 16 February 1383, states that Henry Davy, clerk, was instituted in the person of Dominus Henry de Morewood, Rector of Handsworth, his proxy, to the church of Kirkebroghton (Church Broughton) Derbyshire, vacant by the death of William White, at the presentation of the King, patron for this turn by reason of "the alien Priory of Tittlebury," being in his hands through war. This reverend Henry de Morewood who was either a much maligned man, or a disgrace to his cloth, had been sued (as already chronicled in chapter VIII.) for poaching in the park of Sir John de Botetort at Handsworth. In 1392 he got away from Handsworth by exchanging with John Garton, a Prebendary of Lichfield Cathedral. As to Tutbury Priory, it was a Cluniac house and therefore "alien"; that is to say, it was subordinate to the mother-house of Cluny in France, and consequently whenever this country was at war with France, all Cluniac establishments in England were seized by the King.

Here we emerge from the more picturesque ecclesiasticism of the Middle Ages upon the opening scenes of that stern religious drama of history known as the Reformation. Upon the death of Henry VIII. the statesmen who guided the affairs of the nation for the young monarch, Edward VI., were all zealous Protestants. A commission was sent round to all the parish churches in the Kingdom to take stock of all church fittings and appointments, and particularly of the ornaments and furniture of the high altars. The Roman Mass being abolished, and the Holy Communion of the English Church substituted by Act of Parliament, many of the priestly vestments and altar ornaments were most strictly forbidden; while images, shrines, and pictures were regarded as positively "superstitious." The Royal Commission may have been animated by the purest motives, and actuated by a sincere regard for religious truth; but the fact remains that their chief concern seems to have been to confiscate everything that could most readily be turned into money. In this, however, it was merely a case of official spoliation supplanting private peculation; for in thousands of places the churches had been robbed by their own parishioners, under pretended zeal for the new Protestant faith; and the halls of many country houses were to be found hung with beautiful altar cloths, and the beds quilted with rich copes, while country gentlemen had no compunction about drinking their claret from chalices, or watering their horses from marble coffins.

The Inventories taken by the Commission of 1552 are often defective; here is a copy of that for—

HANSWORTHE.

Fyrste, one challes of sylver with a paten

ij	copes, one of red velvet, the other of whyte damaske
ij	crosses of brasse
ij	candelstyks of brasse
iiij	vestments with all thyngs belongynge to them, one of blew damaske, one of sylke, and one of whyte fustyane
iij	alter clothes
ij	corporas cases
iiij	belles

MEM. That there tooe chalyses in the olde inventorye which ij challeses be now made one challes, and also one vestment was solde by the churchwardens and by the consent of the hole parishe.

For the complete understanding of this inventory some glossarial explanations may be necessary. The Chalice was, of course, the cup to contain the wine administered in the sacrament of the eucharist; and the Paten was a small circular plate for the bread. The Corporas (or Corporal) was the linen cloth on which the consecrated elements were placed during the celebration of the sacrament, and with which they were covered afterwards. The case is now called a Burse. The Vestment here meant was the Chasuble, the chief vestment used in the highest office; it was large and oval in shape with an aperature through which to put the head. The Cope, literally "the cape," was a long cloak worn in sacred ministrations. Damask was a rich silken fabric woven with elaborate designs in it; and Fustian was an imported cotton fabric with a short pile. Brass and silver were relatively far more valuable in those days than they are now; metal altar crosses and candlesticks would then be considered much more precious than we should regard them nowadays.

Within the next thirty-four years occurred all the horrors of the Marian persecution, followed by the re-establishment under Elizabeth of a Protestant state church. But the newly constituted Anglican Church had scarcely been established a quarter of a century ere it was found to be in a most "lamentable" condition. The bishops had made priests of the basest of the people; it was not merely that the new clergy were drawn from the lowest ranks of society, from tailors and shoemakers, from barbers and shepherds, but they were frequently dissolute persons, drunkards, and notorious evil-livers. And as they were invariably without learning, it followed that they were unable to preach, and sometimes indeed scarcely able to deliver the Homilies that had been specially prepared for their use. This being so, the Puritan party rose up in wrath and indignation at such a scandalous state of things. Queen Elizabeth, however, stoutly opposed her influence to theirs; for while they always set great store by preaching, an "exercise" they accounted as equivalent to the sacred "prophesying" of old, her august majesty delivered an opinion that so long as all Popish ordinations were annulled, it would suffice for public worship if there were three or four preachers in each county. In 1586 a "Survey" of the country was made, county by county; and in Staffordshire 83 parishes were found to be without preachers; 18 congregations were served by laymen; while 40 incumbents were scandalous livers. Here is the report upon this parish—

> "HANESWORTH. A parsonage, worth £120 per annum. Patrons, Sir John Bows and Sir Robert Stanford. Some recusants [in the parish]. The parson a bad liver; no preacher."

The name of this "dumb dog" who held the living of Handsworth, this type of minister so profoundly abhorred of the Puritans, is charitably unrecorded.

XVI.—THE BENEFICE.

The first Protestant rector of whom we have knowledge is Wiliam Walter, who signs at the foot of each page of the Registers from 1558 to 1510, appending the term "Curatus"; in the subsequent years to 1603, he styles himself "Rector." He was evidently the parson who succeeded the notorious evil liver of 1586, perhaps chosen for his preaching ability and high scholarship, and who subsequently to 1597 copied the entries into a new parchment Register as already recorded. After him came the Rev. Henry Stamford, as mentioned in chapter xi. (p 44).

The next Rector is commemorated by a mural tablet still fixed on the wall of the church and bearing this inscription—

John Fulnetby, B.D.
Archdeacon of Stafford, Canon of the Cathedral
of Lichfield
And Parson of Handsworth
Deceased September 1636, Aged 71.

Underneath is a small grey tablet, with an incised shield of arms, and a scroll bearing the motto, "Mors mihi lucrum;" beneath which is another scroll with two wings. The Rev. John Fulnetby was Precentor of Lichfield, 1608; Archdeacon of Stafford, 1614; Prebendary of Gaia Major, and Bachelor of Divinity, 1605; as a pluralist he not only held the fat living of Handsworth, but also the neighbouring rectory of Aldridge. His will, proved 1636, and dated 1629, names no place of burial, but it is believed he was interred at Aldridge, he bequeathed the sum of £30 to the poor of Aldridge and Barr, making his wife executrix. (See Prebendary Smith's Aldridge.") During his tenure the Registers contain, attached to an entry of 1615, the signature "W. Harding. curate."

From the Parish Registers the names of succeeding "parsons" may be obtained. In 1699 Thomas Oakes signs as rector; presumably the same as the Rev "Jno. Thos. Oakes, Rector," who was buried here on "October 25th. Anno Dom. 1731."

Then a diocesan record at Lichfield informs us that

" On 18 Novr. 1731 Maria Oakes, patron for this turn, presented John Oakes, clerk, A.M.. of Jesus College, Cambridge, to the Rectory of Hansworth, vacant by the death of Thomas Oakes."

The Parish Registers contain the signature, under date 1754, of this John Oakes, who was the son of the previous rector; the same records disclose his burial on July 9th 1767. The Rev John Birch, uncle to George Birch who became lord of the manor, succeeded; and upon his death in 1776 the Rev. Thomas Lane became rector, presented by the aforesaid

George Birch, Esq., these two gentlemen having married each other's sister. During Mr Lane's time the church was broken open and robbed (1784) and he records that £30 were expended in the purchase of a new communion plate. The Rev. Thomas Lane died and was buried here in October 1802; and on July 4th of the following year the Rev. Thomas Lane Freer, M.A., was inducted to the living. This rector died 25 March 1835, and is commemorated by a Gothic tablet in the church. The Rev. James Hargreaves, M.A. succeeded; he died in 1841 and is similarly commemorated. Mr Freer's mother was a Lane of Bentley Hall; and he also held the living of Wasperton in Warwickshire. One branch of the Freer's lived at the Friary (See Fletcher's "Leicestershire Pedigrees.") The church contains several monuments and memorials of the Freer and Haughton families of Birchfield House.

The Rectory of Handsworth was then held from 1841 to 1847 by the Rev. Hy. R. Woolley; and from 1847 to 1860 by the Rev. Geo. Wm. Murray, who afterwards became rector of Bromsgrove, an Honorary Canon of Worcester, and Proctor for the diocese of Lichfield. His published farewell sermon preached at Handsworth, which shows that he was Rural Dean as well as Rector, is dated from "The Rectory, Stafford, 1860." For the next thirteen years the benefice was held by the Rev. Herbert Richard Peel, M.A., who was a nephew of the great statesman, Sir Robert, being a son of the Very Rev. John Peel, D.D., Dean of Worcester, by his wife Augusta, daughter of John Swinfen of Swinfen in this county. The Rev. H. R. Peel resigned the living in 1873; after years of martyrdom to rheumatic gout the disease eventually attacked the brain, and during a fit of temporary insanity he committed suicide (1885). His father the Dean had held the patronage of the living.

Dr. Randall, in contrast to his predecessor. was a man of a particularly robust mould. His opinions on social questions. too, were also broad, and he never shrank from giving public utterance to them. He was distinctly anti-teetotal, and on one occasion startled the community by saying from a public platform he could see no more harm in a supply of beer being delivered at the people's houses day by day, than in the house to house supply made by the morning milkman—a sentiment, it would appear, in which he merely anticipated by a few years the methods of daily distribution now being followed by some of the local brewers. His famous speech, delivered in 1876 at a congratulatory banquet given at the New Inns to S. C. Allsopp Esq., M.P., the Earl of Dartmouth in the chair, has been printed; it was uttered soon after the notorious "Beer and Bible Election," and the reverend champion protested vehemently "against the denunciations hurled at brewers and licensed victuallers," especially winging his shafts at Mr. J. S. Wright. a departed worthy whose statue now stands in front of the Birmingham Council House. It may have been on account of his deeply-rooted political convictions, or because he could never realise Handsworth as more than the "village" he had first known it; but for years he steadfastly refused to recognise the urgent calls of the parish for a School Board to meet the educational requirements of a rapidly growing urban district. At his initiative several thousands of pounds were raised in voluntary subscriptions, and with this sum "Undenominational Schools" for 700 children were erected in Boulton Road (1883); but the effort was futile, and within ten years the Boulton Road Schools had passed into the hands of a popularly elected School Board. The march of progress is not to be arrested by the methods of an inept clericalism.

With the departure of the breezy Dr. Randall from the picturesque old Rectory house—he resigned in 1892 and retired into private life—a new order of things set in. How the change was brought about, which among other thing, involved the provision of a new parsonage, and a substantial reduction in the rectorial income, will be recorded presently. In 1892 the Rev Robert Hodgson, M.A., was inducted rector of Handsworth, and six years later he was elevated to the dignity of Archdeacon of Stafford. Within the next half-dozen years Mr. Hodgson's health gave way so seriously that in 1904 he resigned his parochial appointment. Happily the breakdown proved to be but temporary, and the Venerable Archdeacon is now a Canon Residentiary of Lichfield. The present holder of the benefice is the Rev. Andrew E. Burn, D.D., who was appointed Prebendary of Gaia Major in Lichfield Cathedral the same year he came to Handsworth. Dr. Burn is also Examining Chaplain to the Bishop of Lichfield.

Here a few words of explanation as to the ecclesiastical status of Handsworth becomes necessary. From the earliest era of the English Church till the constitution of the modern bishopric of Birmingham (1905) Handsworth was within the jurisdiction of the diocese of Lichfield, or of Coventry and Lichfield, as for centuries it was styled. It was a rectory described as within the ancient deanery of Tamworth and Tutbury for almost as long a period; but in the first year of Victoria and under the energetic rule of Bishop Ryder, came a change in this respect.

On August 11, 1837 the Rev. George Fish, A.M. vicar of Walsall, was appointed Rural Dean over the undermentioned parishes: Walsall, Walsall St. Paul, Aldridge, Barr, Rushall, Bloxwich, Bushbury, Darlaston, Wednesbury, West Bromwich, West Bromwich Christ-church, Handsworth and Perry Barr. Bacon's "Liber Regis" which gives this, attaches no title to the new Rural Deanery; but by 1857 at the latest, both a Rural Deanery of Handsworth and a Rural Deanery of Walsall existed. A later change was made by an Order in Council, dated 1894, when (amongst other things) the parishes of West Bromwich, Tipton and Darlaston were transferred from the Rural Deanery of Handsworth to the newly constituted Rural Deanery of Wednesbury.

When the new bishopric of Birmingham was formed a common sense view of the prevailing circumstances recognised that Handsworth was unquestionably part and parcel of the social community of Birmingham; and irrespective of old civil and ecclesiastical boundaries, Handsworth was wisely included in the new diocese. The Birmingham diocese was divided into the two archdeaconries of Birmingham and Aston; the former was then sub-divided into five Rural Deaneries; namely, Birmingham Central, Edgbaston, Harborne, Kings Norton, and Handsworth. The newly constituted Rural Deanery of Handsworth was made to embrace Handsworth old parish church of St. Mary, the three matured daughter churches of St. James, St. Michael, and Holy Trinity (Birchfield); St. John's parish church of Perry Barr, with its mission churches of Christ Church (Aldridge Road), All Saint's (Oscott), and St. Mary Magdalene (Witton); St. Paul's church Hamstead; the projected new church of St. Peter (Grove Lane), St. Andrew (in Oxhill Road—replacing the mission Church of the Good Shepherd), St. Thomas (on a site in Rookery Road), and All Souls in Wenlock Road; and not only these in Handsworth proper but also the following important ecclesiastical districts within the limits of the ancient civil parish of Birmingham—All Saints, St. Chrysostom, St. Cuthbert, St. Peter, and Bishop Latimer's churches. Truly a wide and important deanery, of which the present Rector of Handsworth, Dr. Andrew Ewbank Burn, is Rural Dean.

*   *   *   *   *

Much has already been said in passing as to the earlier history of the Advowson of Handsworth. In Tudor times the right of presentation came to be divided between the Stamfords of Perry Hall and Mr. William Huddleston of Elford. Edward Stamford sold his moiety to Richard Best, who with the consent of his two sons, Richard and William Best, by a deed dated 20 September, 20 Charles II., sold the same to Joseph Ainge and his heirs for £200. Ainge acording to one authority afterwards purchased the other moiety, and conveyed the whole to the Wyrleys.

But a list of successive patrons of Handsworth rectory is given thus in "Bacon's Liber Regis" (1786)—

> "Edward Birch, serjeant-at-law 1692. Humphrey Wurley Birch, esq., patron every third turn; Mr. Ainge every third turn. Walter lord Aston and Sir Edward Littleton, 1636, Mary Oakes, widow, 1731. John Wyrley Esq., 1767, George Birch, Esq., 1776."

The value of the living in mediæval times has already been dealt with (chapter VII). The 1288 valuation held good till the reign of Henry VIII., when we find Handsworth set down in the "King's Book" as worth £13 9s. 2d.—Archidiaconal Synods 7s. 6d. The latter sum was termed a "Synodal."

and was a money tribute payable by the inferior clergy to the Archdeacon at his Easter visitation. In later times the reputed yearly value of the living has been set down as £200 in 1767, £400 in 1776, and £1,000 in 1803; increased land values in the parish being chiefly if not mainly responsible for this growth of revenue. This expansion continued, notwithstanding the deductions made from time to time during the first half of the nineteenth century towards the endowment of the four daughter churches which had to be built to meet the increase of population, till the great change of 1892 to which reference has just been made.

It was in 1891 the Handsworth Rectory Act was passed enabling the Bishop of Lichfield to purchase the advowson from the then rector, the Rev. William Randall, D.D., who was desirous of resigning the incumbency on account of failing health; the price was £20,000.

Under the Handsworth Rectory Act, the Ecclesiastical Commissioners administer the estates of this church, paying to the Rector £1,000 per annum. This is the gross income, and after deducting the customary charges that are obligatory in such cases, the net revenue of the present holder of the benefice is upwards of £800.

The Handsworth Inclosure Act of 1791 (exactly a century previous to this date) had allotted to the rectory certain portions of the "open fields, commons and waste lands of the parish," of which the rector for the time being might grant leases of 21 years, or if for building land, for 99 years. Consequently the endowments, irrespective of surplice fees, the rectory house, tithe rent charges, and the extensive ancient glebe lands, included some increasingly valuable ground rents.

Out of the Tithe Rent charges, however, the following annual amounts are now payable:—

To the Incumbent of St. John's, Perry Barr, £150.

To the Incumbent of St. James's, Handsworth, £80.

To the Incumbent of St Michael's, Handsworth, £50

To the Incumbent of Holy Trinity, Birchfield, £50.

There was acquired for the bishops of Lichfield by the former Act, not only the patronage of Handsworth rectory, but the right of presentation to any new churches which might subsequently be erected within the limits of its ancient jurisdiction. A new rectory house, to replace the old one, was erected at a cost of £2,500; new roads to develop the rectorial building estate were constructed at a cost of £6,000; while the sum of £1,150 was expended in obtaining the Act.

XVII.—THE CHURCH CHARITIES.

During the eighteenth century and for some years afterwards the grossest abuses often prevailed in the administration of many church charities, and this not infrequently with the connivance of those public functionaries who should have been the trusty guardians of the poor. Not a few public charities were diverted to private objects, and in this way a number of old endowments came to be reported as being "lost." It was to put a stop such scandalous cases of malversation that in 1818, through the exertions of Lord Brougham, a Charity Commission was appointed. The Commissioners visited every parish in England, and in due course presented their Report to Parliament. From their official REPORT, dated 1823, are extracted *verbatim* the following particulars of the Handsworth benefactions (omitting here, for the present, The Bridge Trust):—

1.—BROMWICH'S CHARITY.

In an old book belonging to the parish, entitled "Handsworth Charitable Uses," is a copy of a deed of feoffment, dated the 6th February 21st Elizabeth (1579), whereby Thomas Bromwich of Perry Bar in the county of Stafford, granted a close of ground or pasture called the Ruddinges, to William Walter rector of Handsworth, and four others, their heirs and assigns, to such uses as were declared in a schedule thereto annexed; viz. to the intent, that they should distribute yearly, at or before the feast of Christmas, all the rents and profits of the said close, except only 12d. which was given to the feoffees for their pains, unto 45 poor inhabitants of Great Barr, and Perry Barr and Handsworth, viz. to 15 of the poor of each place, such as the said feoffees should think most meet to receive the same.

This land was exchanged in the year 1794, under the provisions of an Inclosure Act for the parish of Handsworth, with George Birch, esq. for an allotment of land on Handsworth common, containing about four acres. The old close did not contain more than one. It was an object to Mr. Birch to possess this land, and the exchange was very favourable to the charity.

This property is under the management of the churchwardens, having been vested in them, as we understand, by the commissioners' award under which the exchange was made.

The land is let to William Ward, as tenant from year to year, at the rent of £8 which is at present the full value. It is cultivated by him as a garden, and would not be worth so much, if not so cultivated. It was inclosed at the expense of the parish. One-third of the rent is paid over to the chapelwardens of Great Barr, one-third to the churchwardens of Perry

Barr which is a division of Handsworth parish, each receiving £1 6s. 8d. half yearly; and the other third forms part of a fund distributed to the poor of the other part of Handsworth parish, in the manner hereafter mentioned.

2.—HODGETT'S CHARITY.

By indenture dated 2nd February 1627, a copy of which is in the old book above mentioned, after reciting (among other things,) that Thomas Hodgett of Handsworth, by his will dated the 11th March 1st Ch. I. (1625), gave an annuity or yearly rent of 40s. for ever to the poor inhabitants of Handsworth, to be issuing out of a close or moorish piece of ground, lying in the parish of West Bromwich in the county of Stafford, which close was by the said will devised to Thomas Milward and his heirs; and farther, that it was by the said will declared, that the said Thomas Milward should, within two years after the decease of the said Thomas Hodgett, make a sufficient feoffment to eight or ten freeholders dwelling within the parish of Handsworth, for the payment of 40s. at Lady-day and Michaelmas, by equal portions, to be yearly distributed by the churchwardens and constables of the said parish, on the said feast days, in the parish church of Handsworth aforesaid; the said Thomas Milward, in accomplishment of the said devise, granted to certain persons therein mentioned, and their heirs, the clear yearly rent of 40s. to be issuing out of the said close or moorish piece of ground, which was known by the name of Wigmore, in West Bromwich aforesaid, to hold the same upon the trusts above mentioned.

This annuity is now paid by Mr. William Bullock, as the proprietor of the land charged therewith, and is added to the general distribution for the Handsworth division, hereafter mentioned.

3.—BIRCH'S CHARITY.

By indenture dated the 22nd April 1663, Thomas Birch the elder, of Harborne in the county of Stafford, for divers good considerations him thereunto moving, and especially for the performance of the payment of twenty shillings yearly, given by George Birch of Wolverhampton, to such uses, intents and purposes as were thereafter declared, granted, enfeoffed and confirmed to William Spencer the elder, and 15 others, their heirs and assigns, two closes, crofts or pastures of land, commonly called the Sling, and the Gorstie Croft, next unto the lane side leading from Gold's Green towards Tipton and being part or parts of the lands called Gold's ground, lying in West Bromwich in the county of Stafford, and then in the tenure of John Tonks or his assigns, upon trust, to permit the said Thomas Birch the elder, and his heirs, to receive the rents and profits of the said premises, for and during the life of the said George Birch of Wolverhampton; and from and after the decease of the said George Birch, then in trust, to permit and suffer the parson, churchwardens and overseers of the poor for the parish of Handsworth, or any two or more of them, to receive the yearly rent and sum of twenty shillings, to be issuing out and yearly paid forth of the said premises, at the feast of St. Michael the Arch-angel, for ever; six shillings and eight-pence, part thereof to be given until the parson of Handsworth aforesaid, for the time being, to preach one sermon in the parish church there upon the 25th day of December, yearly, for ever: and thirteen shillings and four-pence, residue thereof, to be given and distributed unto such and so many of the poor people as should inhabit in that part of the parish of Handsworth, which is commonly called on this side of the water, viz. on this side the river of Tame, by the discretion of the parson, churchwardens and overseers of the poor for the said parish, or any two or more of them, upon the 25th day of December, yearly, for ever; and the deed contained a proviso, that if the said Thomas Birch the elder, his heirs or assigns, should buy, purchase or assign so much land, being within the said parish of Handsworth, as should be worth yearly forty shillings or above, and should settle the same upon the said feoffees, to the uses intents and purposes above limited and declared, that then that deed should be void. In our Fifth Report, will be found an account of a similar benefaction of the same George Birch, to the parish of Wolverhampton, charged on certain premises called Gold's grounds, in the parish of West Bromwich.

It will be seen from the Report, that the estate called Gold's grounds, has been divided among different proprietors, and that three-fourths of it now belong to the family of Danks's, of Wednesbury. The Handsworth dole, after having been for several years unpaid, apparently from some uncertainty as to the parties liable to it, is now received from Mr. Josiah Danks, of Wednesbury; 6s. 8d. is paid to the rector, and 13s. 4d. is added to the Handsworth distribution.

4.—POOR'S LANDS.

There are some parcels of land, containing 5a. 2r. 22p. let to the late Henry Stanley, of Perry Barr, and now held by his widow, Ann Stanley, as yearly tenant, for an annual rent of £8 8s.; one-third of which is paid to the churchwarden of Perry Barr, and the other two-thirds to the churchwarden of Handsworth, and respectively form part of the general distributions hereafter mentioned, in those several divisions of the parish. It is not known from whom this land was derived. It may possibly have been acquired under some of the benefactions to the poor of this parish, mentioned in the old charity book (and hereafter stated), but which, the parishioners are unable to connect with any of their present receipts.

Some incorrectness at present takes place in the division of this rent.

The deduction of the property tax, while it continued, reduced this rent to £7 11s. 6d. and the churchwarden of Perry Barr, who receives the rent, paid over to the churchwarden of Handsworth, two-thirds of this, amounting to £5 1s. Since the cessation of the property tax, the same payment has inadvertently been continued; and the whole of the remainder, being £3 7s. has been carried to the Perry Barr distribution. The division ought to be £5 12s. to Handsworth, and £2 16s. to Perry Barr.

There is also an allotment of land, containing 1a. 2r. 26p. made under the Perry Barr Inclosure Act, in respect of the land held by Stanley, and which is let to Thomas Joiner, as yearly tenant, at a clear rent of £2 9s. of which the churchwarden of Handsworth receives £1 12s. 8d. and the churchwarden of Perry Barr, 16s. 4d.

All these lands appear to be let for their full present value.

There is likewise a piece of land in Handsworth, containing 3r 24p., on part of which some messuages are built for a Workhouse, with gardens; and the residue, about half an acre, is let to John Cope as yearly tenant, at the rent of £2 2s. This land was purchased by the churchwardens and overseers, at the time of the inclosure in 1794, for the use of the poor of Handsworth, and the whole of the rent is carried to the account of the Handsworth distribution.

5.—GRICE'S CHARITY.

By indenture of bargain and sale dated 6th November 1806, and duly enrolled in the court of Chancery on the 8th December in the same year, between Joseph Grice of Handsworth esquire, of the one part; and the Rev. Thomas Lane Freer rector of Handsworth, Henry Piddocke Whately, William Houghton, and six others (trustees for the purposes hereafter mentioned), of the other part; reciting indentures of lease and release, dated 15th and 16th July 1805, whereby John Taylor and others conveyed and assured to the said Joseph Grice, his heirs and assigns, the premises hereafter mentioned, to the use and behoof of such persons, and for such estates, and subject to such provisions as the said Joseph Grice should by any deed executed in the presence of, and attested by two or more credible witnesses, direct, limit or appoint; and further reciting that the said Joseph Grice was desirous to convey the same to the trustees, for the charitable uses hereafter mentioned; it was witnessed, that the said Joseph Grice granted, bargained and sold, directed, limited and appointed, unto the said trustees, their heirs and assigns, all that piece or parcel of land, bounded on the southwest by the Sand Pit Terrace, in or near Birmingham; on the south east by a certain street called Powell Street; on the north east by land, late of Edward Carver, under lease to George Griffith; and on the north west by other land, late of the said Edward Carver, under lease to

John Williams; and containing in breadth in front next to the said terrace, 50 yards, or thereabouts, and carrying the same breadth throughout the whole depth thereof, and containing in depth 50 yards, or thereabouts, and containing in the whole 2,500 square yards or thereabouts: and also all those 10 messuages, tenements or dwelling-houses, with the outbuildings and appurtenances thereunto belonging, built upon part of the said piece of land, and then in the several occupations of Josiah Hipkins, and nine others: and which said piece of land was, by lease, dated March 25th 1778, demised by Henry Carver, esquire, to William Bevans, for 120 years, at the yearly rent of £7 16s. 3d.; all which ground and premises are situate in the parish of St. Martin, in Birmingham to hold the same to the said trustees, their heirs and assigns, on trust, to receive the said ground rent during the remainder of the said lease, and to pay yearly on St. Thomas's-day, to the rector of Handsworth, or to such person as he should appoint, in the said parish church, the sum of two guineas, to preach a sermon on that day properly adapted to the understanding of the poor, inculcating their duty to submit cheerfully and with pious resignation to their present situation, and that though in this life they may have their sufferings, yet in the world to come, there will be no distinction of persons, if they conduct themselves in a truly religious manner; and upon further trust during the continuance of the said lease, to distribute the residue of the said sum of £7 16s. 3d. on St. Thomas's-day, yearly, immediately after divine service, unto and amongst such poor persons, being parishioners and residing within the parish of Handsworth, as they the said trustees should deem the most worthy objects of charity; and from and after the expiration of such lease, then upon trust to receive the rents and profits of the said lands, buildings and premises, and thereout expend yearly, what may be necessary in repairing the said messuages and buildings, or in rebuilding the same, or any part thereof, and for carrying the trust into effect; and after payment thereof, and of two guineas yearly, to the rector of Handsworth, or to such person as he shall appoint to preach such sermon as aforesaid, to pay and distribute the sum of £30 yearly on St. Thomas's-day immediately after divine service; that is to say, £20 to poor persons, parishioners of, and residing within, that part of Handsworth which is not within the hamlet or district of Perry Barr; and £10 to such persons as should be residing within the said hamlet or district of Perry Barr, as the said trustees should think most worthy objects of charity; and upon further trust, out of the residue of the rents and profits, to pay to the rector of Handsworth £2 annually, for ever in lieu of and as a full compensation for the pasturage or herbage of the churchyard belonging to the said parish church, if he should think proper to accept the same, to prevent cattle grazing in the same; and then upon further trust, out of the then residue of the rents, to pay to the organist of Handsworth church, if there should be an organ there, £15 yearly on St. Thomas's-day. towards his salary, and after payment thereof, to pay to the beadle of the parish yearly, on St. Thomas's-day, 10s.; and after payment thereof to retain the sum of 3 guineas yearly, for paying a receiver, for collecting the rents and keeping the trust accounts; and upon further trust (if the rent should be sufficient) to pay to the churchwardens and overseers of the poor of Handsworth the sum of £20 to be by them distributed yearly on Good Friday, after divine service, among the resident poor parishioners; that is to say, £13 6s. 8d. in Handsworth, and £6 13s. 4d. in Perry Barr: and after payment thereof, in the last place to distribute the remainder (if any) to such poor housekeepers residing within the said parish, as the trustees may deem proper objects of charity. The trustees to have power to lease, upon terms not exceeding twenty-one years after the expiration of the said lease, reserving the best yearly rent that can be got, without taking fines. When the trustees should be reduced to three by death, or any declining to act, or ceasing to reside within the parish of Handsworth, the others to nominate out of the then rector, churchwardens and overseers of the parish, so many persons resident therein as shall be necessary to make up the number of nine, the rector always to be one.

Mr. Grice is still living, and receives the rent himself, which he sends to the parish officers, divided into three portions; namely, £2 2s. for the rector, £3 16s. for the poor of Handsworth, and £1 18s. the remainder, for the poor of Perry Barr.

There is a sermon preached regularly on St. Thomas's-day, by the rector, after which the money is distributed (with the other charity monies) by the churchwardens and trustees, to the poor of Handsworth and Perry Barr, each taking their respective shares. Out of the Handsworth share, 5s. is annually given to the beadle, in consequence of a wish expressed to that effect in a letter from the donor.

6.—Charities of Dorothy Huxley and Joseph Stubbs.

By indentures of lease and release, dated the 3rd and 4th February, 1819, between Wyrley Birch, esquire, of the first part; George Barker, gentleman, of the second part; John Crocket and William Cowper, overseers of the poor of the parish of Handsworth, of the third part; the Rev. Thomas Lane Freer, Nathaniel Gooding Clarke, William Haughton, Joseph Grice, and James Underhill, esquires, trustees of the National School in the parish of Handsworth (and which said William Haughton and James Underhill were churchwardens of the said parish), of the fourth part; and William Wills the younger, gentleman, of the fifth part; reciting, that Dorothy Huxley, of Great Barr, by her will, dated the 7th August, 1797, charged certain premises in Handsworth with the payment of £20 to be paid to the churchwardens and overseers of that parish, upon trust, to place out the same at interest, and to apply such interest for the use of such poor persons of the said parish as they should think proper, in buying clothes, or otherwise; and further reciting, that Joseph Stubbs, of Handsworth, by his will, dated 13th February, 1817, desired his trustees, therein named, to settle and secure out of his personal estate, the sum of £2 2s. per annum, for the use of the chanters or singers in Handsworth Church, to be applied for that purpose by the trustees or governors of the National School there, and directed the same to be secured by the investment of a sufficient sum of money in the funds or otherwise, as the said trustees should think proper; and further reciting that the said churchwardens and overseers, parties thereto, had received from the representatives of the said Dorothy Huxley the said sum of £20 with accumulated interest, amounting altogether to £40; and that the executors of the said Joseph Stubbs had agreed to secure the said legacy of £2 2s. a year, by the investment of £52 in the purchase of land, and had paid the said sum of £52 to the parties of the fourth part in discharge of such annual sum, and further that the said Wyrley Birch had contracted with the said parties of the fourth part, for the sale to them of the parcel of land thereafter mentioned, for the sum of £100 composed of the above-mentioned sums of £40 and £52 and the further sum of £8 to be paid by the said parties of the fourth part; It is witnessed, that in pursuance of the said agreement, and in consideration of the said £100 the said Wyrley Birch conveyed to the said Thomas Lane Freer and others of the fourth part, and their heirs, a parcel of land, as the same was then measured, marked and staked out, being Part of a piece of land, called Far Bird's Hill, in the parish of Handsworth, containing by admeasurement one acre, and which piece of land so granted was triangular, and adjoined on the west to land belonging to —— Bary, and to land late of —— Finch, esquire, but then of John Wodhams; on the north, to other land of the said Wyrley Birch, and on the east, to the road leading from Birmingham to Perry bridge; to hold the same upon trust, out of the rents and profits thereof to pay to the governors or trustees of the National School of Handsworth the sum of £2 2s. per annum, for the use of the chanters or singers at Handsworth Church, according to the intent of the said Joseph Stubbs; and upon further trust, to pay the residue of the said rents and profits to the churchwardens and overseers of Handsworth, to be by them applied for the use of such poor persons of that parish, as they should think proper, either in clothing, or otherwise, according to the intent of the said Dorothy Huxley; and it was declared, that when the trustees should be reduced by death to two, the survivors should convey the land to the use of themselves, and three others, and their heirs, with the approbation of the said church wardens and overseers, upon the trusts aforesaid. This land is let to Thomas Stanley, as yearly tenant, at £4 2s. per annum, which is its full value.

Of this rent £2 2s. is paid by the trustees to a fund belonging to the singing boys at the church, for their use; and £2 is carried to the Handsworth distribution fund. This fund consisting of—

Bromwich's charity, one-third	£2	13	4
Hodgett's charity	2	0	0
Birch's charity	13	4	0
Poor's land, viz., Stanley's two-thirds	5	1	0
Joiner's do.	1	12	8
Cope's	2	2	0
Grice's charity, two-thirds (5s. to beadle)	3	11	0
Huxley's charity	2	0	0
	£19	13	4

is distributed by the churchwardens, part on St. Thomas's Day, and part on Good Friday to the poor of Handsworth, not including those of Perry Barr, in sums of from 1s. to 3s., according to a permanent list, the vacancies of which, as they occur, are filled up by the churchwardens. The fund for distribution to the poor of Perry Barr, receives also the two following charities, which belong exclusively to that division of the parish.

7.—GIBBONS'S CHARITY.

In the old charity book it is stated that Humphrey Gibbons and Thomas Gibbons, by their feoffment dated 15th May, 32d. Ch. II. (1680), gave one parcel of land, called Roles Breach lying in Perry Barr, to the use of the poor of Perry Barr only, for ever. The rent is there stated to be £1 5s.

The sum of £1 5s. is annually received by the churchwarden of Perry Barr, from the trustees of the Bridge Charity before mentioned, but they have no other knowledge respecting the origin of this payment, than what is derived from a memorandum in a survey of the bridge land, taken in the year 1778, in which underneath a catalogue of part of the premises belonging to the Bridge Charity called Thickbroom's land (so called from being occupied by a tenant of that name), consisting of 8a. 1r. 17p., is written as follows:—N.B.—The above land has been subject to an annual payment to the poor of £1 5s.

The amount of this payment makes it probable that it originated in the above mentioned benefaction of Humphrey and Thomas Gibbons; but we find no further means of connecting it therewith.

8.—OSBORN'S CHARITY

It is stated in the old charity book that Henry Osborn, by deed of feoffment, dated 4th April, 1670, granted a rent charge of 6s. out of a cottage and land, called Sadler's Farm, lying in Perry Barr, to be distributed to 18 of the poorest householders in Perry Barr.

Neither this charity, nor the premises said to be charged, are now known by name; but a corresponding sum of 6s. is received by the churchwardens of Perry Barr, from the Widow Stanley, who inhabits a cottage in the township, as the rent of a piece of land attached to her garden. In the map of the Bridge lands, we find laid down a small piece of land, called Poor's Land, twenty yards in length, which lies at the back of Widow Stanley's cottage.

The distribution to the poor of Perry Barr is as follows:—

Good Friday.

Share of Bromwich's Charity	£1	6	8				
Do. Poor s land, Stanley's rent	1	13	6				
Do Do. Joiner's rent		16	4				
Payment from Bridge trust (qu.Gibbons)	1	5	0				
Do. from Widow Stanley (qu. Osborn's)		6	0				
				5	7	6	

St. Thomas' Day.

Share of Bromwich's Charity	1	6	8				
Do. Poor's land, Stanley's rent	1	13	6				
Do. of Mr. Grice's charity	1	18	1				
				4	18	3	
			£10	5	9		

These several charities are distributed at these two periods, to poor people belonging to this division of the parish, chiefly those not receiving parochial relief, according to a list previously settled at a parish meeting. The list remains unchanged from year to year, unless from death, or other good cause. The sums given vary from 3s. to 1s.

9.—ANONYMOUS.

In the will of Thomas Osbourne, dated the 26th November 1739, is a devise to his daughter Lydia Osbourne, and her heirs, of a messuage or tenement, with the buildings, gardens and crofts, closes and parcels of land thereto belonging (which parcels of land appear from other instruments to contain three acres), called Undrell's Tenement, in the parish of Handsworth, subject to "the usual and accustomed payment of 20s. a year to the poor of Handsworth."

In four conveyances, subsequent to this will to successive proprietors, the last of whom is Mr. John Richardson, mason, of Handsworth, the premises are conveyed, subject to this payment of 20s. a year to the poor of Handsworth. The name of the original benefactor nowhere appears.

The late proprietor, Mr. Hutton, was accustomed to send 20s. worth of bread, in quartern and half quartern loaves, to the church, on St.

Thomas's-day, to be distributed by the churchwardens to the poor attending there. Since Richardson purchased the premises, he has also generally sent Bread to the church. In the year 1818, he paid to the churchwarden £2 as two year's amount in money, but from that period to the time of our examination the dole had been in arrear.

10.—William Cowper *alias* Piddock's Charity.

The poor of Handsworth are entitled to an annual sum of 6s 8d. out of the rent of a cottage and land, situate in Oldbury, in the parish Hales Owen, and belonging to the trustees for the poor of Harborne, under the benefaction of William Cowper alias Piddock, of which an account will be found in a subsequent part of this Report, among the charities at Harborne.

11.—Sir William Whorwood's Charity.

The poor of Handsworth receive £5 a year, part of the charity of Sir William Whorwood, which is distributed by the churchwardens of West Bromwich, and of which an account will be found in this Report, among the charities in the latter parish. It will there be seen that they were further entitled, under a decree of the Court of Chancery, to some arrears of this annuity, which were ordered to be invested in land for their benefit, but that there is no appearance of this having ever been done.

12.—Lost Charities.

In the old charity book are also mentioned the following benefactions, as to which we were not able to obtain any further information:—

(a) Lane's Charity.—By deed poll dated 24th January 9th James I., William Lane enfeoffed to Roger Stanley and others, and their heirs, a cottage, garden and premises, and three crofts of land, near thereto, lying in West Bromwich and Handsworth, or one of them, adjoining the great pathway leading from Wolverhampton towards Birmingham; also a close or pasture, into two parts divided, being at Bustlehome, in the parish of West Bromwich, adjoining the highway leading towards Walsall, upon trust, among other things, after the death of the said William Lane and Francis Lane, therein mentioned, to distribute among the poor inhabitants of the parish of Handsworth, yearly, on Good Friday, 10s, issuing out of the said cottage, close and premises. These premises cannot be ascertained.

(b) Elizabeth Piddock's Charity.—Elizabeth Piddock, by will bearing date in 1576, appointed the sum of £40 to purchase a piece of land, the rent whereof to be dealed and given amongst the poor at two times in the year, for ever, at the oversight of her sons, and their heirs. It is added, "whereof William Piddock, of Winson Green, doth distribute yearly to the poor of Handsworth 20s."

The loss of this charity seems the more remarkable, as a similar benefaction, given apparently by the will of the same person to the neighbouring parish of Harborne, was secured by a purchase of land, and still remains in activity—[See infra, the charities in Harborne.]

(C) WILLIAM HODGETTS, of Hales Owen, by will dated the 6th June 1617, gave to his brother, Thomas Hodgetts, the house wherein the said Thomas dwelt and all the testators lands in Handsworth, for his life, paying yearly to the poor people of Handsworth 6s. 8d.; and the reversion of the said house and lands he gave to Richard Hodgetts his cousin, John Hodgetts, his son, and his heirs, for ever, paying yearly, for ever, 6s. 8d. to the poor of Handsworth aforesaid. It is added, "Memorandum, the said will above mentioned is in the custody of Nicholas Hodgetts, of the Grove, in Handsworth."

(d) HARRY COOKE, by will, dated 6th May, 1637, willed, that the 12s. by the year, which he had forth of the parish lands, should be for ever thereafter employed in Handsworth only, by his successors, in such manner as he had done; and he willed, that there should be so much money laid forth by his executors, as would buy lands to make up 40s. by the year, for ever, and to be employed as the (   ) was in Handsworth.

(e) HENRY WILLIES, by will, dated 26th August, 1659, gave to the churchwardens and overseers of Handsworth and Perry Barr £4, the use of it to be distributed to the poor.

(f) HENRY BROWN, by will, dated 20th June, 1681, gave to 20 poor families of Handsworth 10s. a year, to be divided 6d. to a family.

XVIII,—A WELL-ENDOWED PARISH.

From the foregoing Report of 1823 it will be seen that Handsworth is a richly endowed parish, notwithstanding that some of its benefactions are now written down as "lost." Shaw, the county historian, writing in 1798, states that the following were at that time the principal benefactions:—

(1) "Sir William Whorwood, knt. gave £15 per annum for ever to charitable uses; of which 5s. to the poor.

(2) "Henry Coke, gent. £2 per annum.

(3) "William Piddock, of Smethwick, gent. (21 James I.) gave 6s. 8d. per annum for 600 years.

(4) "George Birch, gent. to the poor on Handsworth side 13s. 4d. per annum, and 6s 4d. to the minister for a sermon on the 25th of December for ever.

(5) "Henry Gibbons and his brother —— Gibbons, to the poor of Perry Barr for ever, one close, now valued at £25 per annum."

With regard to the Charity of the Whorwoods, of Sandwell Hall, discrepancies in the two accounts will have been observed. Sir William Whorwood, knight, was "seized in fee" of the rectory of West Bromwich, and having devised £6 12s. annually for ten years, and then £10 annually for ever, half to the poor of West Bromwich and the other half to "such of the poor of Handsworth as dwell along the highway near Sandwell," died in 1617, and Thomas Whorwood entered into possession of the rectory. But Thomas was unmindful of the wishes of his predecessor, and for eleven years appropriated the money which should have gone to the poor. But the Court of Chancery compelled him to disgorge £116, to be invested in lands, and so the poor were made eventually to benefit by the unconscious self-denial that had been imposed upon them. But only half the amount was so invested; at any rate the Commissioners only found that the West Bromwich share was represented in land, and the balance was unrepresented by any real estate. Still as the honours' roll of benefactors displayed inside the parish church vestry, records the fact that Sir William Whorwood left to the poor of Handsworth the sum of £5 per annum, to be paid out to the tithes of West Bromwich, the money would appear to be still paid. A new Charity was instituted in 1826 (subsequently to the above quoted Report) by Miss Ann Boulton of Thornhill House. The property bequeathed to the poor consisted of "a part of Tranter Fields, otherwise Tranter Butts" in the parish of Birmingham (now called Sheep Street) and the site whereon the Kyrle Society carries in its beneficent work, then occupied by twenty-two houses. The ground rent therefrom has already grown from £4 11s. 8d. to £47 5s. 10d.

In the course of years some of the properties left for the benefit of the poor have greatly increased in value, and the traditional "twelvepence" of olden times is now often represented by a substantial sum. Then again the Handsworth Churchwardens of 1794, the period when the common lands were enclosed, evinced some slight show of public spirit in acquiring an allotment for the poor, though they might certainly have gone much further, and with perfect justice.

In 1823 (as is recorded in the Huxley and Stubbs Report) Handsworth was distributing £19 13s. 4d. and Perry Barr £10 5s. 9d. By the end of the century this total of £29 19s. 1d had (with the addition of the Boulton Dole) more than doubled, and has since continued to grow at an extraordinary rate of progression. In the general growth of values during the past century a remarkable rate of increase is afforded by this particular Huxley and Stubbs Benefaction. The old Charity Board in the church shows the combined income as formerly amounting to £3 2s. 0d.; but a judicious investment of capital in land at Well Head had by 1890 swollen the income to over £34.

Taking the public bequests of Handsworth as a whole it must be admitted that they have been fairly well safeguarded, and certainly in later times, judiciously administered. In the case of the richest, the Bridge Trust, of which an account will be given in due course, if the intentions of the pious founder have been departed from, it is because the original purpose had become obsolete, and the funds have been discreetly applied to a purpose more in consonance with modern requirements. To the modern mind, imbued with socialistic ideas of manly independence, the 1806 bequest of Mr. Joseph Grice, of Handsworth Hall, so far as it provides for the perpetual "inculcation of pious resignation" in a position of pauperism, is grotesquely preposterous; a redeeming feature may perhaps be found in the subsequent clause which provides for the payment of a church organist. There is something, too, to be said for the Stubbs bequest which provides funds for the payment of "chanters or singers in Handsworth Church."

The ancient book in the Parish Chest, referred to from time to time in the Charity Commissioners' Report, has a parchment cover which is endorsed "Donations for Charitable Uses." A few passages in the text of some of the ancient bequests call for the historian's comment.

The allusion to the two old roads (in the Report on the Lane Charity) is interesting; by one it is shown that the old highway from Handsworth to Walsall went by way of Bustleholm, and by the other that in 1612 the correct description of the road "leading from Wolverhampton towards Birmingham" was "the great pathway;" for it is a fact that the present "main road," as it is now generally called, was for centuries a mere bridle-path, which was first turnpiked as a highroad in 1727.

The references to "the Churchwardens of Perry Barr" in the 1823 Report do not imply the existence of a church there at that period; these officials were extra wardens attached to Handsworth church and specially charged with the care of all parochial affairs in that outlying and extensive hamlet. It is certainly strange in the case of the Poor's Lands that while the benefit has remained, the name of the benefactor had been forgotten. Some little light is thrown upon the subject of such losses by an open letter printed and published in 1841, addressed to the Charities Committee of Handsworth and Perry Barr, by an irate parishioner named Samuel Kendrick, who thus publicly protests against a report which had just previously been issued by the Committee, and which contained statements he vehemently controverts. He asserts that the "Ancient Book of Charitable Uses" had been ingeniously mutilated "in those portions prior to 1806." and leaves the reader to infer that this had been done for some wrong or fraudulent purpose.

Kendrick's pamphlet is rather instructive reading alongside the Parliamentary Report of 1823. The writer complains that he has been misrepresented as saying some 19 acres of land belonging to the Poor of Perry Barr had been filched from them; what he had alleged and now repeats was that 5 acres of land really be longing to the Poor of Perry Barr had been misappropriated by the Trustees of the Bridge Estate; and that there was in existence somewhere an allotment of 9 acres made to the poor at the inclosure of the Common Fields of the township. He refers to records in the Court of Chancery which show that at the Inclosure of Perry Fields in 1738, much of the land was divided up between "Esquires Gough and Wyrley," but that a considerable allotment also fell to the Poor of Perry Barr at that time.

Suppression of important facts relating to Bromwich's Charity is alleged. It is affirmed by Kendrick that originally there were over $4\frac{1}{2}$ acres, and not one acre as reported; and moreover that the Act gave no authority for effecting exchanges. Former churchwardens are charged with neglecting their duty, and the rector's honesty is impugned in that being brother-in-law of the lord of the manor, he knew this charity was not vested in George Birch. The rector is also reproached that, while enjoying an income of £2,000 a year, he is careful to look after his own interests, but does nothing whatever to improve the value of the lands belonging to the Poor of his parish.

Then there seem to have been difficulties not only as to the source from which the Poor's Lands were originally derived, but also as to their identification. Local tradition, says the pamphleteer, pointed to certain fields in the vicinity of Oscott College, and named the benefactor as one Gibbons, which appears to agree with the Report of 1823. But the writer contended that the Poor of Perry Barr are entitled to enjoy the whole of the allotment made at the 1811 Inclosure without sharing it with the Poor of Handsworth.

Passing reference is made to a Pamphlet of the Rev. D. N. Walton, curate of Handsworth, in which it was stated that the rent of £8 8s. 0d. paid by the Widow Stanley (*Vide* Report of 1823) was for $20\frac{1}{2}$ acres; a sum Mr. Kendrick thinks quite inadequate. Also Mr. Kendrick is of opinion that the Broomy Croft which the Bridge Trustees had held for a number of years was originally "the allotment made to the Poor when Walk Mill Field" was inclosed, at the time of the Perry Fields Inclosure. Finally he comes to the conclusion that the Poor of Perry Barr have a right to Thickbroom's land (*Vide* Parliamentary Report on Gibbons' Charity); to the Widow Lowe's "lower field," as shown on map of 1794, about $1\frac{1}{2}$ acres which Wyrley Birch held; and to such share of land inclosed on Perry Barr Common in 1811 as was then allotted to them. Appended to Kendrick's Pamphlet are (1) a Table showing exact areas in the Great Field and the Little Field allotted in 1738 to '"Esquire Gough, Esquire Wyrley, and the Poor of Perry Barr," respectively; and (2) a Sketch Map purporting to identify some of the lands in dispute.

Many other interesting allusions occur in these controversial pages of 1841. It would appear, for instance, that a survey of the Bridge Trust Estate was made in 1778 (as mentioned in the Reports on the Gibbon's and the Osbourn Charities), that a Parish Map was prepared in 1794, and another one by Mr. Fowler in 1840, with a full reference book. And although it is put on record that in 1737 a Mr. Geast had delivered eight Deeds of the Bridge Trust Estate for safe preservation in the Parish Chest, it is alleged that subsequent gross negligence was alone responsible for the loss of all the Estate Rent rolls from 1755 to 1782; though incidentally the Survey of 1778 had shown the fields occupied by Joseph Thickbroom "with house and lands by the Blacksmith's shop at Perry Barr." At this distance of time, however, it is difficult without the proper documents, to judge of the real merits of Mr. Kendrick's case.

The administration of the Charities at the present day is highly commendable. Under a scheme devised by the clerk to the trustees, Mr. W. H. Price, it is sought to make the division of the funds as equitable as possible by taking as a working basis the number of houses within each ecclesiastical district which are assessed at £12 and under. St. James's parish, being the most industrial in its character, benefits most by this arrangement. According to the returns of five years ago, when the amount divisible had further grown from £62 in 1890 to £313 in 1902, the figures governing the distribution were as follows:

In St. James's parish there were no fewer than 3,058 houses of that value or under; in Holy Trinity, Birchfields, 814; in St. Mary's (the mother parish), 643; St. John's, Perry Barr, 565: St. Michael's, 326; and St. Paul's, Hamstead, 271.

Two distributions are made each year (on Good Friday and St.

Thomas's Day) and the amounts which the various parishes received in 1902 were: St. James's, £76 9s. and £95 11s. 3d.; Holy Trinity, £20 7s. and £25 8s. 9d.; St Mary's, £16 1s. 6d. and £20 1s. 10d.; St. John's £14 2s. 6d. and £17 13s.; St. Michael's, £8 3s. and £10 3s. 9d.; and St. Paul's, £6 15s. 6d. and £8 9s 4d.

The fluctuations in the amount to be disposed of will be gathered from the figures on the cheques sent out as follows to the various Incumbents at Christmas 1907: to the Rev. T. S. Cave, St. James's £55 9s.; the Rev. J. T. Jones, Holy Trinity, £17 3s.; Dr. A. E. Burn, St. Mary's, £13 7s.; the Rev. H. A. G. Blomefield, St. John's, Perry Barr, £12; the Rev. H. E. Clatworthy, St. Peter's, £10; the Rev. R. R. Needham, St. Michael's, £6 13s.; and the Vicar of St. Paul's Hamstead, £6.

This did not exhaust the funds at disposal; a sum approaching £100 was set aside as subscriptions to various local hospitals, in return for which notes were acquired for distribution to the sick poor. Other contributions, with a similar object, were made to Nursing Societies, Convalescent Homes, and kindred beneficent institutions of the neighbourhood; food and clothing and other distributions in kind were made, besides contributions towards the outfit of needy young apprentices.

The present method of distribution has another advantage over the old custom which insisted upon the attendance of all recipients at the parish church. The trustees became alive to the hardship which this inflicted upon aged people when, many years ago, an 'old man who had tramped from the distant district of St. James's, was overcome by the effort and expired in the church during the sermon.

The list of Church Charities concludes with that of the late Joshua Horton, who by will founded a Dole at St. James's Church by which thirty widows of the parish, over sixty years of age, receive a sovereign each.

*   *   *   *   *   *   *

Handsworth also boasts—if Doles, with their pauperising influences and their general tendency to undermine habits of self-reliance, are institutions to boast of—a Dissenting Charity. This is associated with the old-established Congregational Church in Union Row. By the will of Matthew Royce Griffin (1878) 50 poor and deserving inhabitants receive Christmas gifts of coal, bread, joints of meat, and parcels of flannel and calico.

"Beneficium accipere libertatem est vendere."

On the Soho Road are the Rhodes Almhouses a pleasing block of building in the Tudor style of architecture, erected in 1871 by Mrs. Rhodes in memory of her husband, John Rhodes esq. Of Waverhill, Handsworth. There are separate sets of rooms for the accommodation of sixteen respectable ladies in reduced circumstances, and who have sufficient means to support themselves. By a Deed dated 7 June 1873 the same benefactress, Matilda Juliana Rhodes, of Waverhill, Handsworth, widow, conveyed to Trustees, two pieces of land situate in Handsworth, one was the site on which she had erected the almshouses, and the other the Trustees were directed to let on lease and apply the rents towards the maintenance of the fabric of the almshouses and for other purposes connected therewith.

Unfortunately the income derived from this source has already been found inadequate for all the objects specified in the trust deed. As the endowment is barely sufficient to keep the houses in repair and provide gas and water for the occupants, the income has had to be augmented by a few private subscriptions The trustees would be glad to see the number of voluntary subscriptions considerably increased, and any one desirous of assisting the institution can obtain full particulars from the Secretary Mr. E. H. Monckton, 27, Waterloo Street, Birmingham.

XIX.—GROWTH OF ANGLICANISM

The record of church progress in Handsworth is good. Very commendably have churchmen tried to keep pace with that remarkable growth of the community which began in the earlier decades of the nineteenth century. Some instructive figures relating to Handsworth Deanery are given in a Diocesan Report of 1869, quoted in Langford's "History of Staffordshire" pp. 494-7.

Perry Barr, the over-river moiety of this extensive parish, and itself an area of very large acreage, was first supplied with a separate centre for public worship. The population has not perhaps grown as rapidly as was anticipated, for to-day the chapelry served by Perry Barr church, and its three little mission churches, does not contain more than 5,000 inhabitants. St. John's, Perry Barr, is still a pretty village church, set in the midst of green fields a quarter of a mile lower down the stream than Perry Hall, and half-hidden even from the intervening high road by clusters of tall trees animated by the presence of a colony of noisy rooks. The church was built in 1833 at the sole expense John Gough, Esq., of Perry Hall, who also provided an endowment fund.

The curate at the old church about this time (under the Rev. H. R. Woolley) was the Rev. D. N. Walton, M.A., and when he left Handsworth in 1842 after a residence of nearly 16 years, special testimony to the effectiveness of his ministrations was borne by a number of those who had been members of the congregation "previous to the existence of St. John's, Perry Barr." This testimony was printed with his farewell sermon, and the list of signatories attached is an interesting record of the first partition of the parish. Among the names are those of John Gough (Perry Hall), John Gisborne (Oscott House), John Wadhams (Well Head), Walter Williams (Ox Hill), and J. L. Proud (churchwarden, of Perry Barr).

Lt.-Gen. the Hon. Somerset Gough-Calthorpe is the present patron of the living, which is a vicarage worth £314 a year. The Incumbents in succession have been the Rev. Arthur Wyatt, M.A. (1834), the Rev. George Braithwaite, M.A., the Rev. Charles B. Snepp, LL.B. (1857), the Rev. Evan J. Rees, M.A. (1880), the Rev. John R. Keble, M.A. (1885), the Rev. G H. Sharpe, M.A. (1890), and the Rev. H. A. G. Blomefield, M.A. (1907).

Each of the seven bells in the tower contains the name of the founder, and the date in the identical terms—"J. Taylor and Co., founders, Loughborough, 1868." Their individual inscriptions, and the diameter of each in inches, run—

(1) Laus Deo in Jesu Christo. (27)
(2) Gloria Patri filioque et spiritui sancto. (28)
(3) In loving remembrance of John Fawkener Winfield (29)
(4) Presented by Mrs. Dickinson. (33)
(5) Presented by R. W. and Mrs. Winfield Revnd. C. B. and Mrs. Snepp
     Revnd Philip and Mrs. Browne. (35)
(6) The Revnd. C. B. Snepp Vicar.
     John Gilbert
     Henry Davenhill
         Churchwardens. (37)
(7) Laus Deo. In memoriam Frederick Lord Calthorpe 1868. This peal
     of six bells erected by friends and parishioners of Perry Bar. (44).

It is not that Perry Barr is crowded with population, but that its
tremendous area stretches over a wide and scattered region which has
recently necessitated the provision of subsidiary churches. The three
mission churches are (1) Christ Church, Aldridge Road, Birchfield, with
300 seats, a chapel-of-ease built at a cost of £800 in 1862 and vested in
private trustees; (2) All Saints Church for the hamlet of Oscott, a small
brick structure to seat 160 worshippers, erected on land given by Lord
Calthorpe, constituted 1893 and vested in the Vicar of Perry Barr, and (3)
St. Mary Magdalene in Holford Road, a brick building seating 220,
provided in 1900, and vested in the Ecclesiastical Commissioners. The site
was given by Mr. Wyrley Birch.

*   *   *   *   *   *   *

It was in 1837 the decision was arrived at by the Rector, the Rev. J.
Hargreaves, to erect a Chapel- of-Ease in the outlying hamlet on the farther
side of Holyhead Road. A site was given by Mr. John Crockett, owner and
landlord of the New Inn, a gentlemanly host of the old school who is
recorded to have conducted his "public-house more like a private house."

The spot selected for the new church was then comparatively rural.
Says St. James's Parish Magazine (1890)—"There was no building on the
main road between New Inn Hall and Bellevue, with the exception of the
old cottages opposite the New Inn. Towards Birmingham no house was
observable on the main road, with the exception of that occupied by
Captain Devey, and that of Mrs. Dunderdales, the old farm in the late
occupation of Joseph Parrish standing close beside the Red Lion, and
'Moorfield.' Towards West Bromwich, there was but one house on this side,
'Woodville.' The rest formed fields and gardens, with an old cottage in the
midst; Albert Street was not made, while Wattville Street was but just
made and it stood for several years devoid of all but a very few houses.

Here St. James's Church was erected to supply the spiritual needs of a
population up to 4,000. The foundation stone was laid in April 1838 by
Mrs. Peel, the wife of the Rev. Dr. John Peel, Canon of Canterbury, and

patron of Handsworth. The edifice having been put up at a debased period, its architecture calls for little note. There were the usual unsightly galleries, and a few uncomfortable "benches for the poor." At first there was no organ, the singing being "led by a musical instrument" of lesser magnitude after the old world fashion. The church was opened in 1840, and its ecclesiastical district was constituted in 1854. An endowment of £40 per annum was secured at the consecration of the building, and another £40 a year from the revenues of the mother church accrued during the rectorship of the Rev. H. R. Peel. The Ecclesiastical Commissioners granted an additional £56 per annum as soon as the population reached the specified 4,000. At first the church was nominally supported by a church-rate levied over the area of the whole parish of Handsworth; but in a very few years popular opposition to the impost grew too strong to warrant further dependence on this source of income. The first appointed curate was the Rev. J Finch Smith (1840) who resigned in 1844, and afterwards became a Prebendary of Lichfield, he erected the first schools for the parish. During the tenure of his successor the Rev. J. W. Fletcher, the vestry was robbed and the Registers taken away; if no transcripts of them had been forwarded to the episcopal registry, all the records from the opening to the date of the robbery appear to be irretrievably lost. In 1851 Mr. Fletcher was succeeded by the Rev. C. Patten Good, and shortly afterwards St. James's ceased to be a chapel-of-ease, becoming by an order in council a District Chapelry, the curate-in-charge taking the title of Incumbent. Some benefactions. including a site for a parsonage, accrued to the church before Mr. Good left in 1856. Three years later a parsonage house was placed on this site, which had been given by Mr. William H. Dawes.

During the tenure of his successor, the Rev. John Sheldon, M.A., an Act of Parliament altered the style of the "Perpetual Curacy " to the "Vicarage of St. James's." The population, according to the 1851 census, was 2,600, and the locality still continued to wear a rural aspect. On the north side of the Soho Road, there were as yet no houses between Rookery Road (then Deadmore Lane) and Grove Lane except those fronting the main road; while to the south side of that road were only the old houses in Nineveh, one terrace in Boulton Road, and a few scattered cottages in Queens-head Lane. About this time the works of Messrs. Fox, Henderson and Co. at Smethwick, the builders of the Great Exhibition of 1851, were closed; and the Smethwick Plate Glass Works, another establishment employing a large amount of labour, were extremely slack, so that there was a very considerable amount of distress among the labouring classes of the neighbourhood. Than these, the only other large centres of employment near the church were Messrs. Muntz, Messrs. James Watt and Co., and the Smethwick Tube Works, all in Smethwick; Messrs. Lloyds' Red Lead Works in Wattville Street being the only one on the Handsworth side of the boundary brook.

Before the Rev. Mr. Sheldon's resignation in 1882 a large scheme of alteration, renovation. and enlargement had been carried out in 1878, at an expenditure of £1,384. In justification of this the 1881 census showed a population of 8,688, a number of large works having been established in the vicinity by this time; though near the church they were, however, all beyond the confines of Handsworth parish, and among them were the Birmingham Wagon Works, The Phoenix Works, Messrs. Moorewood's Works, and the Cornwall Works of Messrs. Tangye Brothers.

The living was held for a brief space in 1882 by the Rev. Henry Lawrence Randall, B.A., afterwards Vicar of St. Michael's, Handsworth; he was succeeded the following year by the present Vicar, the Rev. Thomas Smith Cave, M.A.

In 1895 the church was almost rebuilt, the south aisle was removed and a new nave erected on its site, and a chancel beyond; the old chancel and nave then became respectively a side chapel and north aisle; a new south aisle was built, with south chancel aisle and an organ chamber above it. To effect this very desirable transformation no less a sum than £8,000 was expended. The edifice has now an accommodation for 1,031, and is situated in the midst of a dense population, estimated to have reached 25,000, and which is constantly growing. To meet these growing demands two new churches are projected; St. Peter's, Grove Lane, and St. Thomas's, Rookery Road. Possibly the provision of another church in Anne Road may also have to be undertaken.

There is a burial ground attached to St. James's Church, some land for this purpose having been provided by one of its earliest benefactors. The register of burials commences in 1844; that of marriages not till ten years later. The living is now valued at £325 a year and is in the gift of the Bishop of Birmingham.

St. Andrew's Church, Oxhill Road, will take the place of the mission church of the Good Shepherd which was temporarily provided in Grove Lane; and its new ecclesiastical district will lessen the populous area hitherto served by St. James's Church. Land has already been provided on which to build a parsonage when a separate parish is created. The foundation stone of the new edifice which is to provide seats for 700 worshippers at a cost of £8,000, was laid with much masonic ceremonial, by the Earl of Dartmouth, 19 October 1907.

*   *   *   *   *   *   *

The foundation stone of St. Michael's Church, Soho, which is a pleasing structure with a spire soaring 160 feet in the air from the summit of a hillock which has not unnaturally been dubbed St. Michael's Mount, was laid in the November of 1852, by the last Earl of Dartmouth who resided at Sandwell Hall; and three years were occupied in the erection of the fabric. The Register of Baptisms dates from 1856, and of Marriages from 1863, the ecclesiastical district not having been legally constituted till a year or two later.

The first curate-in-charge was the Rev. C. F. C. Pigott. The second was the Rev. Nicholas T. Garry, M.A., late rector of Taplow, and Canon of Christ Church, Oxford. Then succeeded the Rev. G. D. Boyle who became, upon the formal separation from the mother church and the legal erection of the district into an ecclesiastical parish, December 10th, 1861, the first vicar of St. Michael's. Dr. Boyle, who left a fragrant memory behind him in Handsworth, died Dean of Salisbury. He issued a Parish Magazine for St. Michael's and extant copies for 1862 and thereabout are not without interest to the older parishioners.

A succeeding vicar, the Rev. Ernald Lane, D.D., is the present Dean of Rochester.

The living was afterwards held by the Rev. Osbert Mordaunt, M.A., now rector of Hampton Lucy, and by the Rev. F. A. Macdona, M.A., now rector of Cheadle. There is a curious incident connected with the appointment of the latter. His brother, the Rev. J. C. Macdona was offered, and accepted the living, and held it for one day only just sufficient time to effect an exchange with his brother, who remained at St. Michael's for several years. The Rev. J. C. Macdona subsequently relinquished the Church, and now sits in Parliament as member for Rotherhithe. Among others who have held the living are the Rev. the Hon. Adalbert Anson, subsequently bishop of Qu' Appelle, and now a Canon of Lichfield; the Rev. Walter Thursby, the Rev. W. H. Oswell (1891), and the Rev. H. L. Randall as just mentioned.

St. Michael's Church Choir has honourable traditions, and it has been said that in the past half of the musical families of Handsworth have contributed to its membership.

The living is a vicarage worth £310 a year with residence, in the gift of the Bishop of Birmingham, and held 1900 to 1907 by the Rev. Charles Howard Gough, and now by the Rev. R. R. Needham. St. Michael's Church serves a population of 10,000 and contains accommodation for 900. Possibly the north-west corner of this district may be apportioned to the new church of St. Peter in Grove Lane.

*　　*　　*　　*　　*　　*　　*

Holy Trinity Church, Birchfield, was erected in 1864 at a cost of £5,000, and its district was constituted an ecclesiastical parish in the following year. The living is a vicarage worth £265 per annum in the gift of the Bishop of Birmingham. The church provides accommodation for 650 worshippers; the population of the district is estimated at 17,000, and as it continues to grow rapidly, a new church in Wenlock Road has just been erected. It was at first proposed to dedicate this new fane to St. Matthew, but when attention was directed to the number of churches already called by that name within a radius of two or three miles, the dedication was altered to All Souls.

*   *   *   *   *   *   *

St. Paul's Church, Hamstead, with seating for 450, amply meets the requirements of a somewhat sparse population of about 1,600, chiefly miners employed at Hamstead Colliery. It was built 1892, and the ecclesiastical district was constituted in 1894. The living is of the net value of £140; it is held at the present time by Rev. R. A. Morley, M.A.

XX.—THE RE-PLANTING OF CATHOLICISM.

As already noted the Reformation did not clear Handsworth of "recusants"—those troublesome subjects who denied the monarch's supremacy in matters ecclesiastical. It is interesting to observe that Perry Barr and Oscott lordships long continued to be held by Catholic families, the Wyrleys, Birches, Stamfords and Goughs professing the old faith either openly or secretly for generations afterwards. It was recorded in chapter xvi. that the Rev. Henry Stamford accepted Anglican orders and became "parson of Handsworth" early in the 17th century. In a short time, no doubt after a struggle with his conscience, he evidently thought better of it, and relinquished the living to the Rev. Mr. Furnaby.

As we may read in the history books, "Popish Plots" were rife throughout the seventeenth century. On an Indictment of Grand Jury before the Justices of Middlesex, on December 3rd, 1678, Henry, Lord Arundel of Wardour, was found guilty of high treason. Among the Justices named in the record of indictment, was Humphrey Wirley, Esq., of Handsworth and Tipton.

In the years 1678 to 1680, when Perry Barr seems to have been quite a populous village, no fewer than 37 of its inhabitants—described variously as nailers, blacksmiths, millers, weavers, husbandmen and labourers—were certified into the Exchequer Office as "popish recusants;" and they had the alternative of abjuring or being prosecuted. At the head of this list appeared the name "Andreas Bromwich, *gen.*"

Owing to the notorious Titus Oates' Plot the national excitement against Romanists reached its greatest intensity in 1679; and it was in the frenzied whirl of this religious storm that Andrew Bromwich was caught up and carried away.

The Rev. Andrew Bromwich, born at Longnor and educated abroad, on his return to England settled down in the quiet seclusion of Oscott, proposing not only to minister to the religious wants of the Catholic families in the vicinity, but actually to establish a seminary in a situation he deemed so peculiarly suitable for the purpose. He was discovered, apprehended and brought to trial. The report of the subsequent proceedings is contained in a folio tract entitled "The Tryal of William Bromwich, printed by the sole authority of William Scroggs by Robert Pawlett, at the Bible in Chancery Lane, 1679." Bromwich was brought to trial before Sir William Scroggs, the Lord Chief Justice, at Stafford, on Wednesday, 13 August, 1679, along with another Seminary priest, William

Atkins of Wolverhampton. Before a packed jury, from which all "popishly affected" had been carefully eliminated, the evidence for the crown was solemnly unfolded.

Ann Robinson, "a Catholic, but now converted," was called, and testified that Bromwich had, at the previous Christmas, administered the sacrament at Perry Barr to her and seven or eight others, "twice at Mr. Birch's and twice at Mr. Purcell's." Two other witnesses of the name of Robinson, but who had not been "converted" from their faith, were hectored by the judge into corroborative admissions; so that the jury had little difficulty in finding a verdict of "guilty."

Upon similar evidence the same jury convicted the other prisoner, Atkins, of like practices at Mr. Stamford's at Wolverhampton. also at "Well Head at Ham." Mr. Joseph Hill says "Well Head and Ham would appear to be near Wolverhampton, but there are ancient buildings bearing these names at Perry and Hamstead. . . . At the former place an ancient houses called Well Head belonging to a Catholic trust still stands. It has the reputation of having been formerly a masshouse. and may possibly have been the scene of those rites which so disturbed Judge Scroggs."

The Perry Barr victim having been convicted was condemned, in accordance with the Christian code of penal laws then prevailing, to be hanged, drawn, and quartered. For some reason the sentence was not carried into execution. Bromwich was reprieved and ultimately set at liberty, probably in 1685 on the accession of that most Catholic monarch, James II.

On his release the intrepid Bromwich returned to his little mission in the peaceful vale of Oscott, which in after years Cardinal Newman felicitously re-named Maryvale. He served this mission till his death in 1702; and at the new and magnificent college on the adjacent eminence, which has since grown out of his early efforts, one of the most treasured relics is the old chair used by this worthy pioneer priest of Catholic emancipation.

As at the Reformation there were "recusants" in Handsworth, so at the Hanoverian Succession there were Jacobites. In the government list of Catholics and other non-jurors who refused to take the oath of allegiance to George I. in 1715, and which was published after the Rebellion of 1745, are found the following local names—

	£	s.	d.
William Davies, of Handsworth, yeoman	10	0	0
Robert Hildicke, of West Bromwich, bridle-buckle maker ...	3	0	0
Edward Ferrers, of Baddersley Clinton	1,451	0	$1\frac{1}{2}$

It does not follow these non-jurors were really fined the amounts set against their names—the government merely held this published forfeit over their heads *in terrorem*. Thus, as we have seen, during the seventeenth and eighteenth centuries Catholics were liable to very heavy penalties for practicing their religion; and for a great part of the period the punishment for being a Catholic priest, was death. It was not however the laws alone which Catholics had to fear, but they had often enough to dread the intolerance of their Protestant neighbours. Little wonder then that they so often worshipped in secret rooms hidden away in old country mansions; and when, later, they ventured to set up separate chapels, that they chose buildings in retired localities, well off the beaten tracks; and restraining all inclinations towards ecclesiastical architecture, severely restricted their establishments to the outward form and semblance of ordinary dwelling houses—as at Old Oscott, to wit.

The primitive little Oscott seminary gradually grew in importance after the death of Andrew Bromwich; and in 1752 the Catholic Bishop Hornyold (co-adjutor to Bishop Stonor, Vicar-Apostolic of the Midland District) had the mission house pulled down, and a larger establishment built in its place, to provide a home, if necessary, for the midland bishops of the Catholic Church.

The Rev. Pierce Parry, who was priest of the mission from 1782 to 1785, built a new chapel in 1778 which is practically the one still in use at Maryvale. His successor, the Rev. Joseph Berington (1785–1793) improved the buildings and laid out the grounds. The next priest in charge, the Rev. Anthony Clough, died after a few months' residence.

The severities of the penal laws against "Papists" had till this time made the existence of Romanist educational institutions in this country next to impossible; but when, a little more than a century ago, the rigours of Catholic disabilities began to abate, the adherents of the old faith began to bestir themselves in the establishment of schools for their children. One large Catholic school for boys in the midlands had already been established at Sedgley Park near Wolverhampton in 1763 (an account of which institution will he found in the present writer's work entitled, "Sedgley Researches"); and now the Rev. John Kirk, president of that school being in charge of the Oscott mission, it was determined to develop this one nearer the more populous centre of Birmingham. A committee of Catholic gentlemen in 1794 took in hand the project of making provision not only for the higher education of boys at Oscott, but for the training of students for the priesthood.

From the Reformation to the French Revolution English Catholics had generally been educated abroad, most of them at Douai, St. Omer, or Liege; but the latter event had swept these seminaries away. Such was the period of storm and stress when Oscott Ecclesiastical College was founded for the accommodation of six students, by the midland bishops, Drs. Talbot and C. Berington.

It was a proud day for Catholicism when, in 1805, Francis Martyn, the first Catholic priest who had been entirely educated in England since the Reformation, was ordained and sent forth from Oscott. Entering fervently into his priestly duties, he in the course of an active career started parish missions at Bloxwich and Walsall, West Bromwich and Stourbridge, and at Bilston and Dudley.

The first President of Oscott College was the Rev. Dr. Bew, who had previously been in control of a Paris college, but flying from the horrors of the French Revolution he assumed a like office in the more tranquil atmosphere of Perry Barr. He held the Presidency till 1808, and almost from the first it was decided to admit laymen as well as clerical students. The college sprang at once into favour; in 1800 the building had to be enlarged to accommodate 60 students instead of the six originally contemplated; and four years later this number was increased to 72. The Vicar Apostolic of the Midlands took over the college and all its liabilities in 1810; and soon afterwards, in view of the larger developments contemplated, private enquiries began to be made for a new site of more extensive area. Even then there was a danger of arousing religious bigotry, and the transactions which led up to the establishment of New Oscott had to be conducted with great circumspection.

The Catholics of the midland counties, Warwick, Stafford, Worcester, and Salop took their courage in both hands in 1824, and at a public meeting presided over by Edward Blount Esq., a Staffordshire gentleman, passed a number of resolutions claiming liberty of conscience and the enjoyment of full civic rights for their co-religionists.—(See Langfords "History of Staffordshire" pp. 484-5).

For the new college was acquired a fine breezy site on the edge of the plateau nearer Sutton, and now designated New Oscott, a furzy eminence well out of the range of Birmingham's smoke. The building was commenced in 1835, and completed three years later at a cost of about £52,000. The edifice, designed by Mr. Potter, of Lichfield, on the lines of Wadham College, Oxford, was an eminently successful piece of architecture considering the debased period in which it was carried out. Although it is often asserted to the contrary, Pugin had nothing whatever to do with the main lines of the structure; but the two lodges were his work, and some of the embellishments were added by him; and he practically re-designed the whole of the sanctuary. The historic old buildings in the valley were retained for the purposes of a Convent and Orphanage, while the old college chapel still serves the purpose of a mission church.

One of the chief founders of Maryvale Orphanage was Laura Blount, for a great number of years a sister of mercy at Handsworth. She was the sister of Sir Edward Blount, K.C.B., who, prior to 1827, was himself educated at that old school He has since built for the Orphanage a large school to which Birmingham now sends same four or five hundred Catholic children. Since its erection New Oscott College has educated a number of England's most eminent Catholics, both lay and clerical. In 1889, however, it was closed to laymen, and since then all the bishops of England, by arrangement, have had a voice in the management of the Seminary. The college has also become a veritable treasure-house of relics collected from all quarters of Christendom; costly altar plate, and religious pictures of historic interest; magnificent vestments and church ornaments of the rarest description; and above all an almost unrivalled library of 30,000 volumes.

*   *   *   *   *   *   *

Modern Catholicity in Handsworth has its centre in Hunters Road. The Church of S. Francis there was opened in 1894, though the history of the mission goes back more than half a century. In 1840 the Convent of Our Lady of Mercy ("S. Mary's") in Hunters Lane was founded by Mr. John Hardman. He gave the land, built the convent and equipped it with everything necessary for the use of the sisters at a cost of £5,335. John, the 16th Earl of Shrewsbury, added a gift of £2,000 towards an endowment.

The Convent is, and has been from its foundation, the abode of a community of Sisters of Mercy. The first Superioress was Miss Hardman (in religion, Mother Mary Juliana) a daughter of the founder. She held office for 35 years, and was a woman of great ability and indefatigable energy. M. Mary Juliana erected the conventual chapel, built the almonry for the relief of the poor, and opened the first elementary schools of the mission; she also founded the House of Mercy (a home for servant girls out of place), and established the Poor Law School, now known as S. Joseph's Home. Her death at the age of 70, occurred at the convent, in 1884.

The handsome convent chapel, designed by the celebrated Pugin, was consecrated by Bishop Wareing In 1847, and was used as a public church till superseded by the newer edifice. Its accommodation had been found inadequate for a number of years; the rector, the Rev. F. Hopkins, therefore determined upon a larger church. The site at the corner of Wretham Road was secured, and the new and larger church erected upon it from the designs of the Very Rev. Canon Scoles, was opened with much ceremony in 1894 by the late Cardinal Vaughan. Dedicated to S. Francis of Assisi, the structure received a number of embellishments from time to time, such as a reredos, stained windows, and marble canapies for the statues; and in 1899 the whole of the interior was most effectively decorated in polychrome by Jeffries Hopkins. But as long as any debt remained upon the building the church could not be consecrated; by strenuous and unremitting efforts the rector contrived to clear it of all liabilities within six years of the opening, and in 1900 the ceremony of consecration was duly performed by Dr. Ilsley, Bishop of Birmingham, who commented on the fact, noteworthy in the history of any church, that the same rector who had projected the good work had been enabled to carry it to its final completion. Shortly after the opening the Rev. Francis Hopkins was honoured by being appointed a Canon of the Cathedral Chapter and it was with deep regret his congregation learnt some five or six years ago that he would be compelled by ill-health to resign his cure.

Canon Hopkins was succeeded at S. Francis's by the Rev. Walter Ireland, formerly President of S. Wilfrid's College, Oakamoor; but again in his case a breakdown in health occasioned a speedy retirement. The bishop then appointed the present rector, the Right Rev. Monsignor O'Hanlon, D.D., who is Vicar General of the Diocese of Birmingham, and Provost of the Cathedral Chapter.

To meet the requirements of Catholics living at the other extremity of the parish in the neighbourhood of the New Inns, another church is projected. A site has already been secured upon which to erect one. In the meanwhile Mass is said every Sunday in a temporary chapel in Albert Road, and this is known as "the Succursal Chapel of S. Augustine (of England)"

XXI.—DISSENT AND NONCONFORMITY.

The most prominent name in the history of religious dissent in Handsworth is that of Francis Asbury, the Pioneer Bishop of America, to whom a memorial chapel has been erected on the Holyhead Road within recent years. A fairly long account of this eminent divine has been given in the present writers "History of West Bromwich," and which will be but briefly recapitulated here.

Francis Asbury was born in 1745 near the foot of Hamstead Bridge, Handsworth; but while he was an infant his parents removed into Barr parish. In his "Journal" he writes of the pious atmosphere of his home, and of the cruelty of his schoolmaster at Snails Green, which drove him to take refuge in prayer. His spiritual "awakening" occurred at the early age of fourteen, and he speaks highly of the ministrations at West Bromwich parish church which he attended till, on the recommendation of his mother, he was induced to go to Wednesbury to hear the new sect of Methodists. The devoutness of this people, the deep earnestness of their hymn singing, and the extraordinary power of the preaching without the aid of a sermon-book impressed the receptive mind of the youth that he was drawn irresistibly towards the new Wesleyan brotherhood. In 1760, at the age of fifteen, he joined himself with four other young men who walked to Wednesbury every Sunday morning for a five o'clock service, returned to West Bromwich to attend church twice, and went again to an 8 o'clock evening service at Wednesbury where Mr. Alexander Mather was the great Methodist preacher at that time. Before Francis Asbury was twenty-one he had travelled the four adjacent counties as a local preacher; in 1763 he was appointed leader of the Society Class at West Bromwich Heath, and in 1767 formally entered the ministry. The Conference of 1771 appointed him for America, and he was present at the first American Conference in 1773. John Wesley having decided that the bishops and presbyters of the Primitive Church were of the same order, and having no objection to the appointment of Superintendents, the American brethren (being quite disentangled from the State and from the English hierarchy) proceeded to appoint Methodist bishops or superintendents of whom Asbury and Dr. Coke were the first.

It was thus a native of Handsworth became bishop of Baltimore in the Methodist Episcopal Church of America. In his episcopal career Francis Asbury preached 18,000 sermons, travelled 150,000 miles, presided at 270 Conferences, and is said to have ordained more ministers (nearly 3,000) than any other man ever did. In a letter to Dr. Coke he writes, in 1809, that he was sinking under the weight of labour and infirmity—"last year I had to travel on crutches several hundred miles, the face of the country is such

I cannot use wheels. . . . The annual duty of our Superintendents is great; they have to visit 8 conferences and make arrangements for 620 preachers; they have to ride 6,000 miles in eight months through wildernesses and devious lonely wilds."

Bishop Asbury founded the first Sabbath School in America, which he organised for the slaves of the Southern States in 1786. (The Independence of America had been declared in 1783, and the following year John Wesley had given up his personal authority over the American Wesleyan Societies).

Francis Asbury died near Fredericksburg, Virginia, in 1816. He was conspicuous for his simplicity of manner, his zeal, perseverance, and patient endurance of hardships. The motto engraved on his seal was "Show thyself approved of God." A very full biographical account of this Wesleyan worthy will be found in "The Pioneer Bishop," by W. P. Strickland (Manchester, 1860).

Another notable convert won from this locality to the cause of the despised "Methodies" was Lord Dartmouth of Sandwell Hall. He regularly attended the services at the Wesley Meeting-house at Wednesbury, where he expressly desired to be known as "Brother Dartmouth." John Wesley writing in 1778, designates this pious noble as "a real patriot" and "a friend to truth." The poet Cowper speaks of this minister of state as "one who wears a crown, and prays." William, second Earl of Dartmouth, died in 1801, and it was written of him—

Thy goodness, Dartmouth, makes thee truly great
And virtuous actions are thy coronet.

At that period, as the classes were largely addicted to gaming, duelling, the patronage of "sport," and similar vanities, so were the masses very generally given over to cock-fighting, bullbaiting and the other brutalities which they attempted to dignify by the name of "sport." There was no place more deeply sunk in this form of degradation than the cluster of gun lock-filers' houses along the Handsworth brookside, which on account of its notorious evil doings had been derisively dubbed "Nineveh." Bulls were regularly baited on the open space near the bridge in Bacchus Road; some anecdotal illustrations of Handsworth's delinquencies in this direction have been given by the present writer in his recently published book "Old English Sports."

In 1820 a band of West Bromwich Methodists made a determined attack upon the spiritual iniquities of this modern Nineveh. They held open air meetings an the bridge, and also on the slope now occupied by St. Michael's Church, but then within range of the celebrated Soho Works, and of the workmen's cottages which were dotted about the basin of the watercourse. A Methodist Society was formed, and weekly services were conducted in one or other of the neighbouring cottages, till increasing numbers warranted the renting of a small domiciliary workshop which was situated over a washhouse. By 1822 Nineveh Chapel was built; it has since grown into a useful centre for much religious and social activity; but as it was erected out side the confines of Handsworth parish, nothing more need be said here except to quote the following interesting record from the "Wesleyan Methodist Magazine" of December, 1822:—

"Nov. 3. A new chapel was opened at Nineveh near Birmingham by the Rev. G. Woolmer. Its dimensions are 33 feet by 30. All the pews are let, and there is a prospect of much spiritual good."

The Handsworth Wesleyan Chapels are embraced within the "Birmingham (Wesley) Circuit;" while the Perry Barr Chapel (Aston Lane, founded 1891, at a cost of £2,500) is in the "Aston Park Circuit." In the former are included the Asbury Memorial Church, erected 1885, and the Somerset Road Chapel, the founding of which at Handsworth Wood would appear to be the logical outcome of fixing the College there. For modern Handsworth boasts the latest branch of the Wesleyan Theological Institution, the others being at Richmond, Didsbury and Headingley.

Though John Wesley himself had contemplated the establishment of a seminary for his preachers, it is curious to find in 1833 his followers divided in opinion on the subject, even to the point of secession—it was feared by old fashioned Methodists that college training would deprive young ministers of that simplicity of mind and fervency of spirit which distinguishes the sect.

When, in 1866, the third connexional college was being promoted for Headingley, a considerable opinion was found to prevail in the Wesleyan body that the time was ripe to consider the urgent claims of the Midlands for similar treatment. London had, of course, a number of educational centres, Manchester had its Didsbury College, Leeds its Headingley, Sheffield its Wesley College, Bristol and Bath its Kingswood School for ministers' sons, but Birmingham had no connexional institution of the kind whatever.

The claims thus put forward by the Midlands were not to be slighted; so to make it a more vigorous and important centre of Methodist activity Birmingham was promised the next extension of the Theological Institution. At first a site near Walsall—the Old Park estate, on the Birmingham Road—was suggested; but eventually the more retired and salubrious situation at Handsworth Wood was decided upon. And to the fair-minded Englishmen there was something peculiarly felicitous in this selection, that the same parish which contained the great Catholic seminary of Oscott, should also include an equally important training institution for Protestant ministers, is a living testimony to the deepseatedness of that spirit of religious tolerance which pervades English society at the present day.

The Building Committee, which included the Right Hon. Sir H. H. Fowler, Thomas Barnsley (of Edgbaston), John Brewer (a Mayor of Walsall), William Newburn (father-in-law of R. W. Perks, M.P.), and T. P. Bunting (son of Dr. Bunting, and father of P. W. Bunting, editor of the "Contemporary Review"), held its first meeting at the close of 1878. They were influenced in their selection of Handsworth by the fact that it lay between Birmingham and the Black Country, an area containing a cluster of circuits in which the students would be able most conveniently to exercise their preaching gifts to good purpose. The site, embracing some 12 acres, was purchased at a cost of £7,000, and the designs of Messrs. Ball and Goddard, architects, were accepted. The architecture is fifteenth century Gothic, of the usual collegiate type, with a tall and massive central tower dominating the whole.

The building, the total cost of which was £40,000, was opened in 1881. It accommodates 70 students, and already some 400 have passed through its portals to labour in the field of Wesleyism. The young men learn to preach before they become candidates for the ministry; and their training in college is at once practical and academic.

*   *   *   *   *   *   *   *   *

Another outcome of the preaching of Wesley and Whitefield, and not the least important as far as Handsworth is concerned, was the founding of Union Row Chapel. Two gentlemen, whose zeal had been stimulated by the work of these great revivalists, erected this place of worship at their joint expense in 1789, and maintained it till 1803 as a member of the Countess of Huntingdon's connexion. The building was then closed for two years, but on April 16th, 1805, it was re-opened as a Congregational Church, and has been attached to that denomination ever since. The ministry of the Rev. John Hammond commenced on July 5th of that year, and continued till 1857; long before the termination of that lengthy pastorate the veteran minister came to be widely known as "Father Hammond of Handsworth." His successor, the Rev. Robert Ann, also had such a long tenure of office that the Union Row establishment came to be spoken of as "Ann's Chapel."

There is extant in print a sermon preached at this chapel by the Rev. Robert Ann, December 22, 1861, on the death of the Prince Consort. In 1877 the Rev G. Chetwode Postans became minister, and was succeeded in 1891 by the Rev. Edwin Tongue. Since 1899 the pastorate has been held by the Rev. Granville Sharp, M.A. A Sunday School has been attached to this old-established place of worship since 1807, and at one time it supported a flourishing day school.

Soho Hill Congregational Church is an offshoot of the Highbury Chapel, Graham Street (Birmingham), whose pastor, the Rev. W. F. Callaway, removed to the new chapel. His successors in the ministry have been the Revs. William Pierce, C. Lemoine, A. Geys Howell, and the present pastor, the Rev. James Wylie, who has held office since 1903. At this place of worship was brought up the Rev. Leonard Lucas, a successful worker of many years' standing in India for the London Missionary Society, and the author of several religious volumes.

Westminster Road Congregational Church, Birchfield, was built in 1882, the first pastor being the Rev. Walter Searle. His successor, the Rev. Campbell Morgan, is now well known in the religious world as Dr. Campbell Morgan, of Westminster (London). Since 1897 the pastorate has been held by the Rev. C. Deeble.

The Hamstead Road Baptist Church was built in 1883, at a cost of £7,000, and is a handsome structure, with nave, aisles, and transept, and a spire 120 feet high, all in true ecclesiastical style.

St. George's Presbyterian Church of England, in Heathfield Road, was erected in 1895. The site cost £600, and the building £4,000. The first pastor, the Rev. John McKeown, M.A., had been minister at the old church in New John Street (Birmingham). He retired through ill health in 1907, and was succeeded by the Rev. J. Sime Miller, M.A.

No the least interesting centre for public worship in Handsworth is the "New Church," in Wretham Road, erected by the Swedenborgians, in 1879, at a cost of £11,500. The sect had then been established in Birmingham for over a century, their earliest meetings having been held in a room in Great Charles Street (1774). After occupying a larger building in Temple Row for about sixteen years, they established themselves at Zion Chapel, Newhall Street, where they narrowly escaped the attention of the "Church and King" rioters in 1791. Their pastor, the Rev. Joseph Proud, had been the centre of a discussion in which Priestley had taken a prominent part. From 1830 till they followed the tide of population to Handsworth they were located in Summer Lane. In the vestry of the church on Soho Hill is the pedestal of the font which stood in the Newhall Street chapel. It bears an inscription not devoid of some little historic interest: "This pedestal for the font is the one which was used by the New Church Society of Birmingham from 1791 in the first place of worship built in the world for New Church worship, viz., that in Newhall Street near the corner of Lionel Street, and was thence removed by the society to their subsequent churches and used until 1876. The original basin, which was of cut glass, richly gilt, was replaced in 1833 by the one now inserted in the stone font in this church, which was prepared and presented by the architect, and is of Anglesea marble, as that in the exterior of the Town Hall, Birmingham."

The Rev. R. R. Rodgers, who has just retired from the pastorate after 42 years' continuous service, has been succeeded by the Rev. Harry Deans; and it is noteworthy that Mr. Rodgers' predecessor, the Rev. Charles Madeley, also served the church for 42 years. Although the Swedenborgian Church is not numerically strong, there are two other societies in this district—one at Moseley and one at Kidderminster.

The United Methodist Chapel in Villa Road, opened in 1900, is scarcely an instance of a migratory congregation deserting the business heart of the city for its pleasanter outskirts—for the reader cannot fail to observe how in Handsworth, as a residential suburb of Birmingham, places of worship have sprung up to serve the overflow of the population—although many of the worshippers at Villa Road were formerly attached to Unett Street Chapel.

XXII.—THE BRIDGE TRUST'.

It will be most informative first to quote *verbatim* the Report which the Charity Commissioners presented to Parliament in 1823:

BRIDGE TRUST (1612).

By deed of feoffment, dated 20th October 10th. James I. (as recited in the deed hereafter abstracted), Nicholas Hodgetts, of Handsworth, as cousin and heir of John Hodgetts, then late surviving feoffee of the messuages, lands, etc., hereafter mentioned, theretofore given for the maintenance and reparation of the bridges, within the parish of Handsworth, at the request of Edward Stanforde and others, substantial inhabitants, and that the estates should be settled and continued in persons fitted to dispose of the same, granted, enfeoffed and conveyed unto the said Edward Stanforde and others, inhabitants of the said parish:—

A messuage or tenement, with barns, garden orchard and closes thereto belonging, in Handsworth;

Also a croft or close of ground, called Jesson's Croft, lying between the great way leading from Perry Bridge towards Birmingham:

Also another croft or close, on the other side of the same way;

Also another croft or close called the Breach in which said close the said Edward Stanforde had six sellions or lands, about the middle of the same;

Also a croft or parcel of meadow ground, near Glomesmore;

Also a cottage or tenement. with the barns. buildings, garden, orchard, hemp land, and a little croft or close, lying near the same, between the common there, called Brown's Green;

And also six sellions or lands of arable ground, lying in a pasture in Handsworth, called Ash Croft;

Also a cottage or tenement, with a garden and orchard near the churchyard;

Also a meadow, in Witton. in the county of Warwick.

And also a yearly rent of 2s. 8d., issuing and payable out of a close of land, called Connigrie Croft, lying in Perry Barr:

To hold to the said Edward Stanforde and others, their heirs and assigns, to the intent that they should dispose of the premises in such sort, that a good rent might be received for the same, and that they should employ the rents and profits towards the repairing and maintaining of the said bridges, within the parish of Handsworth, as need should require; and if it should happen there should be any overplus of the rent, that the same should be employed and bestowed upon some good and charitable uses, within the parish of Handsworth, at the direction and appointment of the said feoffees, or the greater part of them, according to the order, use and custom, heretofore in like case used.

By Indenture, dated 4th June. 1745, between Humphrey Wyrley and others, of the one part; and Walter Gough, and six others, of the other part; reciting the deed above abstracted, and reciting further, another deed poll, dated 16th July 1652 whereby Thomas Lane and Thomas Bromwich, the two surviving feoffees in the deed above mentioned granted, enfeoffed and confirmed, unto Sir John Wyrley, knight and others, all and singular the premises before mentioned (except six sellions of land, in the close called the Breach, and also the yearly rent of 2s. 8d. in the said poll particularly mentioned) to hold to them and their heirs, in trust, to and for the use and behoof of the inhabitants of the parish of Handsworth, to and for the necessary reparations and maintenance of all common bridges within the said parish; and reciting further, that by several mesne conveyances, all the premises, except as in the last deed excepted, had become vested in the said Humphrey Wyrley and others, upon the trusts above declared: and further reciting, that by a decretal order dated 1st June, 1743, by the lord chancellor, in a cause wherein the attorney-general at the relation of Jonas Hipkis and John Brown was plaintiff, and the said Humphrey Wyrley and others, the parties of the first part, were defendants; it was ordered amongst other things, that certain trustees therein named, being eight in number, should be discharged from the trust, and that it should be referred to the master to appoint seven substantial inhabitants to be new trustees in their room; who, together with Humphrey Wyrley and William Ashford, should make up the number of nine trustees, to execute the said trust, to whom the said trust estate should be conveyed upon the trusts declared in the deed of 20th October, 10th. James I., with a clause, that when the trustees should be reduced to four, the survivors should out of the most substantial inhabitants, elect new ones, to make up the number of nine, and should make a conveyance of the trust estate to the use of the grantors and grantees, and further reciting, that the master had reported that the said Walter Gough and others were fit persons to be made trustees; It is witnessed, that in pursuance of the said decree, and for executing the trusts according to the true meaning of the deed poll of the 20th October, 10th, James I, the said Humphrey Wyrley and there granted, bargained and sold enfeoffed and confirmed to the said Walter Gough and others, the premises before mentioned (except as before excepted) to hold the same to the said Walter Gough and others, to the use of the said Humphrey Wyrley, Ashford, Gough and others, their heirs and assigns for ever, upon trust as declared in the said deed of the 20th October, 10th James I.

The Trust has been continued by several conveyances, the last of which bears date 25th March, 1807, wherein the premises are described as follows:—

1.—A messuage or tenement, with the buildings and closes thereto belonging, in a place called Birchfield End, otherwise Brisnell-end in the occupation of Matthew Glover, known by the several quantities and descriptions following: A close, called the Home Close, containing together with the garden ground and land on which the buildings stand, 4a. 3r. 12p.; also two other closes called Upper and Lower Linigoe, containing 4a. 1r. 10p.; also a close, containing 1a. and 1r. upon a line with the Home Close; also two other closes called the Breaches, containing together 9a. 1r. 8p.; also two other closes called Jesson's Crofts, containing together 3a. 2r. 26p.; also two other closes called the Meadows, containing 5a. 1r. 2p.; all of which last-mentioned premises and lands contain together 28a. 2r. 18p: also another messuage or tenement, with the garden. etc., thereto belonging, at Birchfield End, adjoining to the first above-mentioned cottage, in the occupation of Josiah Thompson.

2.—Also, two messuages, with the barn, buildings and garden thereto belonging, in the occupation of Joseph Willis and Thomas Jones.

3.—Also, a croft or piece of ground, called Ashford's Croft, in the occupation of John Southern, containing 1a. and 1p. situate at Brown's Green.

4 and 5.—Also a new-erected messuage, with the buildings and garden therto belonging, in the occupation of Solomon Smith, containing 1r. 26p.; also, two small pieces of ground, with the shopping, buildings, and erections thereon late the property of George Birch, esquire, containing by estimation 1r. and 26p., being near to Handsworth church.

6.—Also, a new-erected messuage or tenement, with buildings, garden, etc., and also, a new inclosed piece of land thereto adjoining, and let with the same, containing 4a. 3r. 34p., at or near Birchfield, otherwise Brisnell-end.

7.—Also, three messuages, with the buildings gardens, etc., thereto belonging, in the occupation of Widow Crawthorn, Joseph Moore and William Stanley; and also, another messuage with the buildings and garden, in the occupation of Richard Bromfield.

8.—And also, a croft or piece of land adjoining, called Broomy Croft, containing 2a. 1r. 15p. which said messuages, lands and premises, are near to Perry bridge; also that meadow land or piece of ground, adjoining thereto, called the Little Croft, containing 3r. and 28p., being near Perry bridge; also, those two pieces or closes of land in Perry Barr, commonly called the Far Field, and Near Leasow, containing 4a. 3r. 12p.

9.—Also, a close of meadow ground called Stanley's Meadow, in the occupation of Henry Stanley, containing 2a. and 32p. being in Witton in the parish of Aston, in the county of Warwick; also, a new inclosed piece of land, in the manor of Witton, in the parish of Erdington in the County of Warwick, lately allotted to the said trustees, containing by admeasurement one acre; also all that annual rent of 2s. 8d. issuing out of a certain close in Perry Barr called Conigrie, otherwise Conery Croft, late in the occupation of John Gough esquire.

On this last Indenture is also a Map of every part of the premises as they then were.

The Property therefore consists of these several parcels, of which the rental is as follows:—

No. 1.—Let to Thomas Beeson, by lease, dated 2st March, 1808, for 21 years from Lady-day following at the clear yearly rent of £65 0 0

This is now a very high rent. The messuage described as being in the occupation of Josiah Thompson, is turned into outbuildings, and occupied with the above. This lease is now vested in John Beeson, brother of Thomas.

A part of the Premises described in the deed as the Breache, is now given up in exchange to Mr. William Houghton, for a field, containing 2a. 2r. 21p., lying nearer to the farm-house, and close adjoining southward to Jesson's croft. The trustees gained 21 perches in measurement, and 10s. 6d. was added to the rent. This exchange took place by a regular indenture, dated 23rd April, 1814. The part of the ground called the Beaches, given up by the trustees, was 2a. and 2r. out of 5a. 7p.

No. 2—These messuages are in the occupation of the Widow Willets and Widow Jones, two old poor and needy persons, who have lately become widows. It was ordered, at a meeting of the trustees holden in the present year, that their rents should henceforth be only 1s. each yearly, it appearing to the trustees that they were proper and meritorious objects of the charity 2 0

The rent used to be £3 3s. from each

3.—Let to N. G. Clarke esq. as yearly tenant, at £3 3s. a year,. which is a full rent 3 3 0

4 and 5.—Let to Solomon Smith, as yearly tenant at 15 0 0

The latter part of ground, No. 5, was not part of the property originally given, but was a bit of waste ground adjoining to the plot No. 4, and was demised by George Birch, esq., in consideration of the sum of £3 15s to the trustees for the Bridge Charity for 1,000 years from the 18th March, 1799, at a peppercorn rent.

Upon the ground so demised, the trustees have lately built a National School, as hereafter mentioned, and on account of the ground occupied by it, have given up 1£ of the rent which used to be 16£. The present is a full rent.

No. 6.—By Indenture dated 7th March, 1794, the trustees demised to Isaac Anderton a piece of ground, containing 4a. 3r. 34p., being a new allotment set out on the inclosure; and also a piece of land, containing five perches, adjoining the above mentioned piece; and also a messuage or tenement situate upon Handsworth Heath, containing by statute measure 30 perches or thereabouts; to hold the same for 99 years, paying yearly £10. By the lease, the lessee covenanted within 7 years to build upon the said ground one or more good and substantial dwelling houses, at the expense of £300 and keep the same in repair, and yield up the same at the end of the term.

The lessee has laid out three or four times the amount of 300£ and the lease is now vested in Widow Phillips, by whom the rent is paid. 10 0 0

The situation was very advantageous for building upon. The house mentioned in the deed of 25th March, 1807, has been built under this lease.

No. 7.—For one messuage; widow Crawthorn pays 4 4 0

For another Thomas Bradbury 5 5 0

And for the third William Stanley 2 2 0
                                                                  —————
                                                                  11 11 0

There was a fourth cottage, occupied by one Bromfield, on the opposite side of the road, but which is now dilapidated.

No. 8.—Let to John Lander, as yearly tenant, at .... 16 0 0 which is a fair rent.

No. 9.—Let to Thomas Stanley, as yearly tenant, at .... 5 10 0 which is the fair value.

No. 10.—The trustees have also within these two or three years received an allotment of 3a. 1r. 4p upon Perry Barr Common, in lieu of their common right there. This is let to Thomas Joiner, as yearly tenant for .... 5 0 0 which is a fair rent.

No. 11.—The rent paid by John Gough, esq., out of Conigrie 2 8
                                                                  —————
                                                                  £131 8 8

Besides the above the Trustees are possessed of a mortgage for 500£ secured upon the Church Rates of the parish of Handsworth, having lent that sum to the churchwardens, under the powers of two several acts of Parliament, passed in the 58th and 59th of George III.

The mortgage deed is dated 24th June, 1821, and it appears that the sum advanced was to be paid off by instalments of 83£ 6s. 8d. annually, with interest, at 5 per cent., £25 0s. 0d.

No interest has yet been received for this money.

There are eight Bridges in Handsworth parish of which five are carriage bridges, and three foot bridges, which are repaired wholly or partly out of the trust funds.

One of the carriage bridges and one of the foot bridges being half in the parish of St. Martin, Birmingham, are repaired jointly with that parish; and one of the carriage bridges is repaired jointly with Great Barr, being half in that township.

These Bridges being now in good order, require a very small sum to keep them so. The heavy expenditure used to be on account of two large bridges, which, about 20 years ago, were transferred to the County.

In the year 1807, there was a balance of £637 in hand, a part of which was invested in the purchase of £600 five per cents.; and other dividends, from time to time, were added to the funds of the charity. Some heavy expenses were afterwards incurred for repairing and enlarging the farm-buildings, which are now very complete and good; but still the income exceeded the expenditure.

At a meeting of the Trustees, held 7th January, 1812, it was resolved, That the establishing a School on the national plan of education, would be a proper application of part of the money vested in the funds; and an estimate was ordered to be prepared of the expense of building a school, to contain 200 children. A School was afterwards built on a piece of ground demised to the trustees by George Birch, Esq., at an expense of nearly £800; and £20 was also given to buy Bibles and Prayer-Books for the children. The £600 stock was sold out for this purpose. The School was finished about 1813, and given up to the committee of management of the school, which is supported by voluntary contributions. It was stipulated that the trustees of the Bridge Charity should always be on the committee. Not withstanding this expenditure, the funds have continued to increase in the hands of treasurer; and in 1820, the trustees had directed the sum of £500 to be lent to the Churchwardens (under certain Acts of Parliament for that purpose) for repairing Handsworth church, as before mentioned.

There was at the last settling, 19th October 1822, a balance in hand of £201. 5s. 4d., part of which is to be laid out immediately in building two cottages at Perry Barr, in the place of the one that has fallen down, and of another that is in a ruinous state.

The sums required for repairs of the Bridges are now so small, that it is difficult to draw any average of the expense.

The sum of £1. 5s. is paid regularly out of the rents of the Churchwarden, which is supposed to be payable out of a piece of ground at the back of one of the cottages near Broomy Close. [See Gibbons's Charity Report.]

It appears from the books, that it was formerly the practice to give out of the rents a sum of money to the poor, at Christmas. In the year 1787, £50 was so paid. In 1793, 25 guineas. In 1795, £21 was given to a Medical gentleman for supplying the poor with medicines, for a year: Also £20 in the same year, for binding poor children Apprentices; and £30 for repairing two houses belonging to the poor of the parish, such being then reckoned as the minute entered in the Treasurer's Book expresses it, good and charitable uses, according to the meaning of the donor.

These latter payments were ordered to be continued in the year 1798.

In the year 1799, £50 was given to the Poor in coals, bacon and potatoes. This mode of application being, however, objected to by John Gough, esq. he filed a bill in Chancery against the trustees, for so far misapplying the charity fund, conceiving that payments of this description aided the poor rates merely, and were not proper applications of the charity. The Trustees, in consequence, desisted, and by a minute made in 1801 it appears, that the matter was referred to arbitration, in the rest of which Mr. Gough was ordered to pay costs, and there the matter ended. Since that time, the trustees have not disposed of any money in that manner; and this circumstance, together with that of the two bridges being transferred to the County rates, may account for the accumulation which of late years has taken place.

The Trustees have it in contemplation to apply to the Court of Chancery for instructions as to the application of the accumulating income.

XXIII.—DIVERTED FROM BRIDGES TO EDUCATION.

The ancient common law of England attached certain conditions to the holding of land; irresponsible ownership was absolutely unknown. There was a triple obligation ("*trinoda necessitas*") inseparably attached to all landed property; namely (1) military service; (2) works for the defence of the realm; (3) the maintenance of highways and bridges. Public bridges being for general convenience, and of common right, had to be repaired by the whole inhabitants of the county in which they lay. In each parish waywardens were appointed to see the work carried out by their fellow residents, who had to supply the labour and the team work. But some men are negligent of their duties and others are perverse; and notwithstanding the threats of fine and forfeiture, it was always difficult for unpaid elective officials to compel their neighbours to fulfil their obligations to the community with any amount of goodwill or thoroughness.

Naturally the roads became neglected and the bridges unsafe. Some bridges were then repaired by tenure—it became a condition of tenure (or sometimes an obligation of status) upon some individual to do the work. It thus came about that lands adjacent to a bridge were frequently held burdened with the legal liability to repair that bridge.

An illustration of this is presented by the "Tame Bridge Case," involving a long series of disputes, and recurrent proceedings in the law courts from 1606 to 1894, an account of which forms chapter xxxv. in the present writer's "History of West Bromwich."

Also the Lench Trust in Birmingham was formed to among other worthy objects—repair the Rea Bridge at Digbeth. Such trusts were associated with the charities of the church because pious founders sought by these benefactions to induce a more, godly spirit by removing obstacles to regular attendance at church. Nicholas Hodgetts, as mentioned in the foregoing Report, may or may not have been the actual originator of the Handsworth Bridge Trust, but the foundation was characteristic of the period in which he lived. Perry Bridge was repaired in 1711 by Sir Henry Gough, who is said to have received £200 towards the cost from the county and the neighbouring parishes.

The great fact that stands out is that some fifty acres of land, mainly on the Birchfield side of the parish, were left for the maintenance and reparation of the bridges within the parish; and that this was strictly carried out till the Court of Chancery ruled the practice illegal, except in respect of the Church Bridge, Grove Lane Bridge, Oscott Bridge, Paper Mill Footbridge, Rectors Meadow Bridge, and Barr Brook Bridge.

The lands of this charity largely increased in value as time went on; so that after the due execution of the trust so far as the maintenances of the eight bridges was concerned, funds steadily accumulated. Then, as the Report discloses, from 1787 and subsequently, advantage was taken of the clause in the endowment which permitted the employment of any available surplus upon "good and charitable uses within the parish of Handsworth."

In the exercise of this discretionary power the indigent sick were doctored, and still more doles were distributed to the poor. Indeed, at an early stage, the trustees seem to have so far enlarged upon the original intentions of the fund as to have brought themselves into collision with an interested party, a member of the Gough family, as related at the close of the last chapter. Happily for Handsworth the collective wisdom of the parish early came to recognise the cause of education as the most desirable channel into which to divert the constantly accumulating funds of this beneficent charity.

Thus, as stated in the last chapter, the Church Schools were established in 1812. This first essay in the provision of public elementary schools by no means arrested the growth of the parishioners' zeal for education. And though it has been darkly hinted that the £500 lent about that time on the security of the Church Rates for the renovation of the church was never repaid, the funds in the hands of the trustees still continued steadily to increase—a tendency further encouraged by the progress of nineteenth century legislation, which threw the burden of maintaining bridges upon the local authorities. An enterprising and public spirited Parish Committee was formed which formulated a scheme and presented it to a public meeting of the inhabitants of Handsworth, which was held at the Waggon and Horses Inn, on Thursday, 10 September, 1857.

The scheme proposed that the revenues of the charity, after being used for keeping wholly in repair the five first-named of the bridges, and contributing half the expense or maintaining the Barr Brook Bridge, should be devoted to educational purposes; namely, to erecting and maintaining a charity school "near the Post Office of Handsworth, being the most populous part and therefore the most convenient," for 250 boys and 150 girls; also to erect a school at Perry Barr for 100 boys and 100 girls; and other new schools as wanted and the revenues permitted. All the pupils resident in the parish were to be admitted free; but non-parochial children might also be admitted as long as there was room, at a fee of 6d. or 2d. per week. But that portion of the scheme which excited the greatest hostility was the recommendation that the proposed schools should be "conducted as British Schools."

It is not difficult to imagine the fierce controversy which arose when this scheme was submitted to a Vestry Meeting on April 9th, 1858. The pamphleteer was quickly in the field to denounce the iniquity of such proposals; "the main object of the amended scheme seemed to be to prevent the teaching of the doctrines of the Church of England," wrote that irate individual.

The outcome of a prolonged public agitation was to obtain the permission of the Charity Commissioners for diverting the proceeds of the Bridge Trust, and to apply the major portion of the income, with an amount which has been invested in consols, to give effect to an amended scheme which was eventually agreed upon in 1859. The money was directed to be applied in founding and maintaining a Middle School at Handsworth, with either an elementary or a branch school, at, or near, Perry Barr. The privileges of the Middle School, which is now the Grammar School, were restricted to boys, but the elementary school was to be open to both sexes alike. The funds, however, were never sufficient to justify the trustees in erecting the latter establishment; and the site for the Handsworth School was not fixed "near the Post Office" in Soho Road, but in Grove Lane. This "Middle School" in Grove Lane was formally opened on August 5th, 1862, under the headmastership of the Rev. J. M. Guest, M.A. The Rev. H. R. Peel, Rector of Handsworth, was the first chairman of Governors, and Mr. W. T. Stubbs the first clerk. And this institution went on for nearly 50 years, enjoying a very fair amount of success.

In 1890 a new scheme was formulated and carried into effect whereby the Bridge Trust School was to be known for the future as Handsworth Grammar School. The board of governors was so constituted as to have upon it representatives from the various local bodies. The vested interests of the Head Master, the Rev. James Merrick Guest, who had then held the post for a great number of years, were carefully safeguarded. As "Master of the Middle School of the foundation" he was to continue in office, with the right to take twelve boarders. But otherwise the school was to be for day boarders only, paying tuition fees of £3 to £8 a year; they were to be from 8 to 16 years of age, resident within or near to the parish, of good character and sound health, and admitted by the test of passing an examination. At the same time were established Foundation Scholarships for total or partial exemption from the payment of fees, in the proportion of 1 to 10 boys in the school, and this laudably with the direct intention of attracting the best scholars from the elementary schools. The educational ladder was admirably completed by the creation of Exhibitions tenable at "Mason College"—now the Birmingham University. The scheme was wisely rounded off by the non-imposition of religious tests for the scholars, though again nothing was done towards bringing girls within the benefits of this public benefaction.

A government return of forty years ago, quoted in Langford's county history, states that Handsworth was then in receipt of £705 14s. 5d. a year from charitable endowments; of which £300 was applied towards education, £184 10s. 0d. to "public uses," £159 17s. 11d. was distributed in doles, and £4 14s. 0d. was expended on church purposes. This return is somewhat difficult to understand. The newly constituted Handsworth Grammar School, with accommodation for 150 boys, enjoys an annual income, exclusive of public grants, of about £1,000. This surely is an institution of which any parish might justly be proud. To commemorate the origin of the foundation the school-badge worn by the boys depicts the "zig-zag bridge" at Perry Barr, the picturesque old structure which still spans the murky waters of the Tame there.

A fuller and more detailed history of the school may safely be left to the writers of school magazine, which is appropriately entitled "The Bridge." In fact the foundation already boasts many honourable school traditions and has a very flourishing Old Boys' Club, associated with which is a Lodge of Freemasons—institutions which at least bespeak a love of alma mater, and disclose an amount of success achieved by the scholars in after life.

XXIV.—WARLIKE HANDSWORTH.

In chapter vii. we obtained some insight into the incidence of war taxes; now to see how levies of fighting men were anciently made within the manor.

In 1538 Pope Paul IV. not only excommunicated Henry VIII., but deposed him for his heretical opinions; and as at this juncture effect might possibly have been given to the papal threat owing to the king of France and the Emperor of Germany suddenly settling their differences, and uniting in an unwonted friendship, there was naturally some amount of apprehension in England. Indeed the king and his privy council were so alarmed that they ordered forthwith a muster of the entire armed forces of the kingdom.

The panic, however, died away; and although the levies were never actually called up, the state papers relating to the incident afford some very interesting local information. The Letters Patent appointing Commissioners of Array, (1539) included among the Staffordshire names of nobles and knights thus empowered to raise these territorial forces, that of "William Wyrley the younger, of Hamstead."

These Commissioners had to call up, array, test, and inspect all "defensible men," horse, foot, and archers; and to see that they were properly equipped and armed ready for active service.

In the following list, occur some terms which will need glossarial explanations to their proper understanding. A "jack," be it known, was a doublet, or defensive body garment, well padded and quilted, and covered with strips of thick leather.

"Splents;" or splints, were pieces of armour for the arms, where they were left unprotected by the jack. A "Salet" (French, salade) was a light steel cap, having a projection behind, extending over the nape of the neck.

"Harness" was any kind of armour worn by a soldier, and the term sometimes included the armour worn by war horses.

The "Bill" used by the billman of that period was a weapon no less than 18 feet in length. It was a pike with a long handle; the head was often an axe, but was always a billhook which could be used for dragging a man from his horse.

The list of names on the Muster Roll of 1539 seems rather a lengthy one; but as the words "Hamstead and Handsworth" which head it, have been crossed out, it is not improbable some of the men may have come from outside the manor. Here is the first part of Roll, verbatim:

Hampstede and Handvorth.

William Wyrley esquyer with vi seruants redy furnysshed with horse and harnes

William Coke a billman Jacke Salet splentes horse

Phylyp Osburne bowman Sallett splentes horse

William Hethcote a billman with horse able

Thomas Dokyn Jack Salet splentes bill horse able

Ryc. Osburne a billman Jack Salett and gorget able

John Werley a billman with Salet splentes able

John Hanmore a billman able

Peter Hoffyld Jacke Salet

Hugh Sharratt a billman able

Richard Barebon a billman able

Richard Saunders a billman with Salet splentes able

John Barebon a billman able

John Hateley a billman Jacke Salett and splenttes

John Abbott a billman able

Richard Hodgettes a billman able

Richard Blackhm a byllman able

William Twyst a billman able

Jame Sherrard a billman able

William Parsons a billman able

Thomas Assheford Jacke

William Pedwall a billman able

Summa with horse and hernes xiiij persons.

In this Roll are two other very similar lists; one is reckoned up or summarised at the end with the note—

"Summa billmen xxxvj persons with summe of habillimentes"

and the other list with

"Summa bowmen xxxiiij persons wyth hors or hearnes."

Among the surnames in these lists it is interesting to note some which still linger in the parish or have helped to make its history—Hodgetts, Smalwode, Osburn, Bromwych, Heley, Austyn, Kyndryke, Blackham, Barebon, Spurryar, Freman, Cook, Starley, Saunders, Botte, Tyrley, etc., etc.

The lapse of a century brings us towards a period of greater military activity. The real commencement of the English Revolution dates from the attempt of Archbishop Laud to force the English liturgy upon the Scottish nation. Charles I. tried to impose this on the Covenanters by force, to which end a special muster of troops was made in 1640. The men from

Staffordshire consisted of the "trained bands," who had been embodied the previous year, and 300 men who were "impressed" for the occasion. The service was so unpopular that in many places the men mutinied and murdered their officers. The trained bands were armed partly with pikes and partly with fire-locks, the newly invented arm, many of which were made in the district round Birmingham and South Staffordshire. The pressed men were armed merely with pikes. This was the last attempt at raising men on the old feudal levies; and the muster roll for this parish contains these names:—

	Traine	Presse
Perry Barre	William Hoomer	John Millward
Handswoorthe	Henry Willys	Richard Collyer
	John Dutton	George Bloxum

When actual hostilities between the King and his Parliament broke out shortly afterwards, the part played by Birmingham, Aston, and this immediate neighbourhood is too well known to need more than a brief recapitulation of that which affects Handsworth directly.

It has been mentioned (p. 45) that Edward Stamford of Perry Hall was a colonel in the Royalist army; and that the Roundheads were furnished with 15,000 sword-blades from the grinding-mills of this locality (p. 51). In many of the marchings and counter-marchings between Birmingham and Lichfield, or Birmingham and Walsall or Wolverhampton, troops of both sides were doubtless passing frequently through Handsworth. On October 17, 1642, King Charles passed through on his way from Wolverhampton to Aston Hall; and the following morning it was a picturesque, if somewhat ominous scene, which was presented by the Cavalier troops riding gaily across Perry Bridge to the rendezvous at Kings Standing. On this eminence (to which allusion was made on p. 8) Charles I. addressed the troops which had been raised for the royal cause in and around Shropshire. This site for a bivouacing ground had been selected on account of its commanding position, and its proximity to Aston Hall, where his majesty was resting. From hence the troops moved southwards along the old Chester Road, and on Sunday, the 23rd of month, encounted the enemy near Kineton, where was fought the memorable battle of Edgehill, the first engagement in the great Civil War.

In the following year Queen Henrietta Maria with a very "mixed" company of Cavaliers, among whom were Spaniards, and Frenchmen, Walloons, and Irishmen, collected by her in Holland, marching from Walsall on their way to join the Prince Rupert at Stratford-on-Avon, passed through this parish, coming by way of Tame Bridge, Newton, and Sandwell Lane, and so on towards Kings Norton, where they encamped for the night.

Passing on for a century and a half in the nation's history we read that threats of invasion by revolutionary France in 1794 led to the enrolment of armed citizens as volunteers, while the Yeomanry were formed into Cavalry regiments. Between 1793 and 1804 this force reached a total of 410,000 men. Handsworth was not behind-hand in this patriotic work. The men of Handsworth, Smethwick, and Harborne, enrolled themselves with enthusiasm—even "the Odd Fellows determined to form themselves into a military corps." Each member agreed to clothe and arm himself at his own expense, and to serve without pay; the gentlemen who formed themselves into troops of Cavalry, provided their own mounts, their uniforms as light horse-men, and all the necessary arms and accoutrements.

We read that on George III.'s birthday in 1799 (June 10) the Handsworth Cavalry, the Hales Owen Cavalry and Infantry, and the Bilston horse and foot volunteers, united with the Birmingham Cavalry and Infantry, and the demonstration was also "obligingly joined by the Regiment of Royal North British Dragoons (the Greys);" after parading New Street the whole force proceeded to Birmingham Heath, where they were reviewed in the presence of a vast concourse of people.

Although the French never gave these enthusiastic volunteers any opportunity of displaying their valour, it cannot be said they were never "called out." If never employed to repel a foreign invader, they were occasionally found handy—in those days before the establishment of a regular police force—in assisting the civil authorities to suppress riots and disorders.

Thus in May, 1810, a riot occurred in Birmingham, the origin of the disturbance being nothing more serious than two women quarrelling in the market over the price of potatoes. The disturbance, however, gave an opening for the outbreak of lawlessness, and "the village of Edgbaston, two miles away," was raided by the mob, thirteen of whom were presently arrested by a troop of Dragoon guards which had been called in to the assistance of the town authorities. The plundering of the Edgbaston farms was resumed just as fiercely the following day, till a hastily summoned body of the Warwickshire Yeomanry had made further arrests of the ringleaders. Then we read in the words of a contemporary reporter that in the evening yet "another attempt at disorder was made at the bottom of Snow Hill; but the Handsworth Volunteer Cavalry arriving, prevented any mischief there, except the little which they experienced themselves, by a volley of stones and brickbats, thrown by some villains who had secreted themselves under the canal tunnel"— not a very sanguinary affair. This was not the only time the Handsworth Volunteers assisted in the restoration of civil order; a kind of service in which there may have been some hard knocks but very little of military glory.

Handsworth parochial records have preserved the following item relating to the Militia:

"March 8th, 1808: For the constable and head-borough's loss of time in going round the parish one day, 10s.; paid for a drum and fife to get men for the locle (local) militia, 10s.; paid for ribbonds. £1 13s. 4d. March 10th: For going to Lichfield to swear in the locle militia, 12s.

The parish constable at that time was Jeremiah Needham; and we can imagine him pompously perambulating the parish, halberd in hand, accompanied by drum and fife, to do this annual recruiting for the militia. The halberd with which he armed himself on these state occasions was a formidable weapon, seven feet in height, such as the beef-eaters are wont to carry. It was carefully labelled. "Handsworth Parish 1622.—J.H. 1729."

To explain this Militia business: Under the ancient feudal system the King could always count on a force of 40,000 men to follow him in war for forty days in each year. After the restoration of Charles II. all military tenures were abolished by law, and the ancient militia force was put on a new footing by statute. Then in 1802 all prior acts relating to the militia were repealed, and the local record just quoted discloses some of the military machinery then working.

Of the 41,000 militia men then leviable, 1,133 had to be provided by "the county of Stafford and Lichfield;" the Parish Constables would have to make out yearly lists of men between the ages of 18 and 45 (among the legally exempt from serving were peers, clergymen, teachers, and poor men with more than one child born in wedlock—£50 being the penalty for trying to bribe the constable to make a false return) and affix the parish list to the church door.

Then the deputy lieutenant of the county having appointed the number to be supplied by each parish, a ballot was taken for them, and the men thus chosen were sworn in and enrolled—in this case at Lichfield, as recorded.

It was again the fear of a French Invasion inspired by the Machiavellian policy of Napoleon III. which in 1859 led to the formation of the Rifle Volunteers. Handsworth was the first parish in the county to raise a Volunteer company, and the eighteenth in the whole kingdom; West Bromwich was the twentieth, and Smethwick the thirty-first. When the various companies about the country were formed into battalions, the Handsworth, Smethwick, and West Bromwich Companies were attached to the 3rd Administrative Battalion of the Staffordshire Regiment, the Handsworth Company being known as the first, and Smethwick the thirty-first. The uniform, which was originally gray, with green facing, bore these distinctive numbers.

At a later period the Volunteers were formed into brigades, and the battalion to which Handsworth belonged was attached to the 1st South Staffordshire Regiment raised at Lichfield in 1702. It was this unification of the auxiliary and the regular forces which necessitated the adoption of the traditional "red coat" of the military by the citizen soldiers.

In 1896 the South Staffordshire Regiment was 6,240 strong, and composed of seven Battalions; the 1st located at Aldershot; the 2nd in India; the 3rd and 4th constituted of the Militia; then came the three Volunteer Battalions, the 1st called the Handsworth, the 2nd the Walsall, and the 3rd the Wolverhampton. Thus organised in brigades the seniority of Handsworth was made apparent, by its two companies being designated A and B, and Handsworth being the battalion headquarters.

After an honourable and useful existence of nearly half a century these Volunteer forces have just been merged in the new Territorial Army (1908).

XXV.—THE WORLD OF SOHO.

Space would be lacking in a general history for all that could be chronicled of the great "world of Soho." But never let it be forgotten that the early industrial triumphs with which the name of that place will ever be associated, were achieved within the confines of the parish of Handsworth. The historic Soho Factory was demolished in 1862, but fragmentary vestiges of its foundation are to be seen to this day lying between South Road and Soho Brook. And is it not classic ground here, this precise spot of the earth's entire surface, where it was ordained that steam-power as first harnessed by James Watt should supplant running-water—should supersede for all time, the chief motive power of antiquity?

It was in 1764 that Matthew Boulton fixed his manufactory in this place. He was a Birmingham manufacturer of steel buckles, chains, and other small wares generally known in the trade as "steel toys;" who, finding his premises in Snow Hill too limited in space, bought the lease of this site which seven years earlier had been granted by the lord of the manor of Handsworth to two partners, Rushton and Eaves, with liberty to turn the watercourse and make a storage pool sufficient for the working of a metal rolling-mill. This was effected by diverting and deepening the channel of the brook between Nineveh Road and Piers Road, the latter being originally a pathway leading through a fine avenue of trees towards Boulton's new factory. Soho was then a mere sandy rabbit warren, a part of the wide open common land of Handsworth in which there was but one solitary human habitation, the warrener's hut on the summit of the hill. Here Boulton erected a factory at a cost of £20,000, and capable of finding employment for hundreds of skilled workmen. In a year or two the whole aspect of Soho was changed; the "great captain of industry" built himself a residence, "Soho House," on the site of the hut—it is still standing in Soho Avenue, and in one of the cellars is to be found the warrener's well—while workmen's cottages sprang up everywhere in the vicinity.

It was in 1773 James Watt, "benefactor of the world," joined Matthew Boulton at Soho. In 1777 William Murdock appeared upon the scene, as an applicant for employment at this world-renowned factory. These three names are subjects of national biography, and can be but mentioned here to be summarily dismissed. Another famous name is that of Francis Eginton, who revived the art of glass-staining in England, and was employed in the japanning and other artistic branches of work carried on at Soho. Boulton and Watt's Factory seems to have been regarded as a sort of Mecca for every artisan who possessed a genius for mechanics, or had a taste for any branch of industrial art.

For all that Murdock did not find the place an inventor's paradise. At the outset his services seem to have been somewhat reluctantly accepted by Boulton; and in after years when he was making his experiments with coal-gas his efforts were regarded very coldly, even by Watt. Yet this spot which saw the perfection of the first steam engine was also to see the first successful experiment in gas-lighting. "Aris's Gazette" describing Murdock's novel illumination of the Handsworth Mint for the great national rejoicing over the Peace of Amiens in 1802, said—"For elegance and boldness of design. grandeur of effect, and promptness of execution, they will remain unparalleled amongst the numerous demonstrations of joy displayed on the public occasion of returning peace.

On the top of the roof was a great star, while above the central window was a large transparency showing a female figure in the attitude of giving thanks for the return of Peace. As a contemporary newspaper account states that 2,600 lamps were used, but does not mention, or even hint, that gas was the illuminant employed on that occasion, some doubt has been raised as to whether this was the historic public introduction of gas-lighting. But a fuller acquaintance with the actual facts will not rob Handsworth of the honour of this historical association. It must be confessed, however, that the instalment was a somewhat primitive one.

It would appear that the gas was manufactured at the Soho Foundry, Smethwick, and carried up to the Mint in large bags; while the illuminations were designed by lines of punctures made in stiff cardboard, and having coloured tissue paper pasted over the holes. (The "History of Gas-lighting " by William Mathews will be found informative on this subject.) Imperfect as the display was, it attracted vast crowds of sight-seers. Yet for long afterwards the critics heaped ridicule upon Murdock's idea of obtaining "light from smoke," one "brither Scot" breaking out thus into rhyme—

We thankful are that sun and moon
    Are placed so very high,
That no tempestuous hand may reach
    To tear it from the sky.
Were it not so, we soon should find
    That some reforming ass
Would straight propose to snuff them out
    And light the world with gas.

To describe the varied and novel productions of Soho is beyond the scope of this work. How prolific in the arts of industry this corner of Handsworth parish has really been is scarcely realised—not only in steam-engines and mining-pumps, plated goods and or-molu wares, vases and candelabra, steel toys and ornamental goods, but novelties, improvements, and inventions of many kinds. This genius of James Watt, assisted by some remarks of Dr. Priestley, had perfected the now common "copying machine;" but when Boulton showed specimens of its work to some London M.P.'s, fear was expressed that the process would lead to the forging of bank notes, and for a time prejudice was excited against it.

By another remarkable process carried on at Soho oil paintings were reproduced mechanically. Francis Eginton became a partner with Boulton for the manufacture of polygraphs or "sun-pictures;" these were sun-pictures in name only, being really impressions from copper-plates, engraved in aquatint, and printed at a copper-plate printing press. The venture never paid, and the unprofitable partnership was dissolved in 1780. In this connection it has been suggested that Watt, Wedgwood, and their other friends were quite familiar with the fact that nitrate of silver might be made to receive impressions, though they did not know how to "fix" the sun-pictures so produced—in other words, that modern photography had its birth at Soho. If the suggestion has not withstood the probing of expert research, Handsworth still takes a high position on the rolls of invention.

Francis Eginton, who had been an enamel painter, then began to paint glass on Soho Hill in 1784, and brought his art to great perfection, as many of his existing windows testify— specimens of his craftsmanship are to be found at St. George's Chapel, Windsor, in Lichfield, and St. Asaph's Cathedrals, at Hampton Court and Arundel Castle, and many other notable places, the nearest example perhaps being the east window of St. Paul's Church, Birmingham. Eginton did not practise any of the principles of mediæval glass painting; his designs stretched over the whole light, without antique borderings or geometric forms; they were executed entirely with enamel colour, with little or no outline and few leads—they were in fact pictorial transparencies. In Shaw's "History of Staffordshire" (1798) is a fine engraving of Francis Eginton's residence, Prospect Hill (which occupied the site of the present Soho Hill Chapel) with a long account of his numerous artistic productions in stained glass.

Not the least important department of Soho's industrial hive was the Mint. It is recorded of the middle of the eighteenth century, when coining was a capital offence, that "one of the grimmest sights of these days were the skeletons of convicted coiners dangling from gibbets on Handsworth Heath." But whereas the "Brummagem" of that period had an unenviable reputation for counterfeiting, the Birmingham of to-day can claim a preeminence in the production of perfect coins and artistic medals, and this unquestionably through the triumphs won in this particular line of industry at Boulton's Soho Mint. Between 1797 and 1806 no less than 4,200 tons of copper coin were issued from this establishment, which stood on the other side of South Road from the main factory. In 1799 an Act was passed enabling the exportation of minting machines from Soho to Russia.

The story of Soho is indeed a classical episode in the world's industrial history. It has a voluminous literature of its own, a passing reference to which must suffice for present purposes. The most exhaustive writer on the subject of Soho, its heroes and its industrial achievements, was without doubt the late Sam Timmins.

Among the standard works on the subject is Dr. Smiles's "Lives of the Engineers—Vol IV. Boulton and Watt" It contains a number of interesting wood cuts illustrative of "Old Handsworth;" among them is a capital view of the famous Soho Factory, and another of the adjacent Soho House, Boulton's residence, which is still standing behind St. Michael's Church. There are two pictures of the Waggon and Horses' Inn. One shows the exterior of this old-fashioned bow-windowed tavern which formerly stood on the site of the Council House; and the other depicts the interior of its great kitchen, where foolish Dick Cartwright innocently gave away the secret of James Watt's new rotary engine. There is a picturesque view of old Soho Pool; one of Murdock's residence, Sycamore Hill, and one of Heathfield as it was when James Watt lived there. There is also a picture of the well-known interior of Watt's Workshop in the garret at Heathfield, which remains to this day just as he left it. There is an interesting view of the exterior of Handsworth old church, and also two interiors; one showing Watt's statue in the memorial chapel, and the other the bust of Boulton in the old chancel.

Another book which the patriotic Handsworthian cannot overlook is "James Watt of Soho and Heathfield," by the late T. Edgar Pemberton (Cornish Brothers, 1905). It contains four interesting illustrations, and has manifestly been produced as a work of love by one to whom the memories of old Handsworth were particularly dear. It must suffice here to indicate the nature of its contents by enumerating the titles of its eight ably written chapters—"Concerning Inventors," "Heathfield," "Soho," "Matthew Boulton," "James Watt," "William Murdock," "Francis Eginton," and "The Lunar Society."

The fame of this locality as the centre of that coterie of eighteenth-century intellectuals who called themselves the Lunar Society will never die. Originally founded in 1765 it took its name from the times appointed for its monthly meetings, which were carefully fixed for the nights when the moon was at the full. One imaginative writer has pictured these philosophers taking leave of their host, and dispersing on their several ways from Great Barr Hall, in the light of a brilliant moon. Quite a number of them always had to ride across Handsworth Heath, in one direction or another. Ere it died down as death took its leaders, this famous club included Boulton, Watt, Murdock, Baskerville, Priestley. Dr. Small, Captain Keir (of West Bromwich), Dr. Withering (of Harborne), Samuel Galton (of Great Barr), Richard Lovell Edgeworth, author and philosopher, Thomas Day, Dr. Erasmus Darwin, John Wilkinson, "the father of the iron trade," and other men of note, not a few of whom were Fellows of the Royal Society, and whose names only as regular visitors to a place would add lustre to its reminiscent associations.

Truly the industrial history of Handsworth if somewhat ephemeral in its character, was glorious while it lasted. To visit its famous workshops and admire its artistic and mechanical productions, came sight-seers from all quarters of the civilized world; among the visitors to Soho at this great industrial awakening were included not only soldiers and statesmen, and the bearers of the most illustrious names in literature and art, in science and philosophy, but princes and potentates and the great ones of the earth. Among the former were there not Dr. Johnson and his satellite Boswell, and among the latter the imperious Catherine II. of Russia? For as Boulton humorously put it, did he not sell what all the world desires to have—"Power"?

> Engine of Watt! unrivalled is thy sway.
>   Compared with thine, what is the tyrant's power?
> His might destroys, while thine creates and saves
>   Thy triumphs live and grow like fruit and flower.
> But his are writ in blood, and read on graves.

Local patriotism regards Matthew Boulton with pride alike for his commercialism which made Soho a world-name, as for the warm-hearted hospitality which led him to dub his house "l'hotel d'amitie sur Handsworth Heath." In August, 1767, he wrote: "I had lords and ladies to wait on me yesterday, I have French and Spaniards to-day and to-morrow I shall have Germans, Russians, and Norwegians."

XXVI.—A RESIDENTIAL OASIS.

A few more words on the passing of Soho— just to recall the names of three or four of the minor industrial worthies once associated with that famous Factory. Samuel Clegg in early life was a manager under Boulton and Watt, and was the inventor of the "wet" gas-meter, that clever mechanical contrivance for measuring gas consumption, and which with some modification is still in use. Well known local names are those of William Brown, an engineer who, when the Factory was closed, was moved to the Soho Foundry at Smethwick, and afterwards followed his profession successfully in other parts of the world; and William Frederick Evans, clock manufacturer, whose grandfather, John Houghton, acquired this branch of the illustrious firm's business when, in 1805, they decided to relinquish it.

William Buckle held a responsible position at Soho Works to the year 1851; and on the ground where Watt had created his "giant with one idea"—as Coleridge called it—he built one of the earliest locomotives, an engine which made a journey from Liverpool to Manchester, 15 September, 1830. This worthy died in London, 1863, at the Royal Mint, where he held a position of trust.

So much for the meteoric but ephemeral glories of Soho; after the extinction of which Handsworth relapsed once more into industrial stagnation. Will Handsworth always remain purely residential, or will it again become an industrial community ?

Although modern Handsworth, as noted in our introductory chapter, has practically no manufactures, it is not at all improbable that quite as many business men reside within its confines as within any of the neighbouring parishes. Handsworth may be regarded as a large residential oasis situated in the midst of a vast smoky wilderness of industrial towns—hemmed in as it is by West Bromwich, Smethwick, Birmingham, and Aston Manor, with but one pleasant outlet on the Barr side. How soon this outlet may be closed, if not by manufacturing, by great mining operations, who can foretell?

The possibility must be recognised, remote though it may be, of the colliery district of West Bromwich, Walsall Wood, and Aldridge, some day crowding in upon the Perry Barr side of Handsworth.

Before the era of canals all the coal sent by road from the Black Country into Birmingham had of necessity to pass through Handsworth. It is curious to recall that in 1766 a public complaint was made in Birmingham—it was issued officially from the Vestry Room at the Workhouse—that a weighing machine had been set up in Handsworth to compete with the town machine at the Workhouse. As the profits of the Workhouse weighing machine went to lessen the levies for the relief of the poor, this competition was denounced as "pernicious," and the townspeople of Birmingham were asked to examine their weigh notes, and beware of frauds committed by coal-heavers who got their coals weighed so far out as Handsworth.

Till the turnpiking and improving of the road between Wednesbury and Birmingham, the coal sent from the mines of the former to feed the busy hearths of the latter, were borne in basket panniers slung across the backs of horses, a train of these sturdy animals chained head to tail, working in charge of a single teamster. At that time the site of the Frighted Horse Inn was occupied by a well-known place of call, a sort of depot, known as the Coal Bank Tavern. (Connected with this house a century ago, it may be noted in passing, was a very prosperous sick club or friendly society, known as "The Loyal Britons in Deed." the business of which was conducted with a preposterous amount of ceremonial and secret ritual and the members of which regularly attended the church decked out in their full regalia on the first Monday in each July, when the rector preached them a special sermon.) The Coal Bank Tavern evidently obtained its name from association with the early coal traffic by road; it was a licensed house of some popularity and considerable prosperity. The gradual exhaustion of the famous "thick coal" (as the "ten-yard seam" of South Staffordshire is called where it "crops out" or comes to the surface, as it does round Dudley and Wednesbury) naturally gave serious pause to the commercial interests of the Black Country. It was generally believed at one time that this rich coal-measure ceased towards the east at a line drawn from Swan Village to Halesowen.

How this supposition was falsified in 1874 by that sound geologist, the late Henry Johnson of Dudley, is well known to most people in this district. Inspired by the confident predictions of this bold mining engineer, capital was raised, trials were made, and eventually at a depth of 1,250 feet, the famous seam was reached at Sandwell, a mile and a half east of the supposed limit. This romance of mining industry is told more fully in "Some Records of Smethwick," pp. 100-102. When it is recalled that in June 1874 a thousand guineas were offered for a hundred pound share in the Sandwell Colliery Company, it will be easy to understand the incentive to that further exploration beneath the sandstone rocks, which in 1880 led to the discovery of the same thick coal, 1,836 feet deep, at Hamstead.

But from the outset the Hamstead Colliery, in striking contrast to that at Sandwell from which it is separated but by a mile or so, has been singularly unfortunate. For one thing it is the deepest mine in Staffordshire—yet its 1,750 or 1,860 feet are not to be compared with pits of 3,000 feet depth such as are found in the Manchester district—and it has always been subject to "bumps" and fires. The latter are generated by spontaneous combustion when the temperature of the mine is high and the air is moist, the hard porous coal having the peculiar power of absorbing the oxygen; while the bumps, or crushing of the strata, are occasioned by earth movements to which deep mines are often subject by the weight of the super-incumbent mass. The Hamstead Colliery experienced a disastrous fire in 1898 which involved the temporary closing of the mine, not to mention a series of 180 minor fires that year, as compared with 132 in 1897. Ten years latter occurred the still more disastrous fire of 1908, in which 24 lives were lost, and 700 men were thrown out of work, under circumstances which aroused the sympathy of the whole nation. This encroachment of the miners upon Handsworth, and the exploding of the old idea that the "exposed area" of the old Staffordshire coalfield was the limitation of its resources, has led to the speculation that it is the same seam which is worked at Hamstead as at Nuneaton, and that these two areas are connected by the same depressed seam underlying the Birmingham basin.

That eminent local geologist, Mr. W. Jerome Harrison, in discussing this matter, notes that five beds of red rock are found to rest upon and conceal the coal-measures; he then proceeds—"The main road from West Bromwich to Colmore Row, and thence down New Street and the Bull Ring; along Deritend, and up the Coventry Road, crosses the five bands of Red Rocks.

"The lowest red beds are:—(1) The so-called 'Permians' (these are now known to be really red-coloured Upper Coalmeasures): they are red sandstones and marls 1,500 feet in thickness. and they stretch from West Bromwich to the New Inns.

"Resting upon the 'Permians,' we find (2) the Bunter Conglomerate or Pebble-Bed, about 300 feet thick, extending eastward from New Inns to the point where Villa Road joins Soho Road; the 'Bunter' is a remarkable mass of rounded stones (mostly quartzites), of which a fine section is exposed in the well-known gravelpit adjoining Blackroot Pool, in Sutton Park; when reached in borings, wells, etc., it invariably yields an abundant supply of water.

"Dipping gently to the east, the Bunter passes beneath (3) the Upper Mottled Sandstone, which extends past Hockley Brook and Constitution Hill; this stratum is seen in the excavation now proceeding on the southern side of Hockley Hill, and also, in the cemetery adjoining Hockley Station. and in the deep sand-pits on the northern side of the Parade, etc.: it supplies an excellent sand for moulding purposes: it can be traced eastward to the foot of Snow Hill.

"The Lower Keuper Sandstone (4) forms the high ground of the centre of Birmingham, upon which stand St. Philip's Church, the Town Hall, the Old Library, etc,"

And so our learned authority proceeds eastward of the Rea, where he completes his series with the Keuper Marls, and passes into a region outside the cognizance of the present writer. Mr. Harrison is of opinion that the thick coal would not be found under Birmingham at a less depth than 2.700 feet: while eastward of the Rea boundary "fault" another 500 or 700 feet would have to be added to that figure for the down-throw of all the strata in that direction.

XXVII.—OLD FAMILIES AND NAMES OF NOTE.

Among those who, in the reign of Charles I., suffered to be fined rather than accept the costly honour of knighthood, were—

	£	s.	d.
Roger Stanley, of Handsworth, gent	10	0	0
Henry Willis, of Handsworth	10	0	0
Henry Cookes, of Handsworth, gent.	12	0	0
Charles Stamford, of Handsworth.	20	0	0
William Stamford, of Perry Barr	20	0	0

In 1663 among those who were "disclaimed" or not allowed the honour of using a coat-of-arms, were,

> William Piddock ⎫
> Rich. Smallbrook ⎬ of Handsworth.
> Hen. Cookes ⎭

At the time of this Herald's Visitation, however, Henry Cookes of Handsworth was dead, but his brother was living at Harbury, Warwickshire, and the family pedigree was entered at a later visitation of that county in 1682, when they claimed the same arms as the Cocks family, of Worcestershire. Attention has been called previously to the Cook family of this parish, in 1332 (chapter vii.); to the same family in 1632 in chapter xii., and to Cooke's charity of 1637 in chapter xvii.; also to the Inquisition of 1549 taken on the death of William Cookes who lived on a considerable estate known as Bays Hall (now The Manwoods) to which were attached iron mills and other valuable properties. described on p. 35. At the Herald's Visitation of 1663 Captain Cooke held some 34 acres of land in Hamstead Park.

Another ancient family was that of Squire. of Ley Hall (see p. 31). "Richard Skwyere de Hondesworthe" is named in an old Wyrley deed; while the parish registers contain these allusions:—

> "Isabel Squier of Ley Hall, widow, and mother of Henry Squier, archdeacon.—Henry son of John Squier, gent., of Ley hall. baptized April 5, 1574.—Roger, son of John and Jane Squyer, baptized October 10, 1582. The said Jane was buried the 11th and died in childbed."

Shaw says "this family is now extinct (1798). Mr. Spencer is the present owner of Ley hall, and has lately built a large brick house there between the church and Perry Bridge—the residence which is still standing near the railway in Wood Lane

The Wyrley family have been treated in chapter ix. Of William Wyrley, the herald, mentioned on p. 40, it remains only to say that a full catalogue of his works will be found in Simms' "Bibliotheca Staffordiensis ;" in the same work also appear the academic records of Humphrey Wyrley of Hamstead Hall, born 1574, and of his son, Sir John Wyrley.

Perry Hall and Park were purchased in 1669 by Sir Henry Gough, knight of Old Fallings, Bushbury, who came of the family of the wealthy Wolverhampton woolstapler, who assisted Charles I. with a loan—

> The old Justice Gough
> Who had money enough.

as the doggrell child-rhyme put it.

As mentioned in chapter xi. his son Walter had a son Walter born at Bushbury in 1713, who succeeded, the estates in 1730. The son of this one was another Walter, who succeeded in 1773, and was the eccentric Squire Gough of whom Shaw complained in his history under the heading of Perry Hall. Of his eccentricities the old tale of "the parson and clerk" is not the least entertaining.

Standing on the Gough estate at Streetley (which place, of course, derived its name from being upon the ancient Icknield Street) is an old inn, originally known as the Royal Oak, but which is now more widely known as "The Parson and Clerk," a popular designation obtained through a long and embittered wrangle between the rector of Handsworth, who had some interest in it, and the landlord, the aforesaid Squire Gough, of Perry Hall— the same who went to law with the Bridge Trustees (see p. 113).

During the progress of a lawsuit which raged over it, the latter, to annoy his clerical antagonist as much as possible, always arranged for at least two servants or tenants to attend church, form a congregation, and compel the parson to read the services twice a week. And when he eventually won the suit, he commemorated his victory by having a caricature set up on the disputed property, representing a parson bending his head in the attitude of prayer. and his clerk standing behind him with an uplifted axe about to strike off his head. The litigious parson was the Rev. Thomas Lane who died in 1802.

Among the sons of the Gough family who went to Oxford to be educated were Henry, born at Perry Hall 1744, and killed by a fall from his horse 1769; John, born at Handsworth 1754, and died 1828; and John. born at Handsworth 1780, son of the former John. Richard Gough of the Perry Hall family published "British Topography" 1768; "Some Account of the Alien Priories," 1780; "Sepulchral Monuments of Great Britain," 1779; Ditto in five volumes 1786— 1796. Further information relating to this family is given in "West's Picturesque Views of Staffordshire" (Birmingham 1830) the plates for which were engraved by a Birmingham artist, Charles Radcliffe: a series of which views were privately printed at the expense of Mrs. Gough of Perry Barr.

Of the Brearley family of Handsworth memorials exist, in the church, of the two daughters and co-heiresses of William Brearley esq. and Anne his wife; one a mural tablet commemorates Anne Maria, relict of Charles Chadwick Sacherevell, of New Hall, Warwickshire, who died in her 85th year, January 1795; the other, Jane Gough of Perry Hall, who died in 1781, aged 69. There is an external monument to Martha, wife of Joseph Brearley, 1804.

The Smallwoods are among the oldest of tile yeomen families of Handsworth. In 1663 Thomas Smallwood held "for three lives 126 acres of land in Hamstead Park. The epitaph on Joseph Smallwood who died in 1775, at the age of 56 runs—

This stone can say, what few vain marbles can,
Here lies a social, worthy, honest man;
How poor to this are titles, wealth, and blood,
Since none are truly great but what are good:
Goodness alone will make us truly blest.
Gives endless joy, and everlasting rest.

The Osborne family, as the Index of this work will disclose, has long had a branch settled in Handsworth. In the fabric of the old church there was carved on an oak cornice the names of John Fiddon and Thomas Osborn, as churchwardens in 1701. The name occurs frequently in the parish records of the last century, about the middle of which William Henry Osborne was residing at Perry Pont House. G. H. Osborne, of Perry Barr, contributed a Note on " Stonehenge" to the "Antiquary," vol. iv. p. 86.

Richard Dugdale of Merevale and Blyth Halls, Warwickshire, was born at Handsworth in 1725, the son of Richard Geast, assuming the surname of Dugdale in 1799. He died in 1806: see allusion to Henricus Geast Dugdale on p. 59.

The Geast family (see chapter xix.) were owners of the old mansion and farm buildings at Hamstead known as Cherry Orchard Farm; they were connected by marriage with the Dugdales.

Tablets appear in the church to the memory of John Whateley of the Austins, 1794, and to Henry Piddock Whateley, 1847.

Nathaniel Gooding Clarke, Esq., who is commemorated in the church by a bust executed by the well-known local sculptor, Mr. Hollins, resided at Browns Green, where he died in 1836. He was "one of his Majesty's counsel well learned in the law," Recorder of Walsall. His son Nathaniel Richard Clarke, Sergeant-at-law, was Recorder of Lincoln, Newark, Nottingham, and Walsall, and Judge of the County Courts of Wolverhampton, Oldbury and Walsall. He died in 1859. The Rev. Henry James Clarke, his son, was born at Browns Green 1823, and became Vicar of Great Barr in 1870. At one time he was Assistant in the MS. Department of the British Museum. He has held a number of clerical appointments and is the author of numerous theological works, as will be found recorded by Simms. According to the same authority the Hon. William James Smith, M.A., LL.M., barrister, and Puisne Judge in the Island of Cyprus. was born at Handsworth in 1853.

Among other natives or residents noted by Simms are Isaac Lea, who died at Handsworth in 1868, and Henry Samuel Westwood, matriculated at Worcester College. Oxford. 1886, who was born at Handsworth in 1868.

William Chance, eldest son of James Timmins Chance, High Sheriff of Staffordshire in 1868, was born at Browns Green, Handsworth, 1853. He is a barrister, a J.P. for Surrey, and the author of some legal works.

Richard Walter, gentleman, who died in 1788, and his wife, Anna Maria, who died in 1796, have heraldic monuments in the church. There is also a stone with armonial adornments to "Sergius Swellengrebel, Esq., lately resident in the service of the States of Holland, at their Settlement of Boethecomba and Bowthano in the East Indies, who died in this parish on 15 August 1778, aged 39." Matthew Boulton became associated with the Swellengrebels through his foreign trade.

Thomas Rhodes. according to Manchester Grammar School Register, was born in that city, 1771, but he settled in Handsworth, and in 1805 married Elizabeth, daughter of John Hodges (Boulton and Hodges, Soho); and was buried in Handsworth Church, 1852,

It will be gathered that besides the old landed families of the parish, Handsworth's residential qualifications early attracted not only the wealthy manufacturers of Birmingham on the one side, but those of the Black Country on the other.

In 1838 Mr. James Russell, of the Wednesbury Crown Tube Works, built Endwood Court, Handsworth, at a cost of £7,000. He took up his residence there, but did not live very long to enjoy its beauties. His son, John James Russell, however, resided there till 1860, when the property was sold. The arms and pedigree of the Russells appear in "Miscellanea Genealogica et Heraldica," N.S., iv., 18–19; their interesting trade history is given in "Wednesbury Workshops." In Handsworth Church the Russell monument is a sarcophagus with weeping figures; there is also a memorial to another local iron trade magnate, Walter Williams, of Wednesbury Oak Works, who died 1857 (see "History of Tipton," p. 45).

XXVIII.—TOPOGRAPHY.

The land had but little value at the time (1757) when John Wyrley, lord of the manor, granted a ninety-nine years' lease of the tracts of common land in Handsworth Heath, Moneybank Hill, and Crabtree Hill warrens, to Rushton and Eaves, from whom Matthew Boulton afterwards acquired it. Boulton purchased the lease in 1762 and afterwards the fee simple of the property, together with a considerable area of the adjoining lands.

It is said much of the waste land hereabouts came to be enclosed by long-headed folk, who after years of undisturbed possession went to the expense of title-deeds to make sure of their claims. It was common talk when the Great Western Railway was cut through the heath that the company paid not a single penny for the land they required, since the then owners could produce no legal proofs of their ownership; and it is still believed by old inhabitants that the descendants of Matthew Boulton are unable to sell their land, and can merely grant terminable leases of it.

Boulton's new mansion, Soho House was placed in the midst of extensive and beautiful pleasure grounds—till well into the reign of Victoria the park he constructed was entirely walled in from Hockley Bridge for quite a mile along the main road. It was laid out in the usual classic style of the period, and in one of its prettiest sylvan groves was an urn to the memory of his friend, Dr. William Small, an eminent physician and chemist, who at one time had been a professor of mathematics and natural philosophy in Virginia, but settling down near Birmingham joined the Soho Circle and became a member of the Lunar Society. His name has been perpetuated by another member of that talented circle, Dr. Erasmus Darwin, who was a poet as well as a physician and a naturalist. Another feature in this pleasaunce was the Shell Pool which occupied a depression on a ledge of land well up the hillside above the watercourse, and was originally fed by the spring that drained the rising ground above it. The pool derived its name from a large ornamental shell through which the water ran into it; and when Boulton artificially improved it, the supply of water was augmented by pumping from the brook below, Watts original engine with its massive oak beam being utilised for this purpose. Though an "ornamental water," the overflow was employed by a large water wheel for motive power in the works below. It was in the Shell Pool Boulton's first wife drowned herself—his second partners fate was equally tragic, she being accidentally burnt to death.

Soho Pool, made between 1756 and 1760 by the construction of an embankment round its lower sides, was the largest of these sheets of water, being some 20 acres in extent. After the closing of the factory it was let as a pleasure pool for boating and fishing, and in November, 1864, the launching of the "Birmingham" life-boat was made one of the public attractions to "Boulton's Pool," as it was sometimes called. The site was drained in 1869, and much of its area is now within the London and North-Western Railway's Soho Wharf. The Mill Pool, through the site of which Ashwin Road now runs, was a third sheet of water, the one which provided the power for the first metal mill and which marked the genesis of the famous factory. It has been drained for nearly half-a-century.

Here we are in the region known as Nineveh. In the old bull-baiting days the most celebrated spot in Handsworth for the pursuit of this pastime was near the bridge across the brook at the junction of Bacchus Lane and Nineveh Road. It was an open space which, if not extensive in area, offered points of vantage for the viewing of the sport from the stout branches of a number of tall trees that stood in front of "Ensor's" Cottage—an old landmark tenanted for 200 year's by members of that family till its recent demolition.

Moving still westward we note that the last vestiges of the wild heathland of this parish were to be seen on the near side of the Handsworth railway station; and on the other side, contiguous to Smethwick, was the "Black Patch," that piece of land which lay so long derelict that the gipsies who permanently encamped there came to believe they had acquired legal right to it, and their eviction in 1905 was effected only after the display of considerable force by the authorities. Years ago when these nomads first settled on the spot—so conveniently near to a populous area in which they could ply their petty trading from door to door—they were attracted to it by its green hedgerows and other rural surroundings so congenial to gipsy life. The first comers were the Smiths and the Claytons, typical English gipsies who, on one occasion, successfully resisted the intrusion of a band of Servian refugees who were travelling the country with seventeen performing bears. Later occupants of the Black Patch were the Loveridges, who, though not Romanies in the strictest sense, had with them "Queen Henty", an acknowledged head among these wandering tribes. When this Gipsy Queen died in her caravan there, an amount of sympathy was extended to the nomads that it almost seemed they had come to be regarded as a recognised section of the community. Their presence in the parish was certainly in keeping with the traditions of the locality; for till the era of Boulton and Watt had transformed the appearance of the place, old Handsworth Heath had been dotted with a number of miserable huts, the homes of an idle beggarly people who lived a precarious life by doing as little work as possible, eking out their existence by thieving and poaching all over the country side.

Before Boulton and Watt's invasion of its solitudes, Soho was a vast rabbit warren. The name of the place is really a hunting term; "So" being equivalent to "See" and "Ho" to "Hie after him!"—the word "Soho," in fact, being a cry with which dogs were encouraged in the hunting field. The subject is well illustrated by the following quotation from an ancient work which was thus translated in the fifteenth century: "If ye hounte at the hare, ye shall say atte uncoupling, "Hors de couple, avaunt." And after that, three times, "Sohow! Sohow ! Sohow !"

New Inn Hall the ancient family mansion, stood opposite the public-house to which it lent its name (some speculations on the origin of which were offered in chapter xi.) till about three-quarters of a century ago. The public inn itself is a famous old hostelry. In December 1798 the commissioners appointed by Act of Parliament to divide, allot, and inclose the commonlands on this side of Birmingham, and which were located in the parishes of Birmingham, Handsworth. Harborne, Edgbaston, and Aston, met at this house for the transaction of their public business—a piece of business the ultimate effect of which altered the aspect of the country very materially, and has indeed transform,ed the landscape more than we now are able to realise.

From the portals of this inn, then kept by Mr. Thomas Crockett, the commissioners set forth to ride round the boundaries of this wide stretch of waste land; across which by the time they held another meeting there, in January, 1800. for the hearing of any possible objections to their proposals, they had arranged for the making of a number of new roads, forty feet in width, through Nineveh and Gib Heath, opening up the land between the main road and Winson Green; useful roads that gave access to canal wharfage. How long the inn has existed as a licensed house is not known; but the bowling-green, on which the local justices met for many years to recreate themselves, is a fine piece of old turf laid down in 1780. On this green the celebrated Julien has given performances when he was in the height of his fame for the wonderful open-air orchestral concerts with which his name is associated. The chronicles of this house, if obtainable, would be full of local interest.

Turning our backs upon Smethwick and looking outwards over Barr, we are able to realise how truly pleasant was the neighbourhood, ere the smoke of the Black Country had enshrouded its skies, and blurred the prospect; a fact borne in upon us by the presence of a group of no less than four old family mansions—Hamstead Hall, Sandwell Hall, Perry Hall, and Great Barr Hall.

The old Hamstead Hall which was pulled down by George Birch, Esquire, was an interesting building with a private chapel, the windows of which contained some good heraldic glass. The Park contained upwards of 360 acres, while Perry Hall stood in a park of but some fifty acres.

"The grounds of Hamstead (says "Nightingale's Beauties of England and

Wales," published in 1813), "winding along the banks of the Tame are pleasing and romantic, being covered with a profusion of stately trees. A lime placed on a rocky eminence is particularly remarkable for its uncommon size; at three feet from the ground it measures 23 feet in girth, and its height is 70 feet. The rock beneath the shade of this mighty tree is hollowed into a cavernous cell which has acquired the title of the hermitage."

The presence of running water is always an attraction, and the Tame, ere the polluted drainage of the Black Country had transformed its once pellucid waters into a foul ditch, was no exception to the rule.

> The Tame was foul as it could be,
>   With sewage black as dye;
> It ran with garbage in the wet,
>   And stank when it was dry;
> No fishes lay beneath its bank—
>   There were no fish to lie.

It seems almost incredible that once upon a time the rights of fishing from the Bridge down to Witton were strictly reserved.

The Alanwoods (formerly called Bayes Hall) is a farmhouse situated on the very confines of Handsworth, the field which adjoins the back premises being in the parish of West Bromwich.

Considering the populousness of the two parishes by which it is surrounded the situation is rather remote, being reached by a private road running out of Sandwell Park Lane towards the Handsworth uplands, and which is abruptly brought to a termination by a gated field into which the house fronts. The house lies in a slight dip, surrounded by a low old fashioned, brick-coped wall, with a gate-way opening between two pillars of corresponding style having the usual ball-caps of stone; and from which a short flight of stone steps descends to a path leading across the side of a little lawn to the front entrance. Outside the gateway stands a horse~block, and just inside the wall are three fine old yew-trees which almost screen the whole edifice from view.

The residence is a gabled, red brick, three-storeyed building, cruciform in plan, with all the chimney stacks clustered at the centre. It is totally devoid of architectural ornament, has no noticable feature inside or out (except, perhaps, its heavy-studded doors with great wrought-iron hinges) and possesses associations of interest beyond those connecting it with Dr. Johnson.

The Manwoods was built about 1680 by Henry Ford, great uncle of the famous lexicographer. Ford was then steward to the Whorwoods who lived at Sandwell Hall. Shaw's "Staffordshire" describes the house in 1798 as "stuccoed," and says it passed with an estate of fifty acres, in marriage, to Mr. Abnet, who sold it to the Earl of Dartmouth about 1750; and (continues

Shaw) "it has been of late years inhabited by Mr. Wright, his lordship's steward."

The house is within sight of the Old Forge where Francis Asbury was apprentised. On p. 22 of Brigg's "Life of Bishop Asbury" we read how this great Wesleyan worthy delivered his trial sermon, when first authorised as a local preacher, in "The Manwood's Cottage," described as "a lonely and antique dwelling standing in subordinate relation to an old ecclesiastical building a short distance from it." This is manifestly an error of identification, as the Manwoods was not built till nearly two centuries after Sandwell Priory had been dissolved; the error becomes quite palpable when the picture of the "cottage" given opposite. p. 1 is compared with the building as it yet stands. But probably it is wrong to confuse the "Manwoods" with "Manwood's Cottage," two separate and distinct buildings in the immediate vicinity of the Old Forge, which originally was the corn mill attached to Sandwell Priory, but upon the dissolution of that establishment became an iron-mill. Briggs, writing in 1879, says —"the very cinder field where its scoriæ were deposited, is now as green, as the meadows which surround it." If by scoriæ he means slag, he is on safe ground; but no cinders or ashes of mineral coal were ever deposited there, as all the smelting at Old Forge was done, with charcoal in the pre-Blast Furnace days. Yet the bishop's biographer seems to convey the idea that the trial sermon was delivered in a house of larger dimension,s than those of a mere cottage; for he pictures the youthful preacher "standing behind a chair in the spacious living-room of that

Quaint old gabled place
With church stamped on its face——

to be henceforth invested with an interest of which the founders of Manwoods never dreamed."

The Manwoods at the present day comprises a farm of 184 acres, leased from Lord Dartmouth by Mr. Thomas Wells, of Oscott, and occupied by his son-in-law Mr. Timmings.

Lying midway between Hamstead and Sandwell, those two outlying collieries which almost link up the Black Country with Birmingham, the farm is beginning to wear the smoke blighted appearance characteristic of the locality; and now Borne of its land is threatened with appropriation by the Handsworth Council for the purposes of a Cemetery.

"The Friary" is purely a house-name, and has no connection whatever with any old religious foundation; it has lent its name to a public thoroughfare, as has the Rookery to Rookery Road and the Grove to Grove Lane. The Grove was once the residence of the Hodgetts' family; and, as we shall see in the next chapter, The Friary was so well known as to be named in an Act of Parliament as a 1and-mark—as indeed was the Spout House at Hamstead, and one or two other residences hereabouts.

As to the origin of the place-name Birchfield it has been surmised (chapter iii.) that like Heathfield, Broomfield, and Middlefield it was anciently one of the common fields of the parish. But whether the fore-part of the name was derived from the prevalence of birch trees in the vicinity, or from the family name of the lords of the manor is a moot point. There is mention of a Hugh de Byrchenfield in the record of a local law suit of 1222; and there was a Thomas Birch of Birch Green living at Birchfield in 1565, and buried at Aston in 1613.

XXIX.—THE TURNPIKE ROADS.

Let us glance at Handsworth in the old coaching days, when its turnpike roads rang at frequent and regular intervals all day long with the jangle of harness and the lively tooting of coach-horns; when the coach-road was an institution, and every park and mansion and the other landmarks along its route would be pointed out by the genial guard after he had roused its echoes with the cheery blasts of his horn.

As to the toll-gates, those stern white barriers by which the road was spanned at brief intervals of every two or three miles, let it be premised that tolls for the repairing of manorial roads had been collected as early as the thirteenth century; and that turnpikes—or turn-spikes, a sort of turnstile—were first set up for the same purpose on public highways is 1663. Three turnpike roads from Birmingham towards the north pass through Handsworth The "main road" was for centuries a bridle-path across the Birmingham heathlands to Sandwell Priory, and then across Bromwich Heath into Wednesbury. It was first turnpiked in 1727 as far as High Bullen, Wednesbury. No less than five subsequent Turnpike Acts dealt with this great highway; the fifth, as already described in chapter 1, the most important in developing the great Holyhead Road. The last Act, in 1832, is noteworthy on account of its allusion to the gas and water mains along its route, and to penalties for breaking street lamps—modernities which seem almost out of keeping with turnpikes.

Both the other highways through Handsworth led to Walsall; the first, through Hamstead was turnpiked in 1787; and the other, which runs through Birchfield, and is one of the latest of the turnpike roads, was not made till 1831, actually within the railway era. Taking the Hamstead Road first, we find that in 1787 an Act was passed for repairing and making more commodious the road, then in a ruinous state, from Walsall to Hamstead Bridge. Among the numerous trustees appointed for this turnpike road were George Birch, John Gough, Samuel Galton, and William Withering, "doctor of physick." A new road about 60 feet wide was authorised, starting from Walsall over the lands of James Rann, Jonas Slaney and others, to a place called Lyon's Denn, and from Rogers Brook over other lands to Shustock Meadow, there to communicate with the existing road from Walsall to Hamstead Bridge; then from Shustock Meadow to the Blue Boar, occupied by one Gilbert Haughton, and from thence to join the existing road to Birmingham and from a watercourse running across the last-named road near the Bugle Horns Inn, over other lands, to the said Hamstead Bridge.

The Surveyor of Highways for each parish and township concerned was to supply, for the purpose of executing the work, a list of all inhabitants liable to render statute labour for road repairs; there was however a somewhat remarkable special clause which expressly exempted the inhabitants of Handsworth from any such obligation on this occasion.

The ancient road from Birmingham into Walsall via Handsworth, Stone Cross and Tame Bridge (according to a manorial survey of Walsall in 1610) entered the latter town at Field Gate, otherwise New Street; while the present Birmingham Road was then known as Peak House Lane, sometimes corrupted to Pig Lane. The Peak House stood near the present canal on the Birmingham Road; and the site of Sir E. T. Holden's residence was formerly occupied by Pig Lane Farm House. The place called Lyon's Den was near Gorway, Mr. W. H. Duignan's residence; "den" is a mere interpretive corruption, the old name being "Lyon Fields," from one Simon le Lioun, the ancient owner. Shustock Meadow adjoins the Bell Inn on the Birmingham Road, and was once part of Shustoke Farm, a moated site.

The Bugle Horn, if not the present Beacon Inn, was probably a licensed house nearer the Hamstead estate of the Wyrleys, who charged one of their heraldic shields with "bugle horns."

Another Act was passed in 1809 to renovate the other end of this road where it lay in Handsworth parish. This enactment was declared to be for making and repairing a road from Soho Hill to the Walsall Turnpike Road on the northern side of Hamstead Bridge, and also another road from Brown's Green to a house called the Friary. The reason assigned was the populousness of the locality and the dilapidation of this portion of the old road. Some houses and buildings near the bridge and standing in the line of the intended road were ordered to be taken down; also a part of the old road stretching from Brown's Green to a point 21 yards north of Hamstead Bridge, and such part of the Hawthorn Tree Lane as lay between the Hawthorn Tree and the Friary, as well as a portion of the Carriage Road which led from Hamstead Bridge towards Tower Hill, were all to be stopped up and discontinued.

Hawthorn Tree Lane is between Brown's Green and Hamstead Hall; the "carriage way" mentioned was the Hamstead end of Rocky Lane. The old road passed through Hamstead Park and was much nearer the present Hamstead Hall; a remnant of the old bridge by which it crossed the Tame is still to be seen near the colliery. A description of the beautiful vale of Hamstead in 1745, the year of Francis Asbury's birth there, is given in the life of that good man written by the Rev. F. W. Briggs, M.A. (Wesleyan Conference Office, 1879). The biographer alludes to the new and straighter channel of the stream made when the new bridge was built in 1809, and then proceeds (p.9) "At the point where the present old Walsall Road (for there is a newer one still) diverges from the older one, and at the south end of the old bridge, is a rather large ivy-clad house, with its front towards the former road; and in a corresponding situation across the bridge, stood the house where Asbury first saw the light." On p 344 of the work is given an illustration of the fellow cottage to Astbury's.

Among the Turnpike Trustees appointed were Lord Lewisham, Sir Joseph Scott, Wyrley Birch, Mathew Boulton, Dugdale Stratford Dugdale, John Eginton, Rev. Thomas Lane Freer, George Freer, John Gough, Joseph Grice, William Haughton, William Osborne, Isaac Spooner, John Smallwood, James Watt, Alexander Walker, Christopher Wren, and thirty or forty more local men of standing and substance. The place of meeting specified in the Act for the Trustees, was "the house of Mary Birch, the Lamp Public House, in the said parish of Handsworth."

The high road to Wednesbury, and this road to Walsall, covered the same ground from Birmingham through Snow Hill as far as that point on Soho Hill "near the house of John Eginton," where the latter branched off to the right. The Roebuck Inn at this important junction, with its extensive stabling then so necessary to roadside houses, seems to have been built about this time. The residence of John Eginton which is mentioned as a landmark, stood upon an eminence on the other side of the Hamstead Road, where the Wretham Road has since been made. (In Shaw's county history, dated 1801, will be found a large engraving of "Prospect Hill, Soho, the residence of Francis Eginton).

Both the Wednesbury and the Walsall traffic coming out of Birmingham along this common portion of the road had then to pay at the tollgate which stood in Great Hampton Street just westward of Hockley Street—it was not till about fifty years ago that this toll-gate was removed outside the Birmingham boundaries, a tollgate being found a great hindrance to trade inside a growing town—to Soho Hill near the end of Villa Road.

It was ordered in 1809 that the trustees under the new Act should contribute to the older Turnpike Trust towards the repair of this section of the road which was common to both routes.

At Hamstead a number of footpaths were stopped up and a new bridge was built in the line of the new road to carry it over the Tame; and as the road passed through Hamstead Park, a "give and take" arrangement was made with the owner of this estate, Mr. Wyrley Birch; he being recompensed for the land he gave up by the appropriation of the abandoned road and the stopping of many contiguous footpaths which had run over his land and interfered with his privacy. Similarly a lane from Brown's Green to Heathcotes Farm, belonging to Dugdale Stratford Dugdale, Esq., was stopped, and the site of the discontinued lane conveyed to an adjoining landowner, Nathaniel Gooding Clarke, Esq., of Brown's Green; a new lane 15 feet wide being made to the said farm, and vested in Mr. Dugdale. Further, power was given to remove the Causeway or

Footroad leading from the Crick Lane to the Lamp Inn, from the western to the eastern side of the then existing Walsall Road; and also, after a lapse of three years, to take for the purpose of road-widening a strip of land belonging to the Rev. Thomas Lane Freer, where the road narrowed opposite to the Lamp Inn, in return therefor making a new plantation of equal dimensions.

Hutton's "History of Birmingham" (edition of 1819), dealing with the public roads out of that city, says "The road to Walsall ten miles, is lately made good. That to Wolverhampton thirteen miles, is much improved since the coal teams left it" (that is, after the canal was opened between Birmingham and the South Staffordshire "coalries.")

Again in 1831 an Act was passed for further improving this road between Soho Hill and the farther side of Hamstead Bridge, and the road from Brown's Green to the Friary; the section specified for diversion being that "from Handsworth Rectory to the New Bridge over the river Tame," while the portion leading out of the said diversion and passing by Butler's Coppice, which was to the south of Brown's Green, was to be improved. Among the trustees were W. C. Alston, Henry Fryer Devey, Thomas Hinton Hasluck, Richard Spencer, John Smallwood, John White Unett and Henry Piddock Whateley; the appointed meeting place was the "Handsworth Tavern in Handsworth"—otherwise the Lamp Inn.

By another Act the same year (1831) a new Walsall turnpike road was made through Birchfield. The Act specified this as a road from the summit of the hill on the north side of Quarry House, then in the occupation of Christopher Wren, Esq., in Perry Barr, running into the highway leading from Perry Bridge to Birmingham at a point called Bristnalls End, Handsworth; and from Perry Bridge along such highway to the boundary brook between the parishes of Aston and Birmingham. The former road from Walsall had come as far as the Quarry House, which derived its name from an old stone quarry near by, and is still standing at the junction of the old and the new roads. Bristnalls End was the old name for the northern section of Birchfield Road. The usual large number of Trustees was appointed, chiefly landowners or men of position in the vicinity off the newly projected turnpike road; among them may be noted Wyrley Birch, George Bragg, Francis Finch, W. H. Osborne, Sir Edward Scott, and Sir John Wrottesley.

The appointed meeting place of the Trustees was named as the Gough Arms Inn, Perry Barr; and as the Grand Junction Railway had just been projected, this Act contained a clause with special permission for carrying the turnpike road safely across that line when made, either above or below it—as we know now, it was carried over the railway at Perry Barr Station. The cutting of the railway led to the diversion of the Aldridge Road, bringing it almost to the corner of the Wellington Road. As to the new railway Vauxhall was then the principal station, and the fare to Perry Barr was a shilling each way.

The Boar's Head Inn at Perry Barr, named after the heraldic crest of the Gough family, was formerly known as the Gough Arms—seventy years ago there was another Gough Arms Inn, a mile beyond the Scott Arms, and now called the Beacon Inn.

Another residence mentioned in the Acts as a landmark was the Spout House, located near the lane in which is now Hamstead Colliery. It would derive its name from being near a spring with a spout attached for convenience of use. These spouts were very common, but the springs have in course of time been neglected and polluted and allowed to disappear. They were once regarded as valuable appurtenants to property and not infrequently have formed the subject of costly, even ruinous, litigation.

The Scott Arms was built for an inn by Sir Joseph Scott in the early part of the last century, and was long a well-known house of call. The road which crosses the Walsall road there was a turnpike for the brief space of twenty-one years, and was the direct route from Oldbury, Smethwick and West Bromwich to Lichfield via Streetley and Watford Gap.

The toll-gates were removed at various dates, generally as the Acts expired, or the debts were provided for—many road trusts were insolent. The toll-gate in Birchfield Road, at the corner of Wellington Road was taken off in 1879, that in Hamstead Road about the close of 1874, and the Soho Hill Gate some three years earlier.

XXX.—FROM STAGE COACH TO TRAM CAR.

To an old inhabitant there is nothing mare interesting reminiscently than to recall the changed aspect of a well-known thoroughfare. Let us briefly recall the vicissitudes of the old turnpikes through Handsworth.

The Rev. Stebbing Shaw writing as a road cicerone in his history, published 1798, after describing the Soho establishment, says "the next good house on the left" about half a mile beyond, going towards West Bromwich, "is the seat of H. P. Whateley, Esq., and farther to the right, Mr. Jenkin's and Mr. Ravee's; while in a more retired spot towards Sandwell Park, stands a very pleasant and handsome mansion of —— Clark, Esq, barrister-at-law and late of Derby." Quoting the same historian his description of the highway to Walsall along the Hamstead Road—" Beyond the church on the right is the house of the late Mrs. Walter; also, that of James Reynolds, Esq. Beyond these, on the left, Mr. Hawkin's, and on the right Mrs. Whatley's. Farther on the same side, H. Holding's, Esq., and next on the left Mr. Villiers, and beyond it Mr. Vaughton's." These were the names of some of the principal inhabitants of Handsworth upwards of a century ago. Going over the same ground some twenty years later, with Pye's "Modern Birmingham" (1819) as our guide and companion, we are told—

"At the bottom of the hill you cross a small stream of water, which separates Warwickshire from the county of Stafford. In ascending the opposite hill, on the right hand is Prospect House, where the late Mr. Eginton carried on his manufactory of stained glass. Soon after the road divides, when, turning to the right hand [along Hamstead Road] it leads you by a row of respectable houses, and when through the toll gate, you leave what was once Handsworth common and immediately on the left is a handsome house with a beautiful avenue of lime trees [now Hall Road], once the seat of the ancient family of Sacheverel, but now the property of Joseph Grice, Esq." [This mansion called Handsworth Hall, was demolished half a century ago.]

"A little farther on the right is a simple though tasteful lodge, leading to Heathfield, the elegant mansion of the celebrated James Watt, Esq., who is well known to all scientific men, for the great improvement he has made in steam engines, and various other useful works. A few years back, the adjacent ground was a wild and dreary waste, but it now exhibits all the beauty and luxuriance that art assisted by taste can give it. Woods and groves appear to have started up at command, and it may now vie with any seat in the neighbourhood, for rural elegance and picturesque beauty. Descending the hill, the parish church of Handsworth presents itself to view, and a short distance before you arrive at it, is the parsonage-house, where the Rev. Lane Freer resides. It is a very excellent house, and possesses more conveniences and luxuries than are usually to be met with in the habitations of the clergy. About a mile farther on the right is the elegant residence of N. G. Clarke, Esq. [Brown's Green] one of the king's counsel; a gentleman highly distinguished for acuteness and perspicuity in his profession, and thorough hospitality in his house. Still farther on the left, as you descend a steep hill, there is a fine view, at a considerable distance, of the domains of Hamstead Hall. It is a very elegant and modern-built mansion, the old one having been taken down some years since, which was for many generations the seat of the ancient and respectable family of the Wyrleys, who possessed the manor and very large property in this parish. On the demise of the late John Wyrley, Esq. the whole of this estate was left by will to George Birch, Esq., on whose decease it devolved upon his only son, the present Wyrley Birch, Esq. It is difficult to conceive a more beautiful residence than this, as it contains all that hill and dale, wood and water, aided by extensive views, can do, to make a place delightful and desirable: these seen here to have been combined in the most beautiful manner; for the river Tame meanders through this enchanting and extensive domain; on whose banks are numerous groves of trees, and from a solid rock there arises a lime tree, of unusual magnitude, whose branches spreading in an horizontal direction became so heavy, and injured the trunk to such a degree, that in order to preserve the body, it not only became necessary to lop of the principal branches, but to bind it together with iron in different ways, by hooping of it, and passing a bar of iron through it, in the same manner as buildings are frequently done, to preserve them. At a height of three feet, it girths twenty-three feet, and rises to the height of seventy feet. The rock upon which this tree grows, is of such a nature, that there is a grotto of considerable size cut in it, wherein the roots from this tree spread themselves in different directions. This inestimable estate, although for so many generations the patrimonial possessions of the family has been lately transferred by the proprietor to the Earl of Dartmouth, and is now in the possession of William Wallis, Esq.

"In the valley is a corn mill, worked by the river Tame over which there is a substantial bridge. Near the summit of the opposite hill the road passes close by the residence of Mr. Wren, who is well known in Staffordshire as an agriculturist. Near half a mile farther on the left is an ancient white house, which has been occupied as a school for a number of years.

"From the green opposite, if you face about, there is an extensive view over the country; two of the Birmingham churches and a monument being conspicuous objects.. A very short distance farther is a gravel pit opposite to which is a rich and luxuriant view for a considerable distance."

Such were the views met with along the roads nearly a century ago. Now let us skip some half century, and come upon Handsworth when it is beginning to grow into a well built suburb. There came a time in the "sixties" when the need of some regular communication with the parent city of Birmingham had to be met—and it was met by a service of omnibuses.

At first two rival proprietors monopolised the service, one named Tolley and one named Mayner. From Villa Cross to town there were a half-hourly service, and the fare for the single journey was sixpence in snowy and difficult weather sometimes raised to eightpence or ninepence. There was no particular rivalry, except perhaps on May-day, when the horses, harness, and whips were much be-ribboned, and the drivers and guards were gorgeously arrayed in bright coloured "top-hats"; so that for a number of years competition failed to afford the public increased facilities. As was inevitable, however, the steadily growing requirements of the locality brought competition in due time, first in the shape of rival omnibuses, and later in the form of the more modern tramway. This was just as the toll-gates were beginning to disappear.

The earliest tram lines laid down for passenger traffic in this immediate locality were constructed by the Birmingham and Staffordshire Tramways Company in 1872 for horse traction. The lines starting from the foot of Hockley Hill ran through Handsworth and West Bromwich, thence branching in one direction to Dudley Port, and in the other to Holloway Bank. The following year they were extended from Hockley to the top of Snow Hill; and there was then established a service of cars between Birmingham and Villa Cross for Handsworth. These lines were constructed on the old-style broad gauges of 4 feet $8\frac{1}{2}$ inches, under the Birmingham and Staffordshire Tramways Act of 1870. A chain horse had to be kept to assist the tramcar up Soho Hill.

In 1886 the Birmingham Central Tramways Co. having acquired the Handsworth lines among the others serving the Birmingham suburbs, the old fashioned gauge of 4ft. $8\frac{1}{2}$in. was changed to the almost universal one of 3ft. 6in. The method of traction to be applied on the Handsworth route was at first a matter of difficulty as the residents along it raised objection to the employment of steam-power in consequence of the severity of its gradients. At that time the cable system was extensively in use in America, although there was but one thus equipped in England—that at Highgate, London. It was resolved to adopt it for the Handsworth line, placing the driving station at Hockley Brook, and dividing the line there into two sections. This division, and the use of two separate cables, was necessitated by the Board of Trade requirements stipulating that the speed inside the city boundaries should not exceed six miles an hour, while the Handsworth section might be worked up to eight miles.

The first section constructed was that from Hockley to Birmingham, the two miles five furlongs of which was laid down at a cost of £25,000 or £9,500 per mile. Two engines of 300 horse-power each were laid down, sufficient for both sections, the main driving power being in duplicate for the full seven miles of single cable. The cable specified was one-inch diameter, of six strands of crucible steel (each of 19 strands) round a manilla core and the breaking-strain was to be 90 tons to the square inch. The weight of the cable works out at $4\frac{1}{2}$ tons per mile, or 30 tons altogether; the length of life assumed for it being 24 months.

The horse trams ceased running on the New Inns and Villa Cross routes on March 28th, 1887, the cable line from Birmingham to Hockley starting the next day (March 29) and a temporary service of omnibuses being put on to New Inns. The Villa Cross was abandoned; and the omnibus service to New Inns was discontinued on the 19th April 1889, the cable line to that destination being opened the following day (April 20)..The cable system of traction was thus introduced to the locality by the Birmingham Central Tramways Company, in the two sections and on the dates named. The total length of the two sections is three miles, of which $1\frac{3}{4}$ miles is in Handsworth. The latter section met, at New Inns, the cars of the South Staffordshire Steam Tramway Company, who held a Handsworth Provisional Order for that portion of their line between New Inns and the West Bromwich boundary. The South Staffordshire Co. had laid their line from Handsworth through Wednesbury to Darlaston in 1883.

The cable method was to be used for a period of seven years, and renewed with the consent of the local authority for a further term not exceeding five years. As yet Parliament had not conferred general powers by which local authorities could work their own lines, and they were therefore very much at the mercy of the companies who exploited their districts. Handsworth felt the irksomeness of this position when the nuisances in connection with the cable system began to manifest themselves, as they did when the mechanism began to get worn and out of order. All along the route the noise made by the cable running over the pulleys became so excessive as to become positively injurious to the health of those residing in the adjacent houses, and a great outcry consequently arose against the employment of the cable system. On the other hand the public reaped the advantage of a frequent, regular, and cheap service, the cars running at intervals of one or two minutes, and the fare for the whole three miles being then (1900) one penny. The popularity and great usefulness of the service may be concluded from the fact that in 1900 no less than $12\frac{1}{2}$ million passengers were carried between Birmingham and New Inns, and the traffic has gone on growing since that date.

Among other monopolies bought out by the Birmingham Central Co. in 1886 were those of the Birmingham Tramway and Omnibus Co. along the

Perry Barr route; here as everywhere else opposition omnibuses were got rid of.

The Perry Barr tramway some six furlongs of single line with passing-places, so far as Handsworth parish is concerned, was laid along the Birchfield Road, and opened for traffic 25 November, 1884. It was constructed for steam traction, by the Birmingham Suburban Tramway Company, with a twenty one years' Order from 1882, to expire in 1903. By the inhabitants of the pleasant villa residences along this route, the steam engines employed were always regarded as ugly, cumbersome, and noisy methods of traction,; and a number of prosecutions were instituted from time to time against the company's servants for the emission of steam and smoke; nuisances always obnoxious to proprietors of lawns, shrubberries, and front gardens.

The Perry Barr steam trams ran to the close of the year 1906; and four months of 1907 were devoted to the re-construction of the line for overhead electric traction. When the service came to be resumed on this system such was the confusion of the arrangements made by the local authorities of Handsworth and Aston with the British Electric Traction Company, in whom the running powers had became vested, a retrogressive step had perforce to be taken, to the annoyance of the public and the stultification of the authorities. The steam trams had given a good through service from Birmingham (Old Square) to Perry Barr for a fare of twopence; the electric car service now (1908) runs from Birmingham (Martineau Street) to the Handsworth boundary at Chain Walk for twopence, where a change of car must be effected, and an extra fare of another penny paid for carriage to Perry Barr.

In 1896, it should be explained, the Central Tramway Company was succeeded by the City of Birmingham Tramways Company who acquired the rights of their predecessors for the remaining years of the various Orders. This transference of interests from one company to another, and the varying dates at which different Orders expired on different sections, all tended to complicate matters between 1903 and 1907, notwithstanding that the local authorities granted twelve-month licenses of renewals at varying times for the working of one or other of the otherwise derelict sections.

Handsworth with an area of 3,647 acres and a large population to serve—in 1900 the rateable value was £225,000 and a district rate produced £33,000—can scarcely be said to be overdone in the matter of tramways with but six miles of line. These statistics were given in evidence before a committee of the House of Lords in 1901, when the City of Birmingham Tramways Company, finding the various Orders for the lines they had acquired from the previous owners, whom they bought out, then rapidly expiring, were seeking the sanction of Parliament to an extension of time. They asked that they might have running powers in all the districts they served till 1907, though some of their Acts expired in 1904 and one in 1903. Handsworth, Aston, and some of the other local governing authorities naturally objected to forego the right, then rapidly ripening, to purchase the lines in their respective areas on the terms originally agreed upon when the 21 years' lease was granted to the company's predecessors.

The Handsworth portion consisted mainly of the two suburban lines by which access is given to the city of Birmingham; the one along the Holyhead Road from Hockley Brook to the West Bromwich boundary; the other along the Walsall Road via Birchfield to Perry Barr. A connecting link between these two diverging lines, laid from Lozells Road along Villa Road, was by that time disused. Perhaps in the early future, when progressive ideas shall have dawned upon the authorities of Handsworth, tram lines may offer facilities along cross roads and ceinture routes—say from Perry Barr to New Inns, offering as part of a girdle-line round the city, direct communication between Aston and Smethwick. For a wide-reaching parish like Handsworth its railway accommodation has always been miserably inadequate; now its tramways are found inadequate being either antiquated or in a state of muddle.

XXXI.—HANDSWORTH UNDER VILLAGE GOVERNMENT.

The present day is characterised by its socialistic tendencies, especially in the form of municipalising the public services; a consideration of the local tramway services therefore leads us naturally to the subject of local government. Of the period of Vestrydom when Handsworth was ruled mainly by its Churchwardens and Overseers, we have just a few records. The Churchwardens' Account Books go back to 4th March, 1673. Here are four items from the year 1688:—

For felling the walnut tree	00	,,	01	,,	00
Received for a walnut tree	00	,,	08	,,	00
For the rails at Hamstead Bridge	00	,,	15	,,	04
Paid Audley for a cart	01	,,	10	,,	00

The maintenance of the parish bridges for the next hundred years or so seems to have averaged £10 annually. The parish appears to have had some interest in the river fishing; in the vestry books is "an account of money that was raised of two persons convicted for taking fish in the river of Tame, in the parish of Handsworth, before Humfrey Wyrley, Esq., Anno Domini 1694 ... ... £2 0 0

Among other curious items are these—

"January 11th, 1737. Paid Thomas Bennett for timber and work done at the bridge, and posts and rails betwixt the church and Mr. Pope's House 10 9 5

March 3rd, 1756. Allowed William Ashford for a load of muck, the land being very much beggared 0 5 0

The original "Town Hall" in which the public business of the parish was conducted was (and is) situated in Grove Lane, some hundred yards below the Grove Tavern. It is an ordinary bit of plain domestic architecture of the 16th century, and is known to have served the little community of Handsworth, when it was a mere village, as a workhouse, a lock-up, and a parish office, for at least a century and a half.

As to the history of this old relic, the late Mr. Allen E. Everitt quoted some old deeds which showed that the "messuage or tenement called the Town Hall of Handsworth (in which the testator's sister, Mary Brown, then dwelt, and had a life interest), was bequeathed by will, 30th April, 1709 by one Thomas Brown, a Birmingham writing-master, to his son Henry. This owner dying at Rushall in 1780 left the property, then described as four separate dwelling-houses, though still known as the "Town Hall" to Jacob Smith of Walsall, upon trust for the benefit of certain of his relatives; and there was a proviso that a payment of £20 should be made "to the Churchwardens and Overseers of the parish of Handsworth, upon trust, to place out the same and apply the interest in manner therein directed."

A stone in the gable end of the building which fronts Grove Lane bears the inscription "H. B. Repaired 1794." At this date one of the cottages was occupied by Mary Brown, a well-known character, who is said to have gone round the village selling fruit, one of her cries, which were delivered with a lisp and drawl, being "My mulberries to sell—open my wallet and see—but please give me the money first!" In 1805 the buildings were sold as five tenements, when with the accompanying land upwards of an acre and a half in extent, it was bought by two men named Underhill. One of these, James Underhill occupied the place, and in 1806 was in office as Overseer of the parish.

Immediately afterwards the "Town Hall" passed into the possession of William Houghton, a draper of Birmingham, who in turn sold it to Thomas Slater. a gunlock maker of Handsworth; upon his death in 1851 it was sold by auction. Without further detail as to its various owners, let it suffice to say that the property appears to have been in the hands of the Brown and Blackham families over the longest term of years. It is claimed that Brown's Green borrowed its name from the former family. The Haughton family, it may be added, founded by the Bull Street silk mercer, lived at Birchfield House, the old red brick residence still standing opposite Trinity Church.

Following the occupation of James Underhill came that of Jeremiah Needham, farmer, who rented his land in those days at 7s. an acre. But it is as a public functionary that he was best known, and has already been mentioned on p 122. Mr. G. H. Brown writes of him—

"Besides being a farmer Needham was a parish constable, overseer, coroner's officer, recruiting officer, and workhouse master. Moreover, the building was the temporary gaol and workhouse. It is related of Needham that he once refused an offer which would undoubtedly in after years have enriched his descendants to an enormous extent. One day he met the lord of the manor, Mr. Gough, of Perry Hall, to whom he was well known, near Villa Cross. In the course of conversation Gough pointed out a piece of land—then waste of about ten acres in extent, on part of which the present post office stands, telling Needham if he would fence it in he could have it. Neednam thanked him but declined the offer, saying that he thought it would be hardly worth his while to do so."

At the beginning of the last century Petty Sessions were held by the County Magistrates at the Lamp Tavern, opposite the parish church gates; subsequently at the New Inns, Holyhead Road, where they used the "green room" which opened upon the lawn; and later, some fifty years ago, the business of the court was transferred to West Bromwich. The annual licensing sessions till then had been held at the Scott Arms Hotel, Great Barr, not only for Handsworth, but for West Bromwich, Smethwick, Harborne and several other of the neighbouring parishes.

Needham's accounts disclose charges made by him for attendance upon such occasions. Thus, under date 15th September, 1817, he charges 8s. "for summonsing eight publicans for their licenses" These parochial accounts were vouched for at the monthly meetings of Overseers and Churchwardens; as the same official had also the responsibility of looking after paupers, lunatics and others who became chargeable to the parish, a few more items from his Account Book will throw light on the public affairs of the village as transacted at the Town Hall at that period.

"1811. January 20th.—Caretaking and maintaining of Elizabeth Linch, 7 days in a dying state ... ... 14s.
Paid for Coffin 14s., for shroud ... ... 5s.
Paid Bread and Cheese 3s. 6d, Ale 14s., For fees ... ... 3s.
Paid 6 men for carrying Elizabeth ... ... 6s.
For my attendance and trouble ... ... 5s."

"1817. May 17th.—For going to fetch doctor to a man that had cut his throat, and taking to the Hospital in my cart ... ... 5s."

"1819. January.—For taking Jas. Fulford to Stafford Asylum quite mad ... ... £2 7 0."

Needham was a good example of the parish official of the old type. He kept the Overseers' Accounts from 10 July, 1807, to 1 July, 1819, in clerkly style. He died in 1820 after holding office for 40 years. He was succeeded by Joseph Chillingworth who lived at the corner of Union Row in Grove Lane, and who was the constable who arrested Booth, the notorious banknote forger. His successor, a farmer named Corbett, whose farm occupied the site of the present Destructor Works, was the last of the parish constables of Handsworth.

In addition to the Parish Constable, who was publicly appointed at the annual vestry meetings, a watchman came to be casually employed in later years, as the number of good houses began to increase in Handsworth. The pay being small, only decrepit old men could be secured for the post; the duties being simply to perambulate the more populous parts of the village during the night, armed with a staff and a lantern, and to call out the hours aloud, as a sort of guarantee to his employers that he was on duty, and not snugly sleeping away the time in his box. It may be guessed that the village was but inefficiently policed under such an antiquated system, and that the public really had to protect themselves.

The rules of the Handsworth Association for the Prosecution of Felons, printed in 1829, has at the end of it a list of some sixty subscribing inhabitants. The Committee, which consisted of the Rev. T. L. Freer (chairman), James, Villars, John Vickers, Christopher Wren, and William Houghton, held their meetings at the Lamp Tavern, an important house of assembly in those days.

XXXII.—MODERN LOCAL GOVERNMENT.

It was not till the early "thirties" of the last century that the national legislature turned its serious attention to a reform of local self-government; impelled to it then, first by the economic unsoundness of parochial administration in the face of a growing pauperism, and afterwards by the alarming state of the public health constantly menaced by a recurrence of cholera and other epidemic diseases

Handsworth was first touched by the new order of things when it passed, along with West Bromwich, Wednesbury, Oldbury, and Warley, into the Poor Law Union of West Bromwich, as constituted for more economical administrative purposes by the Poor Law Amendment Act of 1834. The Earl of Dartmouth was first chairman of the West Bromwich Board of Guardians (1835), James Spittle, vice-chairman, and among the 20 or 30 members were Joseph S. Chavasse, Samuel Kenrick, Christopher Wren, and Robert L. Chance. Although Handsworth Workhouse was supposed to be superseded, the new "union" workhouse at West Bromwich—derisively dubbed "the bastille" by the poor—was not opened till 1857.

Equally slow progress marked the development of Handsworth local government under the Public Health Acts, which the inhabitants seemed loth to adopt. Eventually the first Local Board was elected October, 1874; it superseded a patchwork government of three different authorities, each with its own clerk and staff of officers. The West Bromwich Union Rural Sanitary Authority had so far been responsible for the sanitary work, the Handsworth Highway Board for the repair of the highways; and Lighting Inspectors (under the Lighting and Watching Act of 1833) for the public lighting of the streets.

Mr. Henry Ward, clerk to the West Bromwich Guardians, became clerk to the Handsworth Local Board, and guided its destinies for the whole twenty years of its existence; in 1894 he continued to act in a similar capacity for the newer form of authority, the Handsworth Urban District Council a position in which he has recently been succeeded by his son, Mr. Ernest Ward.

The Handsworth Authorities met at the Parish Offices in Baker Street (which was also occupied by the Relieving Officer) till the Council House was built. As the memorial tablet in the entrance hall of the latter testifies, this very essential public building was erected in 1877, Mr. William Aston then being chairman of the Local Board. Among the members named on the tablet, Mr. George Heaton, of the Birmingham Mint, was long the chairman of the Handsworth bench of magistrates. Another name was that of Mr. William Medlicott Ellis, a Birmingham merchant, who died at his residence. The Willows, Perry Barr, in 1892, having been a chairman of the

Handsworth Highway Board, an active magistrate, and for 20 years a guardian of the poor (Birmingham).

The site of the new building (comprising Public Offices, a Lecture Hall and Free Library) about an acre of land in extent, had been previously occupied by the Waggon and Horses Inn. The land. buildings, fittings and furniture, cost about £20,700. It should have been mentioned that the Free Library Act had been adopted, and the buildings put up in 1877 are now well equipped as a temple of literature, and a branch library has been in existence at Birchfield since 1885.

As Handsworth had grown into a really large and populous urban district ere it adopted that modern form of local self-government by which alone the manifold public wants of a large community can be adequately met, there were as a consequence many deficiencies to be made good before the place could be regarded even as a moderately well-equipped town. How far the local authority has succeeded within the space of about a quarter of a century in overtaking the neglect of previous generations, and whether public efficiency has been secured by the sacrifice of economy, are questions which the impartial historian must leave to the judgment of the ratepayers.

The primary duty of the Local Board as a health authority was to overhaul the sanitary arrangements of the parish, and the first report of the Medical Officer of Health, Dr. Welch was not a very flattering one. The houses of the poor were often built "back to back," while the gardens of the well-to~do invariably contained a dumb-well: for there was not a properly constructed sewer in the whole area. As Handsworth could only be properly drained by carrying its sewage through Aston towards the low-lying land at Saltley, an agreement was entered into with Aston Local Board (1876) for the construction, at the joint expense of the two Boards, of a main sewer for this purpose. The work was carried out at an expenditure of £60,000, and almost immediately afterwards handed over, on equitable terms, to a newer and wider control, brought into existence by the force of circumstances.

The Tame, collecting its waters from a number of grimy Black Country towns as a matter of course became a highly polluted stream; and its condition after the Rea had joined it at Saltley, bringing more contaminated water from Birmingham, was infinitely worse lower down. This state of things was resented by riparian landowners, and much litigation resulted. The outcome of it all was the formation in 1877 of the Tame and Rea Drainage Board. This united body, which was instituted to deal with the drainage and sewage treatment of an area of nearly 50,000 acres, is representative of the following local authorities interested in this basin —the City of Birmingham, Aston Manor and Sutton Coldfield

(Warwickshire), Kings Norton (Worcestershire) and Handsworth, Perry Barr, and Smethwick (Staffordshire). In 1883 Handsworth and Smethwick jointly constructed a large sewer for draining 575 acres of the former and 1,120 acres of the latter, the Handsworth Authority contributing to the cost about £5,500 and Smethwick £8,500.

Prior to 1879 every occupier in Handsworth had paid for the removal of his house refuse and the cleansing of his ashpit and privy; in that year the Board undertook the work, executing it through contractors. Some dozen years ago the Cleansing Department established a Destructor for the burning of the refuse in Queen's Head Lane. The improvement in the public health of the parish soon began to reveal itself in the vital statistics; the mortality per thousand fell from 15.9 in 1874 to 12.9 in 1893.

Not far behind the duty of preserving the public health comes that of preventing the outbreak of fire; so early in 1878 came the inauguration of the Handsworth Fire Brigade, followed by the later development of a branch Fire Station at Perry Barr in 1890. The Brigade is technically a volunteer corps of fire-fighters, although the Superintendent is engaged to devote the whole of his time to the organisation of the work.

An enlightened community does not advance very far in the work of public sanitation before encountering the necessity for open breathing-spaces—for providing a town with its "public lungs and children's playground." In 1888 Handsworth set about the work of laying out its first public "pleasure grounds;" and piece by piece, an area of some $60\frac{1}{2}$ acres, was acquired at an approximate outlay of £28,000 for the Victoria Park, now one of the largest and most popular public recreation grounds in the Midland district.

More recently the piece of land known as the "Black Patch," which, as already related, had been lying derelict and occupied as a permanent gipsy encampment for many years, has been acquired by the public for similar purposes. Its situation at the meeting point of three populous parishes has induced the respective authorities of those places to combine in the purchase of the land. The price was £12,749 towards which Birmingham contributed £4,000, Smethwick £1,000, and Handsworth £1,000, the Open Spaces Society gave £5,279, and the rest has been provided by public subscription.

Within the last few years municipal developments have come upon Handsworth "thick and threefold." It may be mentioned that when the Urban District Council came to be formed under the Local Government Act of 1894, the parish was for greater convenience divided into five electoral wards, and the number of members constituting the local authority wee increased from 12 to 15.

As already recorded (p. 69) the constitution of an education authority for this parish was delayed for a number of years after the population had begun to grow at so rapid a rate. Consequently a large number of Handsworth children could not find school accommodation here, and had to be educated outside the parish chiefly at the cost of the neighbouring authorities. It was not till July, 1892, that the first Handsworth School Board was elected; a body which, while it lasted, did its work admirably. In 1902, however, the duties and responsibilities of the School Board were passed on, under a new Education Act, to a Committee of the District Council.

The Local Board in 1892 took advantage of the Technical Instruction Acts, and appointed a Committee to carry out this branch of the public work; how well the work has since been directed is evidenced by the present sound condition of the Handsworth Technical School.

It was a distinct advance on the work of the old lighting authority when Handsworth Public Electricity Supply was inaugurated at the close of 1905. Mains were laid in a central block of streets stretching from the Generating Station to the Birchfield and Trinity Roads, where the largest proportion of private consumers might be expected. Only the main thoroughfares were lighted by electricity, 120 standards being erected at an average distance apart of 66 yards. The cost of the undertaking had already reached £70,000. The Generating Works are situated on the site of the old mill-pool which Edward Rushton formed in 1756 for supplying power to the small mill he had erected on Soho Brook, and which as previously related passed into the hands of Boulton. These modern municipal works are to supply power as well as light.

There will certainly be a call very shortly for power to work the street tramways; in which connection opportunity may be seized to correct the impression that the tramways were "leased" to the companies. This was not the case. The companies originally interested were authorised by Provisional Orders granted by the Board of Trade to construct the lines through the streets, and the only way the Local Authority can get rid of the companies is by purchasing from them the parts of the undertakings lying within the parish boundaries, and this under the terms of the Tramways Act 1870 on the expiration of the 21 years from the date of the Act confirming the Order.

The last public undertaking brought to a completion was the Public Baths in Grove Lane, opened in 1907. This institution includes Turkish and Swimming Baths, and although by no means in a central situation, has had the large sum of £21,000 lavished upon it.

Although some half-dozen years ago a Birmingham company established a public Crematorium at Perry Barr, the populous and extensive district of Handsworth has hitherto depended mainly upon the ancient churchyard for the disposal of its dead; but the churchyard, enlarged from time to time as it has been, can no longer cope with the requirements of the growing population. The provision of a municipal burial ground now being imperative, some 70 acres of the Leveretts Estate have recently been acquired at a cost of upwards of £21,000. To drain the 1and? lay it out and erect chapels for a Public Cemetery is expected to cost £10,000 more before the work is completed.

All these large undertakings coming so closely upon each other already threaten to become a drain upon the public purse, notwithstanding that the rateable value of Handsworth now stands at £285,000, and that a rate at 3s. 4d. in the £ has just produced £43,000. There is a feeling abroad among the ratepayers that owing to the presence of a certain disquieting factor in the governing body, economy is often wilfully sacrificed; and the most recent record of local self-government in Handsworth does not warrant optimistic views as to its future.

A short time ago a proposal to incorporate Handsworth as a municipal borough was brought before the public. That it was received very coldly is not a matter for surprise when the circumstances of the case are considered. Handsworth is a large residential suburb attached to a great city, and has grown rapidly to its present swollen proportions within a decade or two. Consequently its population is alien or imported rather than native, attracted to the spot chiefly, if not solely by economic reasons. Such a population is merely an aggregation of residents, moved by no common interest except the convenience of locality combined with a comparative cheapness of living; it is certainly not a community which can be actuated by the sentiment of local patriotism or inspired to great enterprise by any depth of public spirit. The probability is that the introduction of a higher form of local government, if the maintenance of its enhanced dignity called for the levying of high rates, might have the effect not only of checking the natural growth and development of the district, but of replacing its present prosperity by a disastrous deterioration of house property. For a suburb like Handsworth must always stand in competition with the other residential districts by which Birmingham is surrounded, many of them offering that greatest desideratum, a comparative cheapness of living, with the facility of access to business which is practically common to them all.

When thousands of Birmingham business men can say, half jokingly and half in truth, that they"do not live in Handsworth only sleep there," we get one of those verbal quips which afford us serious food for reflection. The fact here forced upon the mind of the hearer is that such men are not attached to the soil of Handsworth by the ties of birth, the sentiment of local patriotism, or anything else that cannot be readily overborne in minds so purely dominated by the spirit of commercialism.

        *   *   *   *   *   *   *

For many centuries Perry Barr was an ancient Manor included within the parish of Handsworth, as were also its hamlets of Oscott and Queeslet. As we have seen (chapter xix.) Perry Barr Church was built in 1833, but it was not till 1862 that Perry Barr was formed into a separate ecclesiastical parish.

As to its civil government it was part of the West Bromwich Rural district from about 1866 till the new legislative requirements of 1894 offered facilities for an improved status. In 1841 the village had 983 inhabitants, and the census of 1891 had shown a population of only 2,310, scattered over its wide area of 4,033 acres.

There being. however, a number of advantages in the urban as against the rural form of government, rather than the township should be transferred to the Walsall Rural district, and notwithstanding the comparative smallness of the population, the Perry Barr Urban District Council was constituted. This body meets at its offices in Hamstead, and Mr. Henry Ward; the Clerk to the West Bromwich Guardians, acts as its Clerk also.

At the last census (1901) the population of Perry Barr had only increased to 2,348. In 1842 the township was assessed at £6,685 to the property tax, for rating purposes Perry Barr is now assessed at about £14,000, chiefly agricultural.

XXXIII.—FOLK LORE, CUSTOMS AND HABITS.

Little is known of the Folk Lore of Handsworth and Perry Barr, for no local discoverer seems ever to have laboured in this vast area of research. When we use the term Folk Lore we mean that ocean of the people's life which no man can sound, which has never been fully mapped out, and which few writers have scarcely scanned.

The meadows of old Handsworth had their Fairy Rings; those circles of rank dry grass which the good folks said were made by the feet of trooping fairies dancing round and round in the moonlight; but which sober science informs us are produced by a fungus below the surface which has seeded in a circular range and prevented the grass roots absorbing their requisite moisture. Dr. Plot, speaking of "fairy rings" in his Natural History of this county, says a Ring "at Handsworth having been observed for divers years by the Rev. Mr. Ange, rector of the place, he seriously told me, that when he first knew it it exceeded not four yards diameter at most; whereas when I measured it anno 1680, it was increased almost to forty, having run through the hedges into another field. As that other at Perry Hall, being in a field near the river, so increased from a smaller to a larger extent, till at length it came to be of near 50 yards diameter, and to run into the water!"

Perry Barr is still rural of aspect, and some of the old-world garden lore lingers there yet. While it is considered "luck" to find a four leaved clover, or to gather a large bunch of snowdrops with which to decorate a room, there are many things the doing of which exercise anything but a benign influence. Thus, it is just as distinctly "unlucky" to decorate the house with "May"—to bring hawthorn blossoms into the house being to invite an attack of fever upon some members of the household. If one, "greatly daring," ventures on the transplanting of parsley, he may expect broken bones in his family before long; and if he wishes his cabbages to grow good hearts he must certainly not fail to plant them in the wane of the moon. It is considered to be exceedingly unlucky to burn elder, a tree in which it is very generally believed a vengeful spirit dwells. Tradition has it that some of Charles I.'s soldiers, when they bivouacked at King's Standing in 1643, lighted their camp fires with faggots of the elder bushes, in consequence of which there was much headshaking among the superstitious natives, who could not restrain their muttered forebodings of coming disasters.

The bee-keepers of Handsworth and Perry Barr were not free from some of the superstitions common to the rest of the country. It was customary to notify the bees by whispering into the hive, of the death of the head of the family, and sometimes to drape the hive with crape; and when a hive or a swarm of bees was sold, it was always insisted that the price should be paid in gold—generally half-a sovereign—and not in silver.

Coming to old church customs, one common to many parts of the country, not omitting Birmingham, is recorded to have been regularly observed every Eastertide in Handsworth. This was the curious custom of "Clipping the Church." Every Easter Monday it was customary for the school children, with others of the adult parishioners, to gather in the churchyard, and when sufficient were assembled to join hands in a ring round the church. They first danced gleefully round the sacred edifice facing inwards; but presently facing outwards the fun became more boisterous as the dance became faster, and particularly when any of the linked ones loosed hands, and went flying off among the grave mounds. The symbolic significance of this old custom has been traced to the setting of the watch round the sepulchre of Christ by Pilate. The custom prevailed also at Wolverhampton and other parts of Staffordshire. In the eighteenth century it was customary for the school children at Walsall to assemble on Easter Monday morning and walk in procession to the Church, followed by a crowd of people, and on arriving at the sacred edifice, to lay hold of each others hands, and with their backs to the building completely encircle it—the last child in the procession joining hands with the first. When circling round it they sang the following verse—

> Round about Thy Temple Lord,
> Throw Thine own protecting arm,
> Keep it from the fire and sword,
> Keep it safe from every harm.

At the conclusion of this ceremony the children were regaled with hot cross buns at the expense of the parish. The custom fell into disuse early in the nineteenth century.

Modern Handsworth, as the up-to-date suburb of a large city, has its votaries of every form of social recreation, both mental and physical. Clubs and combinations flourish for the pursuit of athletics in various forms; for cricket and football, the latter under both codes, Rugby and Association; for lawn tennis, hockey and golf, for swimming and cycling, in all five of which the female section now participates; while in the sport of cross-country running, there is no combination of amateur runners in the world more famous than the Birchfield Harriers—a club which has been contesting championship honours for three decades.

While thus glancing momentarily at the sports of the people sight must not be lost of the fact that the renowned Aston Villa Football Club was at its birth, and during its earlier years, more of a Handsworth than an Aston institution. At that time Aston Manor was more directly represented both in cricket and football by the Aston Unity Club. The Aston Villa Club was originally constituted of youths attached to the chapel of that name, whose cricket club took up football as a winter sport when the latter game was beginning to become popular some thirty years ago. They played their football in various parts of Handsworth, wherever a suitable field could be found; at one time in Westminster Road, at another on a field between Birchfield Road and Leonard Road; but the club's earliest national triumphs were won on the ground in Wellington Road, opposite the Old Crown and Cushion Inn, which was opened September, 1878, with a match against the Wednesbury Strollers. For nearly twenty years the Aston Villa Football Club played at Perry Barr—as evidence of which were they not known among their supporters as the "Perry Pets"—the Wellington Road ground finally closing its gates in 1897.

Neither must it be forgotten, passing from the physical to the intellectual, that the Perry Barr Institute was one of the earliest of the suburban societies established around Birmingham for the holding of lectures and entertainments, and for affording other forms of mental recreation. The Institute building is the one now adopted as the Birchfield Branch Free Library. The Institute, no doubt, met a want at the time it was established; ten or twenty years ago social recreation was sought more in the way of public assemblages than at the present time when it has become the fashion to beguile the tedium of winter evenings by holding bridge parties or whist drives at each other's private residences.

In a population of seventy thousand, made up largely of that middle-class element which, of all our English grades of society, is perhaps the most "clubable" and the most inclined towards sociability, there are naturally various coteries for the cultivation of art or the study of science, to say nothing of the opportunities for joining together in religious and educational work, or taking part in social, political, or philanthropic movements. Not the least useful work undertaken in combination is that of the Photographic Society, the members of which are engaged in a pictorial survey of Handsworth, and whose photographs of local scenes will in time to come prove a far more valuable record than the verbal description of an historian can ever hope to be.

XXXIV.—MISCELLANEA.

Towards tile end of a lengthy work involving research in many directions, there generally remain in the chronicler's note-book a number of odd memoranda which he has so far failed to introduce; into his compilation, but which are not entirely negligible because of some inherent interest they possess. Not to waste or jettison a number of such notes in this instance it is proposed to huddle the heterogeneous mass together in a sort of literary olla podrida to form a penultimate chapter.

The garrulous Doctor Plot ("Natural History of Staffordshire" 1686) mentions the "trunks, ,&c. of trees being found buried in the moors at Handsworth." Likewise in his chapter upon antiquities, he describes the brass head of the bolt of a catapulta, found at Handsworth which has been engraved; he also notices the traces of the Roman road running through Handsworth and Perry Barr. The worthy doctor also records the existence of a curious local echo. He says that "near Hamstead (the seat of the much honoured, and my truly noble patron, the right worshipful Sir John Wyrley. Kt.) on a bank side in a field south-easterly from the house, that from a quadruple object answers distinctly four times."

Shaw records that in the tremendous thunderstorm on Sunday. July 6. 1794. the lightning threw down the chimney of Joseph Latchford's house, at Handsworth, and forged its way into the lower room, where it killed a boy lying near the door. Nine persons were in the house, but none were hurt, except one slightly in his foot; the windows were broken, and part of the tiling carried to some distance.

Among the manorial rights of Perry Barr in olden times, in the one known as that of "turbary" (the privilege of cutting turf) it was necessary to obtain a licence in writing from the lord of the manor before a tenant could cut peat—a most unusual restriction.

With regard to The Friary, the residence of Mr. Walter G. Griffiths, if this old house really marked the site of a religious establishment, it could have had no connection with Sandwell. Sandwell was a Benedictine house, and the Benedictines were monks, not friars. And yet it is curious to observe that on this side of Sandwell we have The Friary, and on the farther side, near to Wednesbury, Friar's Park, although there is no record of friars ever having been settled in this locality. The Friary might possibly have been the Grange or home farm of the Priory, and through some confusion of terms, the name "Priory Grange" may have been shortened and altered to "Friary."

Again, the friars, being before all things mendicants, usually made their abode in or near a populous district, which in mediæval times this was not. This fact, however, does not place it outside the bounds of possibility that The Friary (as also some cell in Friar's Park) may have been an anchorhold or reclusorium in connection with the Priory. Such a building consisted sometimes of three or four cells, together with a little chapel, but in connection with a priory would be used only for self-inflicted discipline, and not as an establishment penitentiary.

In Handsworth Churchyard is buried one of the most notorious criminals of modern times. William Booth, a century ago, was farming some 200 acres at Queslett, and at the same time was taking advantage of the secluded situation of his house to follow systematically the nefarious practices of a forger and coiner. Long suspected by the Birmingham police, his arrest was at last resolved upon, and knowing the defensive and other secret arrangements of his retreat—walled-up staircases, barricaded doors, and upper rooms approachable only by trap-doors and movable ladders—the constables felt justified in requisitioning the services of a troop of soldiers to assist them. The arrest was made, although a brief halt of the cavalcade at the Boars Head Inn, Perry Barr, nearly led to a frustration of the police plans. Booth and his accomplices were duly brought to trial at Stafford and found guilty. The chief culprit was hanged there August 15th, 1812, and his body afterwards given over to his relatives for interment. Relics of his criminal practices, in the shape of counterfeit coin and copper plates for engraving bank notes have since turned up at intervals in the vicinity of his farm. the last discovery being made a quarter of a century ago.

For the maintenance of the Watt Chapel the rent of two cottages opposite in Hamstead Road was set apart, but in some way unknown the property has been lost sight of, and is now reckoned among the "lost charities" of Handsworth. During Chantreys lifetime it was his practice to come down from London at certain times and see the Watt statue, which he regarded as one of his best works, cleaned under his personal supervision.

There is extant an interesting printed Programme of a Choir Sermon preached at Handsworth Church on Sunday morning, June 10th, 1827, by the Rev. Humphrey Pountney, B.A.. (Curate of Oldbury, when selections of sacred music were performed by Miss Heaton, Mr. Heaton, and Mr. Machin, and other members of the Birmingham Oratorio Choral Society.

Our next note constitutes a correction to one of the most popular anecdotes in the literature of Soho. The well-known story about Murdock's wooden hat, related in Smiles's "Lives of the Engineers" is said by Miss Emily Murdock Walton, a great-granddaughter of the inventor, to be a pure fabrication. The conversation between Murdock and Boulton on the subject is quite imaginary. Dr. Smiles was correctly informed that William Murdock did turn a wooden hat as a specimen of his skill, but the tale as generally related he thought too good to alter—and everybody now believes the anecdote, or prefers not to disbelieve it. A collection of Murdock's drawings and papers are in the possession of Mr. George Tangye, at Heathfield.

At the beginning of the nineteenth century it was the complaint of the author of "English Bards" that a new reading public had arisen to buy books according to their own tastes.

> Each country book-club bows the knee to Baal,
> And hurling lawful genius from the throne,
> Erects a shrine and idol of its own.

Handsworth was among the places boasting one of those Book Clubs which in our grandfathers' days supplied the place of public libraries.

About 1822 "The Handsworth English and Foreign Book Society" was in existence. The members in the year named were Mr. Matthew Robinson Boulton and Mr. James Watt, of Soho, sons of the great engineers; Mr. Samuel Tertius Galton and Mr. Samuel Galton, the bankers, of Steelhouse Lane; Mr. H. Galton and Mr. J. H. Galton. members of the same family; Mr. Molliett, a banker in Cherry Street, who resided at Hamstead Hall; the Rev. Thomas Lane Freer, who was rector of Handsworth from 1803 to 1835, the Rev. G. Holbrook, his curate; the Rev. J. Corrie, pastor of the Old Meeting House; Dr. Johnstone, one of the first physicians of the Birmingham General Hospital, and Nathaniel Gooding Clarke, the eminent King's Counsellor, who resided at Browne's Green House. Seven days were allowed for each volume, and threepence was the forfeiture for each day over—the institution was a private circulating library among a number of friends with literary tastes.

For a number of years Handsworth was the adopted home of the Rev. Arthur O'Neill, of Chartist fame, whose portrait is enshrined in Birmingham Art Gallery as one of our local worthies. Arthur O'Neill was born at Chelmsford, about 1820, the son of a proscribed Irish refugee. He was born to troublous times; though a man of peace he was forced by fate into conflict, his tender mild blue eyes often flashed in a dauntless defence of the undying principles of liberty and justice. Having entered Glasgow University in 1835 he was three years later attracted by the Chartist agitation; he was, indeed, fascinated by it and became enthusiastic in the cause. In July, 1840, he was sent from Glasgow to Birmingham to take part in a public welcome to two political prisoners on their release from Warwick gaol; his was the character to be appreciated in the Birmingham of those days, and he was invited to take up the pastorate of a chapel in Newhall Street, and here he also acted as Secretary to the Christian Chartists. When the second Chartist persecution began in 1842, Birmingham was placarded for an open-air meeting to be held in Summer

Lane on August 22nd, to petition the Queen to consider the distressed state of the country— that was in "the hungry forties." The four men who carried round the placards were arrested. For addressing a meeting at Cradley on August 22nd the Rev. Arthur O'Neill was arrested and committed to Stafford gaol for "holding an unlawful meeting," and in the following October he was indicted for sedition. After several trials as a political prisoner he was sent a second time to Stafford gaol, and was a prisoner there for one whole year with Joseph Linney, of Bilston, and another Chartist hero. In 1846 his ministry was removed to Zion Chapel, the building mentioned chapter xxi. Always in the van of political reform and never flinching in his long-maintained fight with oppression, the career of Arthur O'Neill is one to be recalled when it is needful to remind the people of the price which has been paid for their present-day liberties and immunities.

One of the later efforts for an improved street lighting in Handsworth, before the introduction of electric lighting, was by means of a lantern with four convex lenses, which had the effect of intensifying as well as diffusing the light from the gas jets. This was a Handsworth invention —Mr. Loftus, the inventor, died in this parish a few years ago.

Three other Handsworth names are worthy of mention. William Bragge, an engineer and antiquary, who died at Hallwood, Handsworth, in 1884, was an authority on pipes and tobacco, his collection in this line being valued at £4,000; his collection of illuminated MSS. sold for upwards of £12,000 in 1878.

Whitworth Wallis, F.S.A., K.C., and knight of several continental orders of chivalry, Director of the Birmingham Museum and Art Gallery, was born at Handsworth in 1856.

In December, 1907, Pope Pius X. conferred the Cross pro Ecclesia et Pontifice upon Mrs. Hopwood, of Lea Hall, Handsworth, in recognition of her earnest services on behalf of her co-religionists, and particularly the poorer section of them.

XXXV.—BIBLIOGRAPHY.

Besides those who have distinguished themselves in the more active walks of life, there are others who have achieved something in the quieter world of letters whose names must not be forgotten. A goodly number of Handsworth names are here extracted from Simms' "Bibliotheca Staffordiensis," that vast treasure-house of all that pertains to the writing and production of books, to everything connected with the literature and learning of this county. Let it be understood that the following items are condensed from Simms' exhaustive work, to which reference must be made for details of literary work produced, or of academic distinctions gained at the Universities. Naturally, the clerical element will be found to preponderate in a list of this kind, to begin with these, we have interesting local records of—

Rev. John Waltham Fletcher, M.A., born at Birmingham Heath 1816, who was Minister of St. James's, Handsworth, 1844-51; Rev. James Michael John Fletcher, and the Rev. William George Dimock Fletcher (born at Handsworth, 1851) his two sons, both with a number of literary productions to their credit.

Rev. Thomas Lane Freer, Rector of Handsworth, who died 1835, and his son, the Rev. Richard Lane Freer, born at Handsworth in 1806, were connected with the Lanes of Bentley Hall; there was also George Lane Freer, surgeon, of the Friary, Handsworth, who died 1823. Rev. Charles Patten Good, of St. James' parish. 1854-56, who became Vicar and Rural Dean of Eccleshall; Rev. Alexander Gordon, M.A., born at Handsworth, 1854, son of William Francis Gordon, Esq.; Rev. James George Edward Hasluck, born at Handsworth, 1820; the Venerable Ernald Lane, sometime Vicar of St. Michaels (p. 93) and a Proctor to Convocation for archdeaconry of Stoke; the Right Rev. and Hon. Augustus Legge, Bishop of Lichfield, who was Curate at Handsworth 1864-66; Rev. Gilbert Littleton who succeeded the Rev. J. Fulnetby as Rector of Handsworth in 1636, Sir Edward Littleton being a joint-patron of the living at that date, as recorded on p. 70; Rev. Osbert Mordaunt, who was at St. Michael's from 1869 to 1875; the Rev. H. R. Peel, Rector of Handsworth 1860-73; Rev. Alan Gordon Smith, B.A., born at Handsworth, 1863; Rev. Jeremiah Finch Smith, M.A., F.S.A., Incumbent of St. James's 1840-44, afterwards Rural Dean of Walsall and Prebendary of Wellington; Rev. Henry Rushworth Woolley, Rector of Handsworth 1841 to his death in 1847

The Rev. Joseph Hill Grice, M.A., born 1809, and died at Upton-on-Severn in 1867, and the Rev. William Grice, M.A., who died Lay Clerk of New College in 1845, were both sons of Joseph Grice, Esq., J.P., of Handsworth Hall, who died in 1833, and is commemorated in the old church by a bust of Peter Hollins. (A later occupant of Handsworth Hall was Joseph Barrows, born 1831, who was long resident there prior its demolition.)

To this section also may perhaps be added William Robert Sheldon, barrister, who was born at St. James's Vicarage 1857 (see p. 91); William Francis Walton, B.A., born at Handsworth, 1865, son of the Rev. Daniel Nathaniel Walton, a prominent Curate of the parish mentioned on pp. 86 and 89; and last in this category, the Rt. Hon. John Veysey (or Harmon) Bishop of Exeter 1519, the donor of Sutton Park, and builder of Moor Hall, who was the son of William Harmon by his wife Joan, daughter of Henry Squeir, of Handsworth.

Turning to the local literature of Nonconformity the pages of the "Wesleyan Magazine" will show obituary memoirs of Henry Foxall who died at Handsworth, December 1823; of John Fryer of Nineveh, 1841; and Anne Hardman of this parish, 1843. (See also p. 91 of the present writer's "History of West Bromwich.") The first-named (Foxall) in his boyhood and through his life was a friend of Francis Asbury, his father being young Asbury's employer at the forge at Hamstead. In Brigg's "Life of Bishop Asbury" will be found an account of the Foxalls, and of the Old Forge in Sandwell Park Lane, where Asbury and Foxall were engaged. The frontispiece to this work is a portrait of the Bishop, which shews him a tall, slender, and sinewy man

By the establishment of the Wesleyan Theological College at Handsworth Wood no inconsiderable volume of free church erudition has been imported into the parish. The Governors (or Principals) in succession have been (1881) Rev. John Hartley, (1892) Rev Robert Young, D.D., (1897) Rev. Thomas Allen:, D.D., and (1906) Rev. Silvester Whitehead. The Theological Tutors have been, (1881) Rev. F. W. Macdonald, (1891) Rev. W. T. Davison, M.A., D.D., and (1904) Rev. J. G. Tasker, D.D.; while the Classical Tutorship has been held (1881) by the Rev. Robert Newton Young, (1892) Rev. J. G. Tasker, and (1904) Rev. W. W. Holdsworth, M,A. Drs. Young, Davison, and Tasker, and the Rev. F. W. Macdonald have each held the position of Fernley Lecturer—the lectureship founded by John Fernley of Southport, some forty years ago, and being the highest aspiration in Methodism for scholars in Theology and related subjects. Five of the College staff have also filled the responsible position of President of Conference, namely, Dr. Young in 1886, Rev. F. W. Macdonald 1899, Rev. T. Allen 1900, Rev. Dr. Davison 1901, and Rev. S. Whitehead (a distinguished China Missionary) in 1904.

The Rev. F. W. Macdonald is a litterateur of the widest range, an orator, and a theologian. It has been said of him that "profound as are his theological attainments, their depth is concealed by the splendour of his style and diction." During his tenure of the chair of Theology he was the means of raising funds with which to purchase some 3,000 volumes, the nucleus of the present college library; and since his retirement from that post his own theological library has been presented to the college collection by the liberality of a friend. The works actually produced by Mr. Macdonald during his residence in Handsworth were "The Dogmatic Principle in Relation to Theology." (1881) "Life of Fletcher of Madeley," (1884); "Life of William Morley Punshon," (1887).

Dr. Tasker is distinguished in German theology, his researches in which gained him his D.D. Whilst at Handsworth Dr. Davison published "The Praises of Israel," an introduction to the study of the Psalms, and "The Wisdom and Literature of the Old Testament."

The Rev. Henry Bonner, born at Bilston 1846, became Pastor of Hamstead Road Baptist Church in 1883, and has made contributions to theological literature.

The bibliography of Handsworth could not fail to he further enriched if so notable a seat of learning as Oscott College could be claimed for this parish. Although "Old Oscott" was, and is, well within the confines of the ancient parish, the new college at Erdington is just outside the boundaries—boundary-lines are erratic.

Hutton, the historian of Birmingham, dealing with Witton, states that a jury of knights in the time of Henry III. was called upon to settle the disputed boundary line between Perry and Witton. "There is a road," says the chronicler, "where foot seldom treads, mounded on each side, leading over the Coldfield, from Perry Bridge towards the Newlands, undoubtedly the work of this venerable band of discreet knights."

The eminence on which the new college was erected at Erdington was known as Gibbet Hill from the fact of a gibbet having formerly stood there. As Handsworth's chief poetaster puts it (of whom, more presently)—

On yonder hill, where once the gibbet swung,
Now made more sacred by the popish throng
A gothic pile, with recent honours crowned
Rises majestic from its classic ground.

Granting we may claim both the new and the old colleges we have a lengthy list of names identified with the Roman Catholic Church. Simms no doubt found a prolific source of information in "The Oscotian; or Literary Gazette of St. Mary's," a college magazine which appeared in 1828-29, edited by the students; a new series was issued from 1881 to 1888, edited by the Rev. Michael F. Glancey, one of the professors, and it is still issued, but is again under the management of students.

Among the Catholic names of note are Dr. Wiseman, President of the college (appointed 1840) and afterwards Cardinal Archbishop of Westminster, and a prolific writer; John Henry Newman (subsequently

Cardinal) who went to Oscott after his reception into the Catholic Church and remained there until his ordination; Henry Howard, grandfather of the present Duke of Norfolk; Henry Weedall, a student at Oscott in his youth and afterwards President; the Rt. Rev. Dr. Ilsley, Bishop of Birmingham, and a former Rector of Oscott College, in which he was trained, 1853-61; Very Rev. James Spencer Northcote, D.D., President of the college 1860-77; the Rev. Thomas Potts, Vice-President of the college to 1808, and then President till his death in 1819; the Rev. Francis Hopkins, college choirmaster, afterwards the indefatigable Rector of St. Francis's, Hunter's Road, whose exertions have been recognised on p. 100; Rev. F. C. Husenbeth, who was at the college from 1814 to 1820 and was a voluminous writer; the learned and advanced, if not quite orthodox Rev. Joseph Berington (a member of the Soho Circle and a frequent guest rather then a member of the Lunar Society) sometime Priest-in-Charge of the Old Oscott Mission; the Rev. Francis Martyn, a noteworthy alumnus also previously mentioned (p. 98); the Rev. William Jones who died at Oulton Nunnery, near Stone, in 1868; the Rev. James Jones, a Vicar-General and Provost, who died at Worksop in 1861; the Rev. Samuel Jones, who died at Walsall in 1833; and the Rev. Robert Simpson, a clergyman of the Church of England who went to study at Oscott, where he was ordained 1851, ending his days at Dartmouth in 1887.

Passing from theology to physic the first literary effort to notice is that of James Vose Solomon, Professor of Ophthalmic Surgery at Queen's College, Birmingham, who was long in residence and practice in Handsworth; he contributed many technical papers on the " Eye" to medical journals from the year 1861. Dr. Joseph Quirke, a native of Ireland, and now long resident in Handsworth as a medical practitioner, was Ingleby Examiner in Midwifery at Queen's College, Birmingham, 1887; he is the author of several medical works of standing.

One of the latest works emanating from Handsworth is a "School Hygiene" by R. A. Lyster, M.B., B.Ch., B.Sc., D.P.H., Medical Officer of Health for Handsworth, and Lecturer on Hygiene at the University of Birmingham. It is published by the University Tutorial Press, Ld., London, at 3s. 6d., and is an admirable text-book for teachers, school managers, and those who have to study the subject for professional purposes.

In the domain of natural science, E. Sheriff Tye, of Handsworth, who died half-a-dozen years ago, was an eminent authority on Conchology, on which subject he contributed many learned papers to scientific journals. His collection of shells was large and valuable.

The late William Richard Hughes, of Handsworth Wood, the City Treasurer of Birmingham, was also a naturalist, but better known as a "Dicken's lover" and a contributor to Dickensiana; his daughter, too, Edith Rose Hughes, born at Handsworth 1872, has claims to literary distinction.

The world-famed establishment of Soho has a literature of its own; it only remains here to mention an account of "The Inventions of James Watt and his Models preserved at Handsworth and South Kensington," by Edward A. Cowper, which appeared in the Proceedings of the Mechanical Engineers' Institute, 1883. Simms contains a full and detailed bibliography of Watts.

Of those who have cultivated the poetic muse only two Handsworth names appear on the roll of local fame. In 1847 Joseph Parkes Jones, of this place, published a Poem, which was printed by T. Ragg, of Birmingham. Then we have the Rev. Harry Howells Horton, who was assistant minister at St. Michael's from 1858 to 1860; he dates the Preface of the third edition of his poem "Sutton Park," from "Handsworth, February, 1846." The work, from which we have already made one extract, begins—

> Sweet Sutton! once again thy woods I view.
> Which o'er my childhood's dreams a magic threw;
> Whose charms have beam'd so bright on memory's page,
> In spite of cares that haunt maturer age.

There are many descriptive allusions; thus he apostrophises the "Parson and Clerk"—

> You lonely Inn, to wintry winds exposed
> Where the lost traveller often has reposed.

In allusion to the tragedy of Mary Ashford he says of her betrayer—

> In the gay circle of the dance he met
> The maid on whom his lustful eye was set;
> He drew his victim from the festal throng,
> And o'er the widening Coldfield wandered long.

In conclusion it may be claimed that the present work is practically the first complete history of Handsworth which has been published. The Rev. Stebbing Shaw's "History and Antiquities of the County of Stafford" was published in London in two (unfinished) volumes in 1798 and 1801, at 15 guineas; copies cold in recent times have fetched as much as £68. In 1812 was published by Swinney and Ferrall of Birmingham, "The History and Antiquities of Handsworth," a folio of 15 pages with 5 plates, which was merely a reprint of that section of Shaw's "Staffordshire" which related to this parish.

Mr. Edward J. Timings, of Handsworth Wood, has in recent years published a number of interesting articles on "Handsworth and Neighbourhood in the Olden Times." Mr. Edward Swift, too, has contributed to the columns of the "Handsworth Herald" from time to time, a number of valuable researchful papers on "Bygone Handsworth."

INDEX

ABNET 140
ADAM 24
ADDYS 49
ADVOWSON 24, 25, 29, 33, 35, 63, 70, 71
AILVERD 16
AINGE 70
ALDRIDGE 6
ALLESTREY 52, 53, 55, 56
ALWIN 16, 32
ANSCULF 16, 17, 18, 42
ANSUN 93
ARDEN 26
ARRAY, COMMISSION OF 118
ARUNDEL 35, 95
ASBURY 101, 103, 141, 144, 171
ASHFORD 109, 119, 154, 174
ASTON 1, 13, 23, 31, 39, 56, 58, 59, 70, 103, 120, 129, 139, 142, 146, 158, 164
ASTON, LITTLE 4, 8, 37
ATTELBERG 31, 33
AUSTIN 119

BARR 32, 33, 38, 39, 42, 43, 44, 45, 71, 72, 114, 115, 127, 139
BARROWS 171
BAYSHALL 35, 140
BELLS 60
BENEFICE 29
BENTLEY 68
BERINGTON 97, 173
BEST 45, 70
BILSTON 98, 169
BIRCH 40, 51, 52, 67, 68, 70, 72, 73, 74, 78, 83, 85, 86, 90, 95, 109, 110, 112, 139, 142, 143, 145, 146
BIRCHFIELD 13, 68, 70, 93, 105, 109, 114, 142, 146, 153, 155, 165
BLACKHAM 119
BLACK PATCH 138
BLOMEFIELD 87, 89
BLOUNT 98
BLOXWICH 98
BONNER 172
BOOTH 44, 52, 53, 55, 56, 156, 167
BOTETORT 30, 31, 32, 34, 36, 63
BOULTON 4, 59, 83, 84, 124, 126, 127, 129, 136, 137, 138, 145, 167, 168

BOYLE 93
BRAGGE 169
BREARLEY 135
BRIDGE, THE 7, 31, 33, 42, 43, 86, 107, 108, 111, 112, 114, 115, 116
BRISNEL END 109, 146
BROMWICH 72, 73, 79, 80, 95, 96, 97, 98, 119
BROOMFIELD 13, 53, 109, 111, 142
BROWN 55, 82, 108, 129, 154, 155
BROWN'S GREEN 109, 135, 136, 144, 145, 149, 155, 168
BUCKLE 129
BURN 69
BURNELL 34
BUSTLEHOLM 81, 84
BUTLER 35

CALTHORPE 46, 90
CANNOCK 1, 19, 31
CAVE 87, 92
CEMETERY 141, 161
CHANCE 136, 157
CHANTERS 78
CHILLINGWORTH 156
CHURCH RATES 111
CHURCHWARDENS 57, 72, 73, 74, 75, 77, 78, 80, 85, 89, 90, 154, 156
CHURCHYARD 76, 167
CIVIL WAR 25, 45, 120, 163
CLARKE 57, 77, 110, 135, 148, 149, 168
CLEGG 129
CLENT 34
CLIFFORD, DE 25, 46
COLEFIELD 37, 38, 42, 51, 172
COLLYER 120
COMBERFORD 29
COMMON LANDS 2, 84, 85
COOK 82, 119, 133
CORBETT 156
COWPER 77, 81
CROCKETT 77, 90, 139
CRUSADERS 28, 29
CUSTOMS, & Co 50, 51, 53, 113, 114, 163–165

DANKS 74
DAPIFER 19, 33
DARTMOUTH 40, 52, 68, 92, 102, 140

DELVES 8, 47
DESTRUCTOR 156
DEVEY 146
DROGO 16, 17, 18, 20, 42
DRUIDISM 9
DUDLEY 1, 16, 18, 19, 20, 25, 42, 98, 130
DUGDALE 135, 145

EDGBASTON 46, 52, 56, 121, 139
EGINTON 124, 126, 127, 145, 148
ENCLOSURE ACTS 2, 14, 71, 72, 75, 84, 85, 86
ERDINGTON 31, 53, 54, 55, 172
ETYMOLOGY 6, 11, 12, 13, 14, 15
EVERITT 60, 154

FIELD NAMES 13, 39, 43, 48, 53, 54, 55, 79, 80, 85, 86, 107, 109, 110, 113, 138, 142, 146
FINCHPATH 48
FITZHERBERT 43, 49
FLETCHER 170
FOLEY 3, 51
FOWKES 3
FRANCHISES 26, 33, 36, 53, 54
FREER 57, 68, 75, 77, 145, 156, 168, 170
FRIARY 68, 142, 146, 166
FULNETBY (FURNABY) 44, 67, 95, 170

GALTON 168
GEAST 59, 135
GIBBONS 79, 83, 85, 86, 113
GIB HEATH 139
GOLDS GROUND 73, 74
GORDON 170
GOUGH 39, 45, 46, 59, 85, 86, 89, 93, 95, 108, 110, 111, 113, 114, 115, 134, 145, 146, 147, 155
GRICE 57, 75, 77, 84, 145, 148, 170
GRIFFIN 87
GRIFFITH 166
GROVE(S) 44, 82, 116
GUEST 116

HALESOWEN 81, 82
HAMON 26
HAMSTEAD 31, 32, 34, 35, 36, 37, 38, 39, 41, 49, 50, 56, 61, 118, 119, 130, 131, 133, 134, 135, 139, 145, 146, 154, 162, 166, 168
HARBORNE 25, 40, 70, 73, 81, 82, 121, 139, 155

HARGREAVES 68, 90
HARMAN 38, 170
HASLUCK 57, 170
HAUGHTON 57, 68, 75, 77, 110, 143, 156
HAYES 50, 54
HEATHFIELD 13, 53, 54, 55, 127, 142, 148, 168
HEATON 157, 167
HERONVILLE 41
HILL 52, 96
HODGES 136
HODGETT S 54, 73, 79, 82, 107, 114. 119, 141
HODGSON 69
HOLFORD 4, 43, 48, 51, 90
HOLTE 38, 39, 55
HOPWOOD 169
HORTON 87
HUDDLESTON 70
HUGHES 173
HUXLEY 77, 78, 79, 84

ICKNIELD PORT 8, 47
INDUSTRIES 49-51, 56, 91, 92, 95, 120, 124-128
INQUISITIONS 33
INNS AND TAVERNS 115, 127, 130, 145, 146, 147, 154, 155, 156, 158

JENNENS 3
JOHNSON 130, 140

KENDRICK 85, 86, 119, 157
KEY HILL 6, 11
KINGS NORTON 1, 70, 120, 159
KING'S STANDING 8, 120,163

LANE 40, 67, 68, 81, 84, 92, 93, 105, 133, 134
LENTON 25, 34, 63
LETTERS PATENT 118
LEVETT 52, 53, 56
LEY HALL 133, 169
LICHFIELD 23, 27, 34, 36, 52, 63, 64, 69, 71, 98, 120, 122, 123, 126
LITTLETON 70, 170
LUNAR SOCIETY 127, 137, 173
LYSTER 173

MACDONA 93
MACDONALD 171
MANWOODS 133, 140, 141

MARTYN 98, 173
MARYVALE 96, 97, 99
MERE 34
MIDDLEFIELD 13, 54
MIDDLEMORE 46
MILLS 35, 37, 48-51, 114, 120, 124
MOILLIETT 168
MORWOOD 34, 63, 64
MOTTE HOUSE 39
MURDOCK 59, 124, 125, 127, 167, 168
MURRAY 64, 68

NECHELLS 23, 52, 55
NEEDEAM 87, 93, 122, 155, 156
NEWMAN 172
NEW INN 44, 45, 46, 47, 90, 100, 131, 151
NEWTON 47, 58, 120
NINEVEH 91, 102, 103, 124, 138, 139, 171

OAKES 60, 62, 67, 70
OLDBURY 81, 135, 157, 167
OFFLOW 16, 18, 25, 26
OLD FORGE 141, 171
O'NIELL 168
ORGAN 76, 91
OSBORNE 60, 61, 79, 80, 86, 119, 135, 145, 146
OSCOT 4, 15, 37, 70, 85, 89, 90, 95-99, 114, 141, 162, 172, 175
OVERSEERS 75, 77, 78, 154, 155, 156

PAGANEL 19, 20
PARISH, THE 76, 77, 80, 81, 82, 157, 158, 159, 160, 162
PARKINSON 3
PARLES 19, 20, 21, 23, 24, 25, 26, 27, 34, 57, 63
"PARSON AND CLARK" 134, 174
PEEL 68, 90, 91, 116, 170
PETER DE BIRMINGHAM 19
PIDDOCK 60, 75, 81, 83, 133, 135, 146
PRICE 62, 86
PRIESTLEY 126, 127

QUEEN ANNE'S BOUNTY 29
QUESLETT 15, 162, 167
QUIRKE 173

RANDALL 68, 71, 92
RAILWAYS 137, 138, 146
REA 45, 47, 114, 158

RECTORS 25, 31, 34, 36, 40, 60, 63, 64, 67, 68, 74, 75, 76, 77, 86, 87, 90-92, 95
RED LION INN 90
REFORMATION 29, 58, 63-66, 95-97
RHODES 57, 87, 136
ROADS, &c. 2-5, 81, 84, 121, 124, 166, 167
RUSHALL 22, 26
RUSHTON 124, 137, 160
RUSSELL 136
RYKNIELD 6, 7, 8, 9

SACHEVERELL 59, 135
ST. LEGER 35
SANDWELL 2, 8, 24, 47, 48, 63, 64, 83, 92, 102, 120, 139, 140, 141, 143, 166, 171
SCHOOLS 69, 78, 90, 97-99, 104, 112, 115, 116, 117, 160
SCHRAFFORD 43
SCOTT 145, 146, 147
SHERIFF 26, 27, 40
SMALLBROOK 133
SMALLWOOD 50, 119, 135, 145, 146
SMETHWICK 1, 2, 91, 121, 122, 129, 130, 138, 139, 155, 159
SMITH 43, 57, 60, 61, 109, 110, 136, 170
SNEPP 90
SOHO 4, 5, 105, 116, 124-128, 137-139, 145, 146, 150, 174
SOHO CIRCLE 173
SOMERY 25, 27, 28, 31, 33, 34, 42, 58, 63
SPENCER 73, 133
SQUIRE 31, 133
STAFFORD 35
STAMFORD 35, 38, 42-47, 67, 70, 95, 97, 120, 133
STANLEY 133
STONE 49
STONE CROSS 48
STREETLEY 9, 134
STUBBS 77, 78, 84, 116
SUTTON 13, 31, 37, 51, 52, 56, 158, 174
SWELLENGREBEL 136
SWIFT 174
SWYNFEN 36, 68

TAME 1, 3, 6, 7, 35, 42, 43, 48, 51, 53-56, 114, 117, 120, 140, 149, 154, 158
TANGYE 92, 168

TASKER   171
TIMINGS   174
TIPPIN   53
TIPTON   37, 64, 69, 73, 95
TITHES   37, 64, 71, 83
TUTBURY   64, 69
TYE   173

UNDERHILL   57, 77, 155
UNION ROW   87

VALOR ECCLESIASTICUS   29
VAUGHTON   148
VESEY   38, 171
VESTRY   115, 129, 154, 156
VICTORIA PARK   20
VILLA CROSS   3, 106, 131, 145, 150,
                         152, 155
VISITATION   133
VOLUNTEERS   121, 122, 123

WAGGON AND HORSES 115, 127, 158
WALLIS   169
WALSALL   3, 47, 48, 49, 69, 81, 84, 98,
              120, 123, 129, 135, 143,
              144-146, 148, 154, 162
WALTER   18, 67, 72, 136
WALTON   86, 89, 167, 171
WARD   157, 162
WARLEY   28, 157
WATT   58, 59, 60, 91, 124-127,
              129, 145, 167, 168, 174

WEDDINGTON   24
WEDNESBURY   1, 3, 4, 34, 41, 48, 49,
              69, 74, 136, 143, 145, 151,
                         157, 163, 166
WELL HEAD   6, 7, 84, 96
WELLS   141
WEOLEY   28, 34
WEST BROMWICH   1, 3, 18, 45, 57, 63,
              69, 73, 74, 81, 83, 96, 98, 101,
              102, 114, 122, 129, 131, 150,
                         151, 155, 157
WHATELEY   75, 135, 146, 148
WHORWOOD   81, 83, 140
WILLIAMS   136
WILLIES   82, 109, 120, 133
WINSON GREEN   81
WISEMAN   172
WITTON   31, 52, 53, 54, 55, 56, 70,
                         110, 172
WOOLLEY   68, 89, 170
WORKHOUSE   75, 130, 157
WREN   145, 146, 149, 156, 157
WRETHAM   40
WRIGHT   68, 141
WROTTESLEY   35, 63, 146
WYRLEY   2, 32, 34-41, 43, 49-51, 58,
              59, 61, 64, 70, 95, 108, 118, 119,
                         133, 134, 137, 154

YARDLEY   52
YEOMANRY   121
YOUNG   171